THE NEW DEMOCRATS, 1961-1986

Canadiana Reprint Series

J.L. Granatstein — General Editor

Copp Clark Pitman is pleased to republish selected titles
that have contributed to the understanding of Canada.
In many cases, new material has been added to bring the
works up to date and reflect the recent research.

AVAILABLE TITLES:

Broken Promises — J.L. Granatstein and J.M. Hitsman
Canada and the Burden of Unity — David J. Bercuson
Canada and the French-Canadian Question — Ramsay Cook
The Maple Leaf Forever — Ramsay Cook
The Office of the Lieutenant Governor — John T. Saywell
The Politics of Chaos — H. Blair Neatby

THE NEW DEMOCRATS 1961-1986
The Politics of Change

Desmond Morton

Copp Clark Pitman Ltd.
A Longman Company

To Ruth and Terry Grier

First published in 1974 under the title *NDP: the Dream of Power;* second edition published in 1977 under the title *NDP: Social Democracy in Canada* by A. M. Hakkert (Toronto) and Samuel Stevens (Sarasota).

Editing: Barbara Tessman, Maureen Lee
Cover design: Julia Veenstra
Cover photo: Kathy Cloutier
Printing and binding: John Deyell

ISBN: 0-7730-4618-6

Canadian Cataloguing in Publication Data

Morton, Desmond, 1937-
   The New Democrats, 1961-1986: The politics of change

(Canadiana reprint series)
First ed. published 1974 under title: N D P : the
dream of power; 2nd ed. published 1977 under title:
N D P : social democracy in Canada.

Bibliography: p.
Includes index.
ISBN 0-7730-4618-6

1. New Democratic Party. I. Title. II. Title:
N D P : social democracy in Canada. III. Series:
Canadiana reprint series (Toronto, Ont.).

JL197.N4M67 1986   324.27107   C86-094125-6

53,899

Copp Clark Pitman Ltd.
495 Wellington Street West
Toronto, Ontario
M5V 1E9

Associated companies:
   Longman Group Ltd., London
   Longman Inc., New York
   Longman Cheshire Pty., Melbourne
   Longman Paul Pty., Auckland

Printed and bound in Canada.

Contents

	Introduction	vii
I.	Background	3
II.	Foundation	19
III.	Setbacks	33
IV.	Elections	53
V.	Conflict	75
VI.	Progress	99
VII.	Clarification	119
VIII.	Performance	145
IX.	Frustrations	169
X.	Reappraisal	185
XI.	Regionalism	201
XII.	Prospects	221
Appendix.	Structure	229
	Further Reading	236
	Index	242

Photo credits

An honest attempt has been made to secure permission for all material used, and if there are any errors or omissions, these are wholly unintentional and the Publisher will be grateful to learn of them.

Ontario NDP (pp. viii, 43, 136); Public Archives of Canada C56365 (p. 2); Federal NDP (pp. 16, 26, 74, 175, 182); Gaby of Montreal (p. 58); Manitoba NDP (p. 102); Saskatchewan NDP (p. 112); Information Canada (p. 118); United Steelworkers (pp. 144, 212, 224); Nova Scotia NDP (p. 203); Photo Features Ltd., Ottawa, courtesy of Mr. Broadbent's office (p. 218).

Cover photo

The buttons depict the three logos used by the Federal NDP over its twenty-five year history. The bottom logo, representing the Parliament Buildings, was in use from the founding convention in 1961 until 1973. The middle logo, a stylised version of the Parliament Buildings, was in use from the 1974 election until 1983–84. The top logo was introduced during the 1984 election and is currently in use.

All logos are reproduced by permission of the Federal NDP.

Introduction

Conventional wisdom and academic political science have generally agreed that democratic socialism has no real future as a political option in North America. In the new world, the twin socialist ideals of liberty and equality could be achieved without the old world doctrine of the class struggle.

Since 1961, like its predecessor, the Co-operative Commonwealth Federation, Canada's New Democratic Party has attempted to defy that dogma. Launched in the enthusiasm of the largest, longest political convention in Canadian history to that time, the NDP soon learned that it was not destined for easy victories or early triumphs. It took time to come to terms with the urban working class constituency it was specially designed to attract. In the process, the NDP had much to learn about the values and ideals that late twentieth-century Canadians could be persuaded to share.

A quarter-century from its creation, New Democrats claim the support of a fifth of the Canadian electorate. The NDP has formed governments in three provinces and the Yukon and it has elected members in almost every province in Confederation. From Victoria to St. John's, it has elected aldermen, councillors, and big-city mayors. The party has survived disillusionment, disappointment, divisions, and occasional obituaries. Like other major institutions, the

Tommy Douglas at an NDP candidates' meeting. Shrewd, realistic, passionate, Douglas was the party's major asset in its early years.

NDP continues to change; more than some of them, it is likely to survive.

This study of twenty-five years of the New Democratic Party is built on a succession of books that appeared more than a decade ago. Like its predecessors, this one spends more time in the backrooms of the party than on its public platforms. Since the NDP, more than its rivals, remains a federation of provincial organizations, the focus shifts often in a search for a pattern to the electoral struggles that mark Canada's political calendar.

Historians who tread too closely on the heels of the present are likely to get kicked in the teeth. The dead cannot be libelled; the living are easily aroused. The present work is not a study in objectivity because the author lacks the pre-requisites: ignorance and omniscience. I have had the benefit of interviews, letters, minutes, records, and the transitory wisdom of print journalism. When wisdom counselled delay, enthusiasm urged speed because Canadians deserve a current insight into a major political institution and New Democrats should plan their future in the context of their own collective experience.

Less than a quarter-century ago, I spent a couple of the busiest and most fascinating years of my life on the staff of the NDP. Then and since my image of social democracy in Canada has been shaped by the remarkable men and women I encountered in the NDP's ranks. Anita Devillez, Gord Brigden, Bob Mackenzie, Martha Miike, the late "Doc" Ames are not mentioned in the text. They and countless others know that Canada is a more humane and caring community because of the political cause to which they gave their hours, days and lives.

In writing this book, I have pre-empted the task which someday may properly be done by Terry Grier. Armed with imagination, rare common sense, and a self-effacing style, he has played a more consistently creative role throughout the first quarter-century of the NDP than anyone, this side of posterity, will acknowledge. This book includes traces of his wisdom and, doubtless, much more that he will someday correct. To him, to Kenneth McNaught, Marion Bryden, Ed Broadbent, Gordon Vichert, and Norman Allen the inspiration for this book is due. My students at Erindale College, University of Toronto, have been a source of inspiration and a pressure for completion. So have colleagues who have relieved me of labour, shared ideas and made their own contribution. Paul Fox, Steven Jaunszems, Laurel MacDowell, Clara Stewart, and Georgie Anderson may all recognize their share. Only the author is responsible for the lapses.

Mississauga, June 1986

THE NEW DEMOCRATS, 1961-1986

James Shaver Woodsworth was the father of Canadian democratic socialism as a serious political movement.

I. Background

"... I am convinced that we may develop in Canada a distinctive type of Socialism. I refuse to follow slavishly the British model or the American model or the Russian model. We in Canada will solve our problems along our own lines."

(J. S. Woodsworth in Regina, 1933)

What is the New Democratic Party? How did it get that way?

The answers depend on your point of view. To a political scientist, the NDP is a party of the democratic Left, advocating moderate socialist solutions for the problems of an advanced capitalist society. It is also a sectional party, winning the bulk of its support, in geographic terms, from four of the provinces west of the Ottawa river and, sociologically, from lower and middle-income Canadians, particularly those from a trade union background.

To its own members, the NDP is both an electoral organization and a political movement, pledged to the eventual transformation of society. If few members could describe either the nature or the process of the transformation, they could still dream that people might be

3

able to live in a better, more humane relationship with each other. NDP voters, on the other hand, when asked, tend to identify the party as speaking up for Canadian working people and the less well-off. Opponents insist that the NDP is merely the mouthpiece for the trade unions or for irresponsible critics of the free enterprise system. A few condemn the party as "reformist," a major barrier to a true socialist revolution in Canada.

Another and perhaps more valid way of looking at the New Democratic Party is to see it as the product of more than ninety years of working class and radical political experience and, therefore, as an indigenous Canadian institution. From trial and error came the realization that Canadian working people and their allies needed their own distinct political party, that it had to be controlled and financed, so far as possible, by its own members, that its principal battles, though by no means all of them, would be fought within democratic parliamentary structures, and that its ideology would be a broad, undoctrinaire socialism.

Of course, not everyone draws the same lessons from history. If the New Democratic Party has undoubtedly become the dominant institution of the political Left in Canada, there has never been a full consensus inside or outside its ranks about correct strategy or tactics. Some radicals have always had a taste for revolutions. Syndicalism, the doctrine that labour struggle can short-circuit the familiar institutions of parliament and government, was discredited by the Winnipeg General Strike of 1919 only to reappear in the Quebec strikes of 1972 — with comparable consequences. Lenin's success in using a tiny revolutionary elite to overthrow the Russian government in 1917 has spawned a whole spectrum of conspiratorial sects around the democratic world, including several in Canada.

What the NDP represents, therefore, is only a majority view of what the Left can and must accomplish in Canada. Its existence, like that of its predecessor, the CCF, transforms a party system which, otherwise, might be almost indistinguishable from that of the United States. Those who find Canada's distinctiveness in her conservative tradition might find just as valuable evidence in the strength of the country's radical political party.

The need for a separate party was by no means apparent to Canadian workers when, in the late 1860s, they began to form enduring labour organizations. Certainly legislative goals ranked high on their agenda: it must have seemed easier to bully politicians than their own hard-faced employers. It could also be more fun. For a time, the traditional Liberal and Conservative parties were able to accommodate the pressures. Sir John A. Macdonald's Trade Union Act of 1872 and the promised employment opportunities of his National Policy of 1878 helped to keep most of the workers in the Tory ranks during the 1870s: factory legislation from the provincial Liberal administrations of Honoré Mercier in Quebec and Oliver Mowat in Ontario helped pull the labour vote to the Grits during the 1880s. As early as 1873, union leaders had begun presenting their views to governments in what are still known as "cap-in-hand" sessions.

For reasons which still have force in broad sectors of the Canadian labour movement, many labour leaders were content with this version of brokerage politics. Political debate could be hopelessly divisive within unions, most members accepted one or other of the established parties as well as the prevailing free enterprise ideology, and union leaders might claim minor patronage rewards for delivering the vote. When more radical labour organizations like the Knights of Labour collapsed in the 1880s, the conservative craft unions, based on high dues and the scarcity of skilled labour, survived. Most took their political philosophy from Samuel Gompers, an ex-socialist who presided over the American Federation of Labor from 1886 to 1924. "Stand faithfully by our friends and reward them," insisted Gompers, "oppose our enemies and defeat them." For the AFL and its Canadian counterpart, the Trades and Labour Congress (TLC), that meant, in effect, a minimum of independent political action and as close an integration as possible into the prevailing social and economic system.

In the United States, where individual congressmen could more easily be pressured to ignore party lines, the Gompers formula might have some validity; in the Canadian parliamentary system, it did not. Canadian union leaders found that winning the sympathy of individual politicans made little difference. Under the tight caucus discipline imposed by Canada's form of responsible government, these individuals had little influence. Thus entire parties and governments had to be converted and, in practice, that was rarely possible. A growing number of labour radicals had no difficulty in explaining why: in Canadian politics, the division of labour was as complete as in a factory. Professional elites provided the candidates, businessmen furnished the money and working people served only in the cheering section or, as the property franchise was gradually lowered, provided a share of the votes. From their political frustrations, a small minority of working people developed a sharp class-consciousness.

There was another problem with the two-party system which was more slowly perceived. It was *not*, as left-wing slogans still proclaim, that the Liberals and Conservatives were identical. In fact, they reflected very real historical and sociological differences. By the 1890s, after a major shift in allegiances, the Liberals had become, predominantly, the party of Quebec, the West and Catholicism, while their rivals were closely identified with Ontario and

Protestantism. This helped to ensure that the bitterest debates in Canadian politics seemed to focus on issues of race, culture and religion. This obsession has regularly helped to obscure a broad agreement among Liberals and Conservatives that the economic system was best controlled by private businessmen, that workers would be paid as much as their employers felt able to give them and that poverty was usually the punishment for improvidence, self-indulgence or laziness. The limitations of a party system united on key economic issues are obvious.

Any party system reflects chosen priorities. Loyalties may be based on religion, ethnicity or even, as some apparently might wish, on sex. In Canada, a primary preoccupation of left-wing politics has been to shift political debate away from issues like language, sectionalism and nationalism to the divisions between rich and poor, between those with economic power and those with none. In the United States, partly because language and cultural differences have mattered less as a basis for party allegiance, partly because of the near-accident of the New Deal, it proved possible to convert a wing of the Democratic Party into a political vehicle for organized labour and the poor. In Canada, that has never happened.

Instead, as early as 1874, independent labour candidates began seeking and occasionally winning election to Parliament and provincial legislatures. In the 1880s and 1890s, thanks to a few labour intellectuals like Phillips Thompson, the author of *The Politics of Labor*, and to the influx of working class socialists from Great Britain, trade unions and labour candidates began to acquire a specific ideology. Obstacles inside and outside the infant Canadian trade union movement were enormous. Early labour M.P.s like A. T. Lépine (elected in 1888), Ralph Smith (1900), A. W. Puttee (1900) and Alphonse Verville (1906) drifted into alliances with the established parties merely to achieve a few tangible gains. Despite repeated resolutions, not until 1917 did the Trades and Labour Congress launch a vigorous attempt at electoral action (in anger at the government's imposition of wartime conscription) and it failed miserably. However, the seeds took root in a number of small labour parties in Ontario and the western provinces and postwar Canadian parliaments were never without a contingent, however small, of labour members. In 1921, they were joined by sixty-five Progressives, spokesmen for a movement of rural protest which had swept across Canada from the foothills of the Rockies to rural Ontario. The Progressives soon faded but the survivors joined with the labour members to form a third force in the House of Commons, the so-called Ginger Group, whose chief spokesman was the bearded, austere former-clergyman from Winnipeg, J. S. Woodsworth. Oddly enough, though a few political scientists still teach that a two-party system is the parliamentary norm, Canada has not known that blessed estate for more than half a century.

Reluctantly and hesitantly, trade unionists had pioneered the concept of a class party. Farmers, beginning with the Patrons of Industry in the 1890s and continuing through a succession of political and economic organizations, helped promote the same notion, though their chief mentor, Henry Wise Wood of Alberta, shrewdly described his supporters as an "economic group." Perhaps the most important contribution of the farmers' movement to the tradition of the Canadian left, in addition to a tradition of successful co-operative enterprise, was an intense emphasis on democratic control and on broadly-based financial support. In part, it was an infusion of the American populist experience, in part it reflected the intense individualism characteristic of the small farmer. But both pressures enforced a pattern of delegate democracy, regular consultation and strict accountability of leaders to followers which would characterize the Co-operative Commonwealth Federation (CCF) and, by inheritance, the NDP.

What the farmers lacked was a unifying ideology. William Lyon Mackenzie King, the Liberal prime minister after 1921, insisted that the Progressives were merely Liberals in a hurry and, as he discovered, he did not have to hustle very fast to catch them. Farmer and labour radicals failed to collaborate very effectively in the Twenties, largely because the trade unionists had developed a political programme, increasingly expressed as a theoretical and uncompromising socialism. Labour activists had long since moved past the TLC's "Platform of Principles," with its demands for free compulsory education, abolition of the Senate and exclusion of Chinese immigrants. Instead, in various accents and with varying degrees of vehemence, they preached the overthrow of the capitalist system.

Nowhere did early Canadian socialism strike deeper roots than in British Columbia, partly because of the influx of radical British workers, partly, as Martin Robin has argued, because of the resource-based economy of the province. Employees of the west coast lumber and coal barons could find a special relevance in the doctrine of the class struggle: they lived it daily. The socialism preached in the company towns of British Columbia and in major cities across Canada tended to be a dogmatic Marxism, attracting few converts but educating a generation of union leaders and organizers. Early socialism in Canada was uncompromisingly proletarian: it was also, visiting comrades complained, intellectually sterile and hopelessly out of touch with Canadian realities.

Part of the problem of Canadian socialists was that, like their comrades elsewhere, they really had no idea about how their philosophy might be implemented. Marx's assurances about the ineluctable processes of history were a poor guide to daily tactics. Did one push history or did one wait? The issue was seriously debated. Some socialists, particularly in British Columbia, contested and won elections in the early years of the century, only to fall foul of their more revolutionary associates. J. H. Hawthornthwaite and Parker Williams, as socialists, represented Vancouver Island constituencies in the British Columbia legislature but both eventually found it impossible to reconcile parliamentary responsibilities and the demands of their doctrinaire supporters. Many radicals abandoned politics altogether, turning to syndicalism and its weapon, the general strike. It was a strategy especially favoured by the Industrial Workers of the World (IWW), the romantic, venturesome labour organization which flourished in the western United States and Canada before the First World War, but syndicalist ideas were discussed in trade union circles everywhere. Though active syndicalists were not actually involved, Winnipeg trade unionists attempted a general strike in 1919. It was a failure. Tactics were muddled and uncertain. Strike leaders failed to understand that, by bringing the entire city to a standstill, they were challenging government authority as well as selected employers. Anti-strike citizens ensured that the authorities shared no such illusion. After two months, a major riot and two deaths, the strike was crushed.

Among the leaders imprisoned after the strike was a former Methodist minister and product of the social gospel movement, James Shaver Woodsworth. He did not need further evidence of the futility of syndicalist tactics. While some socialists had found their model in Lenin's 1917 revolution, Woodsworth had found his in the newly radicalized British Labour Party and its 1918 programme for parliamentary socialism. While fellow socialists now preached the revolutionary overthrow of the hated capitalist system, Woodsworth insisted that change could be achieved in Canada "by means of education, organization and the securing by the workers of the machinery of government." In 1921, he won a seat in Parliament for the Winnipeg constituency he would represent until his death in 1942. As one of the tiny contingent of labour members, he watched with dismay the floundering, division and eventual disappearance of the Progressives as a political force. Learning their lesson, Woodsworth became a master of House of Commons procedure, rejected a Liberal offer of a cabinet portfolio, and used his bargaining power with a minority government to extort Canada's first old age pension legislation. His ally, another former clergyman, was William Irvine, elected as a labour M.P. from Calgary. The two became the nucleus of the Ginger Group, a loose alliance which soon included Agnes Macphail, Canada's first woman M.P.

By no means all the Canadian Left had followed Woodsworth's lead. On May 23rd, 1921, the Communist Party of Canada was formed at an almost cloak and dagger meeting in a barn near Guelph. Seven months later, the Communists gave themselves a public front by forming a Workers' Party of Canada for which they pulled the strings. Though the Communists resembled the innumerable sects and fractions which splintered the Canadian Left, their discipline and conspiratorial tactics gave them enormous advantages in disposing of left-wing rivals. Impeded only by contradictory and ill-conceived orders from Moscow, a tiny handful of militants destroyed an enfeebled Canadian Labour Party and infiltrated a number of unions before being expelled.

The Twenties were a desperate period for Canadian unions and radicals. Dismal poverty and low wages persisted but almost no-one seemed to care. Labour was on the defensive against a form of industrial democracy pioneered by Mackenzie King in his days as a Rockefeller employee — the company union. The farmers' movements were disillusioned by politics and disintegrating under the solvent of high prices. When the economic blizzard swept across Canada in the Thirties, capitalism tottered but its sworn opponents were too busy trying to rescue the victims to try to complete its overthrow. There was one benefit. Radical farmers and workers slowly realized that they had more in common than their destitution. Conferences of the scattered, quarrelsome western labour parties had begun in 1929 and, at Calgary in 1932, they finally found unity with farm groups in proposing "a co-operative commonwealth, in which the basic principle regulating production, distribution and exchange will be the supplying of human needs instead of the making of profits." The Co-operative Commonwealth Federation was born.

In the East, a group of academics formed the League for Social Reconstruction (LSR) and provided the Canadian Left with a version of socialism in tune with the Fabian parliamentary tradition and, to some extent, with Canadian economic and social circumstances. At Regina, in 1933, the CCF's original eight-point programme was replaced by a lengthy manifesto prepared by an LSR committee and drafted by a Toronto academic, Frank Underhill. It emphasized economic planning, nationalization of financial institutions, public utilities and natural resources, security of tenure for farmers, a national labour code, socialized health services and greatly increased economic powers for the central government. To suit its fervid mood, the Regina convention added a conclusion asserting that: "No C.C.F. Government will rest content unitl it has eradicated capitalism and put into operation the full programme of socialized planning which will lead to the establishment in Canada of the Co-operative Commonwealth."

Despite its aggressive ending, veteran radicals like Ernest Winch from Vancouver complained that the statement was no more than pale pink, if only because it explicitly rejected violence and guaranteed compensation to dispossessed owners. On the other hand, rural leaders from Ontario and Alberta complained that the convention had been captured by doctrinaire socialists and that the Manifesto was "not the language best understood by Ontario farmers." At Calgary, a lone trade union leader, A. R. Mosher of the All-Canadian Confederation of Labour (ACCL), had appeared but he did not come back to Regina. Boldly, the CCF had subtitled itself "Farmer-Labour-Socialist" but none of the constituent elements seemed really happy. In 1934, continued flirtation of socialist groups with the Communists forced Woodsworth to dissolve the Ontario CCF but factionalism continued to wrack the party from coast to coast. In 1935, William Aberhart's Social Credit landslide engulfed the mildly sympathetic farmer government of Alberta and what had once seemed one of the most radical provinces of Canada rapidly became the most conspicuously conservative. Only in Saskatchewan, during the depression years, did the CCF find significant electoral support.

Paradoxically, it took a world war and returning prosperity to make the CCF grow. A younger, more pragmatic generation of leaders emerged in the wake of J. S. Woodsworth's refusal to compromise his pacifist principles in 1939. M. J. Coldwell, an English-born Regina school teacher, became the CCF's second national leader. David Lewis, a Rhodes Scholar, lawyer and dramatically effective speaker, became national secretary at a meagre $1,200 a year. T. C. Douglas, a young Baptist minister who had been elected to Parliament, returned to Saskatchewan to lead the CCF to its first provincial victory in 1944. For many Canadians, the war hammered home the CCF's depression message — that resources could be found to sustain full employment and a booming economy if only the will and the planning were available. In 1942, a CCF candidate upset the Conservative party leader in a by-election in the traditionally Tory Toronto riding of York South. Overnight, the CCF became an electoral force. In 1943, an Ontario provincial election boosted the party's share of the vote from five to thirty-one per cent and the CCF narrowly missed forming the government. A year later, it was in office in Saskatchewan and a Gallup Poll had indicated that the national CCF had more popular support than either of its rivals.

It seemed like the verge of victory for Canadian socialism. Instead, it was the top of the mushroom. Mackenzie King's Liberals, threatened with defeat and caucus defections to the CCF, hurried family allowances and a generous veterans' charter into law and promised much more. The Conservatives added "Progressive" to their name and strained, a little unconvincingly, to deserve the title. The business community financed a vitriolic anti-socialist campaign which did not hesitate to link the CCF to Hitler's Nazis. Even the Communists got into the act. Terrified lest democratic socialists make major gains, the Communists formed an odd, clandestine alliance with the Liberals, working effectively to split the left-wing vote in major industrial centres like Vancouver, Windsor, St. Catherines and Hamilton. In the 1945 federal election, the CCF advance was stopped in its tracks. In Ontario, where its popular support slipped back to twenty-two per cent, its legislative representation fell from thirty-four to eight.

Never again would the CCF recover the momentum of the war years. In Ottawa and in provincial legislatures from Nova Scotia to British Columbia, it provided contingents of able representatives, offering much of the inspiration and innovation to be found in Canadian politics in the stagnant postwar years. It was not enough. Falling membership, tired leaders, financial crises and declining electoral support were all symptoms of what a sympathetic sociologist, Leo Zakuta, described as "a protest movement becalmed."

Only in Saskatchewan had the CCF achieved power and only there did it survive as a major force. A unique socialist outpost in North America, it was, to the party's unmixed delight, a success story. In 1944, the province had been almost bankrupt, harder hit than any other by the combined onslaught of drought, rust, grasshoppers and depression prices. In twenty years in office, the CCF did not transform Saskatchewan into a Garden of Eden or even a socialist utopia, but it did fulfil virtually all its promises. It collected a team of brilliant civil servants and put them to work to restore and diversify the province's economy, setting firsts in Canada for hospital, health and automobile insurance and in welfare and labour legislation, creating publicly-owned industries, some of which failed, most of which proved to be successful. Moreover, the CCF in Saskatchewan managed to maintain the unique grassroots organization which had carried it to power and, probably to a greater degree than any other democratic socialist party, the CCF in government remained accountable to its members and supporters.

Try as it might, the CCF could not make Saskatchewan a launching pad for a fresh attempt to spread its strength across Canada. In Alberta, the party made almost as little headway as Social Credit made in Saskatchewan. In British Columbia, the CCF seemed to be permanently installed as the official opposition regardless of who formed the government. In Ontario, after virtual annihilation in the 1952 election, all that proved possible was a painfully slow recovery. In Quebec, where the CCF had suffered under ecclesiastical ban during its ten formative years, there was

When T.C. Douglas took a bankrupt Saskatchewan and made it prosper after Liberal and Tory failures, no one could claim that socialism meant economic ruin.

virtually nothing beyond the courageous personal leadership of Thérèse Casgrain. In Atlantic Canada, the only oasis of support for a wandering CCFer was the coal mining community on Cape Breton Island, already in sharp economic decline. Perhaps the political scientists were right about left-wing politicial parties in North America.

There was only one other possibility — a fresh look at Woodsworth's own political model, the British Labour Party. Nowhere in the world had democratic socialist parties made headway without a direct, organic link to their trade union movements. That had certainly been the case in Britain and western Europe, in Australia and New Zealand. The CCF had envisaged the possibility of effective links but, in the 1930s, most Canadian trade unionists were either tied to the Gompers tradition of the TLC or to the Communist-controlled Workers' Unity League. Not until 1938 did any labour organization — District 26 of the United Mineworkers of America, stormy petrel of the Cape Breton coal fields — affiliate with the CCF. Its move was a reflection of a wider movement in the United States, the launching, under Mineworkers' leadership, of the Congress of Industrial Organizations. Under the magic letters CIO, American unionism finally battered its way into huge, hitherto impregnable industrial plants. In Canada, the CIO mystique inspired young activists in both the CCF and the Communist party and, although initial progress was slow, wartime brought a flood of organizing victories and a massive growth in the ranks of organized labour across the country. In 1940, a merger of the national unions in the ACCL and the new CIO unions created the Canadian Congress of Labour (CCL), a rival for the more conservative TLC. Three years later, the new Congress broke with all precedent by endorsing the CCF as "the political arm of labour." A Political Action Committee (PAC) was authorized to give practical effect to the motion of support.

The CCL endorsement was a precedent of enormous importance but of little immediate value. Within the CCL and in all its major industrial unions, a bitter, remorseless struggle for control was soon raging between Communist leaders and their opponents — most of them militant CCFers like Charles Millard, Larry Sefton, William Mahoney and Fred Dowling. While they held control, the Communists effectively prevented support for their CCF rivals — often with arguments that Sam Gompers would have admired. Even when they had been defeated in all but a handful of unions, the scars remained. Victory had come too late to help the CCF at the peak of its strength and, when aid was forthcoming during the Fifties from big industrial unions like the Steelworkers, Packinghouse Workers and United Auto Workers, it could only replace the party's own failing financial resources.

In 1954, the negotiations for the merger of the TLC and the CCL began. An obvious stumbling block was the divergent attitude of the two congresses to political action. Deliberately, the CCF supporters held back from forcing the issue. Old leaders were retiring and even in the TLC a few active CCFers were rising to positions of influence. When the new Canadian Labour Congress formally came into existence in 1956, an agreed policy had been evolved in consultation with CCF leaders. Within two years, under leadership from men like Stanley Knowles and the Steelworkers' Eamon Park, the Congress would move to create a new alliance of the political Left in Canada. For the first time, most of organized labour in Canada would be invited to get involved.

In 1871, the Toronto Trades Assembly had come into being to help workers fight for a nine-hour day in a six-day week. Ninety years later, the descendants of those Toronto workers could create their own political party.

II. Foundation

In 1957, the CCF celebrated its twenty-fifth anniversary. A committee gathered photographs, recollections and a scattering of advertisements and published a souvenir booklet. To some, it looked like a slightly premature obituary. In that year's election, the vagaries of the system had given the CCF twenty-five seats – more than at any time since 1945 – but popular vote had slipped again to 9.7 per cent, the lowest point since 1940. Since 1945, the CCF had turned from thoughts of power to congratulating itself on its internal democracy, the value of its contribution, and the benevolence of its influence on legislation. Now there were doubts that the CCF could even survive as the nation's conscience. They were confirmed less than a year later. Reinforcing John Diefenbaker's mandate to govern, Canadian voters left the CCF only eight seats and a mere nine per cent of the vote. The party's most respected leaders, Coldwell and Stanley Knowles, were defeated.

The CCF's problem was no longer a secret. Where did a solution lie? To the party's left wing, the invariable answer was a return to a purer, less compromised socialism. To Colin Cameron or H. W. Herridge, the old enemies were still alive. The face of capitalism had not changed. The dominant leaders – Coldwell, Knowles, Lewis, F. R. Scott, the Montreal lawyer and poet — thought differently. The CCF could not appeal to Canadians in the prosperous Fifties with slogans and rhetoric redolent of the great depression. In 1956, after a number of false starts and a great deal of ill-feeling among CCF fundamentalists, the Regina Manifesto was supplanted by the Winnipeg Declaration, a statement which suggested that the CCF had come to terms with the reality of a mixed economy and that its concerns were with a wider world, not merely with Canada. However, as the 1957 and 1958 elections demonstrated, party images are not changed by mere prose. The handful of Liberal or Conservative voters who might burst from their parties in a rage were not in search of moderation. Veteran CCF voters could only wonder whether their cherished party had sacrificed its teeth. It was not simply the Regina Manifesto which tied the CCF to the Thirties; it was the name, the faces, the utterances, the ever-present righteousness — the entire image of the party.

A year before the 1958 electoral debacle after initiatives from CCF leaders, the Canadian Labour Congress executive had begun to decide its stand. At Winnipeg in April, 1958, the CLC convention endorsed, with barely a dissenting voice, a call for "a fundamental realignment of political forces in Canada in . . . a broadly based people's political movement which embraces the CCF, the labour movement, farmer organizations, professional people and other liberally minded persons interested in basic social reform and reconstruction through our parliamentary system of government." Three months later, a shaken, demoralized CCF almost unanimously accepted the invitation. A joint CLC-CCF committee, soon rechristened the National Committee for the New Party (NCNP), was formed with ten members each from the party and the Congress. In due course, ten more members were appointed, representing the other elements that had been invited to participate. When the farm organizations bluntly announced that they were not interested, the NCNP promptly dreamed up the institution of the "New Party club" which farmers could organize on their own. The device was even more appropriate for the professionals and "liberally-minded." Staff and organizers were appointed and, by the summer of 1961, a newsletter optimistically claimed 8,500 members in three hundred clubs, most of them clustered in Ontario and Quebec but one as far away as London, England. Of the ten "club" members added to the NCNP, four represented agriculture and the rest were middle class professionals.

Three years is a long period of gestation, even for a national political party. It was, a later NDP pamphlet grandiloquently put it, "the longest, largest nation-wide teach-in in our history." In the unions and in the growing New Party clubs there was enthusiasm. Canadian politics were becoming interesting. Economic recession brought rapid disillusionment with the Diefenbaker government. Workers were dismayed by rising unemployment, reaching half a million jobless in the winter of 1960. The urban middle class deplored the government's perennial indecision. Union leaders saw little improvement in the Liberals, particularly after the Smallwood government in Newfoundland crushed a loggers' strike and virtually drove free trade unionism from the province without protest from the federal Liberals.

Only among CCFers was there a growing resistance. "It seems to me," complained a leading member in Nova Scotia, "that the principle we believe in and have fought for these many years is worth a little dignity and not to have to be crawling for help from people that should be with us." In British Columbia, the provincial secretary complained that New Party members were being admitted regardless of their ideology. Alberta CCFers grudgingly acquiesced in the arrangement only after they had founded a "Woodsworth-Irvine Fellowship" to promote true socialism. In Saskatchewan, where the trade union alliance promised trouble among an already dwindling force of rural supporters, the name CCF was to survive as the title for the "Saskatchewan Section" of the new party. Even in Ontario and Quebec, provinces which apparently had most to gain from a formal alliance with labour, persistent suspicions of trade unionism grumbled at the edges of party meetings. Douglas Fisher, one of the few CCF newcomers to Parliament in the 1957 and 1958 elections, predicted that the alliance would deliver few votes and that the unions would sit on their financial resources.

The problem for Fisher and other doubting CCFers was that they really had no alternative. The New Party movement now had a momentum of its own — it had been endorsed almost unanimously. In the absence of any other constructive choice for the CCF, denunciations of corrupt unions or allegations of abandoned principles merely provided hostile editors with welcome ammunition.

Moreover, there was just enough success to hint that the idea might work. In federal by-elections on October 31st, 1960, a boyish Walter Pitman, running as a New Party candidate, captured Peterborough. If a small, conservative Ontario manufacturing town could be captured, the movement was on target. Early in 1961, the Quebec Federation of Labour endorsed the New Party by a margin of 507 to 5. To a movement perennially shut-out of Quebec, the news sounded incredible. On June 28th, T. C. Douglas, the diminutive Saskatchewan premier, finally announced that he would be a candidate for the New Party leadership. The man the organizers had always wanted was available.

CCF conventions had been gatherings of only a few

hundred delegates, meeting annually in hotel ballrooms and halls. For the Founding Convention, trade unionists contributed their organizing expertise. From the decorations to the labour troubadour, improvising folk songs for the occasion, it looked and was professional. The new image was being fashioned. Cautiously NCNP and labour leaders attempted to ensure that it was not an image of trade union domination. The labour members of the NCNP had collected $175,000 for a New Party Founding Fund; most of it helped pay travelling expenses for non-union delegates. Careful predictions about attendance helped ensure that union delegates were outnumbered by CCF and New Party club representatives. Of the 1,801 accredited delegates, 631 came from union locals, 710 from the CCF and 318 from the clubs. The balance included M.Ps, M.L.As, members of CCF councils, labour federations and the NCNP.

For five days, in 1961, 2,084 delegates, alternates, guests and officials filled the sweltering Ottawa Coliseum. Between speeches from prominent well-wishers and procedural battles, issues which had been in flux had finally to be settled. Programme, structure, leadership and even the party's name had been debated in pamphlets, magazine articles and even a book, *Social Purpose for Canada*, published by the University of Toronto Press on the convention eve. A series of New Party seminars had been conducted across Canada as a vehicle for publicity and for genuine influence on the forthcoming meeting.

Inevitably, if the convention was far from a rubber stamp, it predominantly shared the sense of direction which the organizing committee had set. The draft programme, adopted with little amendment, was in sharp contrast with the rhetoric of the Regina Manifesto (though not with what the CCF had actually been saying for the previous fifteen years). Mindful of recent unemployment, it promised jobs, economic planning and the organized mobilization of social capital which would generate orderly growth. It proposed a Canadian Development Fund and a list of measures to regain control over foreign-owned corporations. National programmes of health insurance, portable pensions and sickness benefits, free education "at all levels to all who can benefit from it" and a steeply progressive tax system reflected the socialist commitment to equality. Elsewhere, the new party pledged itself to protect the family farm, fishermen, credit unions and even, to the dismay of veteran socialists, small business. Patriotically, it agreed to encourage Canadian culture, strengthen the CBC and give the country its own flag and anthem.

Only in two areas was there bitter debate. By the 1960s, the Canadian democratic Left was withdrawing from even its reluctant acquiescence in the Cold War and collective security. The well-advertised horrors of nuclear weapons led to demands for unilateral disarmament, first in Britain, and later, in the United States and Canada. Nuclear disarmament buttons proliferated at the convention, forming one of the few common bonds between many New Party club members and the CCF left wing. The draft programme called for Canada to abandon NORAD but to stay in NATO. It was, frankly, a compromise and it was soon subjected to a bitter, emotional attack from the floor. As they had done in so many CCF conventions, Coldwell, Douglas and Lewis came to the microphones to hammer back the unilateralists. Whatever they may privately have felt, the successors of Woodsworth would not allow the new party to go back to his isolationist pacifism.

They showed less caution in a new area. In 1960, it seemed that the ice had broken in Quebec and, by the summer of 1961, the Quiet Revolution had even reached the New Party convention. The Quebec delegation, 167 strong, was almost as large as British Columbia's. The QFL resolution had meant something. If they were to stay, there was a price, already spelled out in an article in *Social Purpose for Canada* by a prominent law professor named Pierre Elliott Trudeau. If the new party wanted support in Quebec, it would have to be genuinely federalist and responsive to the cultural demands of French Canada. Accordingly, the draft programme had promised "equal recognition and respect" for the two national languages and cultures and a new doctrine of "co-operative federalism."

For the Quebec delegates, that was not enough. By the third day of the convention, they had persuaded the gathering to abandon the word "national" and substitute "federal" wherever it had appeared. On the fourth day, they enforced the logic of this demand by insisting that the convention agree that Canada had been created by the association of two nations. Whatever the historical nonsense of this claim, as pointed out by the CLC's research director, Dr. Eugene Forsey, the delegates overwhelmingly agreed.

Only two issues remained: the leadership and the name. Douglas's only challenger was the CCF's sole Saskatchewan M.P., Hazen Argue. His campaign reflected ill-feeling within the CCF's caucus about the New Party development and the snub Argue himself had felt when he had had to persuade the CCF's last national convention to elect him as leader. By no means a left-winger, Argue became the spokesman for those at the convention who wanted to protest, as Gad Horowitz has suggested, "against the liberalization of the party's image, against 'labour domination' and, in a sense, against the new party idea itself." The vote — 1,391 to 380 — was a predictable victory for the Saskatchewan premier and an indication of the strength of the unreconciled element in the convention.

The overheated ecstasy of the NDP's founding convention in 1961 persuaded many delegates that victory would come early and easily.

The liveliest pre-convention debate had centred on the choice of a title. Some diehards had pleaded for retention of the CCF initials; others campaigned for "Social Democratic Party" and many came to like "New Party," the almost accidental name under which the three year campaign had been waged. It was short, non-committal, accurate (at least for the time being) and impossible to abbreviate into barbarous-sounding initials. Their judgement did not prevail. In the only major grassroots uprising of the convention, a handful of Ontario CCFers pushed, lobbied and manipulated their way past procedural roadblocks and won acceptance for their favourite — "New Democratic Party". It was adopted by 784 votes to 743.

By the afternoon of August 4th, weary delegates could go home, their ears ringing with appeals to work their hearts out for what they had created. Journalists filed final copy while editorial writers consulted the entrails and decided that something significant had happened. "Nobody in his right senses," warned the Montreal *Star*, "should end this week without recognizing that a new and powerful voice has been developed in the left wing of Canadian politics." Prime Minister Diefenbaker had already warned that the next election would be fought on the issue of "socialism versus free enterprise." In October, the Canadian Chambers of Commerce launched "Operation Freedom," a crude campaign, reminiscent of the Forties, directed at service clubs and school children. It would, promoters hoped, "rouse Canadians from apathy and indifference into action against the growing threats of socialism and communism."

The Founding Convention had been a success. For once, the Canadian Left had appeared in the major leagues — confident, strong, efficient, yet retaining the idealism and the basic democracy which had given it distinction. Yet, in retrospect, it had diverted attention from some basic problems; it had not resolved them. And, for many, the convention had been the end, not the beginning of their efforts. Throughout, Claude Jodoin, the president of the Canadian Labour Congress, had emphasized that the responsibility of the Congress was to bring the party to birth. Thereafter, its relations would be like those of the British Trades Union Congress and the Labour Party — sympathetic independence. It was up to individual local unions to affiliate to the party as they did to the Congress. Simultaneously, both the National Committee for the New Party and the New Party clubs dissolved. They had completed their work; the party was in existence; constitutionally they were irrelevant and even harmful to its progress.

In practice, these decisions left the party floundering for the critical first six months of its existence. The tiny CCF and New Party staffs, harried to exhaustion by convention preparations, had made no plans for the future. The money collected for the Founding Fund was gone and only a fluttering of CCF membership revenue could keep the federal organization alive. After the convention, the party leadership scattered. Douglas rushed back to Saskatchewan and the increasingly bitter battle to introduce North America's first government health insurance scheme. Michael Oliver, the new president, was in Montreal; David Lewis, the chief architect of the party, was in Toronto and Stanley Knowles was in Winnipeg, struggling to win back his seat. Only Argue and a small, slightly mutinous caucus remained in Ottawa. In Ontario, the biggest challenge for the new party, energies were reserved for a provincial founding convention at Niagara Falls on October 7th to 9th. After Ottawa, the meeting was an inevitable anticlimax.

Dissolution of the New Party clubs left hundreds of members to find their way into NDP constituency associations. Many never made the journey. Those who did too often found organizations dominated by veteran CCFers who sometimes had little patience with the newcomers. In rural areas and in Quebec, where the CCF had barely existed, the club members could presumably create their own riding associations but little in their New Party indoctrination had prepared them for that challenge. For many in the New Party movement, the attraction had been the notion of a shapeless party which they could mould to their own taste. Once the clay had set and they found themselves in a more moderate reincarnation of the CCF, they left. The bulk of those New Party people who remained active in the NDP would probably have been recruited by a revived and more relevant CCF.

In the pre-convention period, it was the trade unions that had been euphoric; the CCFers who had appeared reluctant. In the aftermath, the roles were reversed. Political involvement gave business leaders and editorial writers a fresh stick to attack the unions. Liberal, Conservative and Social Credit politicians, threatened by the new development, showed their teeth. If unions get into politics, warned Ontario's Premier Leslie Frost, they must expect to be treated politically. The Canadian Construction Association urged the federal government to consider whether the union right to check-off of dues might be cancelled since the money was to be used for a political party. In Victoria, Premier W. A. C. Bennett pushed Bill 42 into law, banning the use of union dues for any political party and abolishing check-off for any union which refused to conform. Challenged in the courts, the new law was solemnly upheld, the judges insisting that political contributions were purely an individual matter. Perhaps oddly, the courts did not extend this principle to contributions from business corporations. Meanwhile, Bennett could enjoy the consequences of his blow to the prospects of his most powerful opponents.

Bill 42 was only one of a number of examples of legislation which seemed to cut into trade union rights in the early Sixties. Having launched into politics to defend its interests, organized labour suddenly found itself more vulnerable than ever. Internally, too, there were problems. Progress toward a merger of the CLC with the Quebec-based Catholic unions was impeded not only by reviving French Canadian nationalism but also by the Liberal links of Jean Marchand and many of the leaders of the newly re-structured Confederation of National Trade Unions (CNTU). Within international unions, new strains also developed. The Steelworkers in Canada ignored opposition from their American president, David Macdonald, and affiliated; in the United Autoworkers, Walter Reuther, a former socialist, was evidently more sympathetic to the NDP than his Canadian director, George Burt, a one-time Liberal candidate. In the business-minded construction unions, there was little inclination to divert funds and energies to quixotic political ventures and some unions, notably the Teamsters and the Seafarers' International Union, had long since developed comfortable, if discreet, links with the Liberals.

Another problem affected both the labour movement and the party — inter-union conflict. To the exasperation of NDP leaders, Tim Buck, the venerable Communist Party leader, claimed that his followers would be joining the NDP and taking it over. That was unlikely. The inevitable election-time embrace from the far left still upset a few unsophisticated voters, particularly in eastern Canada but, if anything, the NDP suffered more from the attentions of youthful Trotskyites with their indefatigable conspiracies. The real Communist problem for the NDP lay in their control of a number of important unions — notably the big UAW locals in St. Catherines and Windsor, the United

Electrical Workers, with strength in Hamilton, Toronto and Peterborough, and the Mine, Mill and Smelter Workers strongholds in Sudbury, Trail and Kitimat. In each of these centres, NDP organizing was frustrated by influential Communist leaders, complicated by raids from non-Communist unions and, in some cases, utterly stopped.

Sudbury, a tough, working class city, was an example. It boasted the largest union local in North America, Local 598 of Mine-Mill — 17,000 members and over a million dollars in assets. To an outsider, the situation could only be described as bewildering. Since 1958, Local 598 had been in a state of revolt against the Mine-Mill leadership but, according to the CLC, if it wished to rejoin the main body of Canadian labour, it would have to join the Steelworkers. The local's rebel president, Don Gillis, refused. To add complications, the Steelworkers launched successful raids on Mine-Mill locals in Port Colborne, Ontario and Thompson, Manitoba, Gillis ran for the Tories in 1962 and Mine-Mill recaptured the allegiance of Local 598, all in quick succession. As long as Sudbury was preoccupied with that battle, prospects for the NDP were dim. Overall, the party's loyalty was unequivocally with its Steelworker allies; locally, solid party activists could be found on both sides of the battle. Not until 1966, when a negotiated settlement ended the struggle, could the NDP make progress.

It took time for New Democrats to understand the complex problems of its new ally. Meanwhile, the charge of labour domination supplanted the older bogeys of socialism as a favourite weapon for opponents. In the autum of 1961, nervous NDPers summoned Claude Jodoin to calm local fears and antipathies in Western Canada. Bluff good will and a few speeches could not overcome a lifetime exposure to anti-union prejudice. With their usual excessive faith in human reason, the NDP leadership had designed a constitutional structure which refuted any logical charge of trade union tyranny and assumed that that would suffice. Indeed, it was the union leaders themselves who seemed most upset by the criticism. Whatever their own views, they recognized that most Canadians, from the judges deciding on Bill 42 to many devout socialists, shared the liberal myth that politics was a matter of purely private concern in which formally constituted economic organizations were somehow illegitimate.

Few NDP leaders could have anticipated what seemed at the time almost an act of deliberate treachery. On January 18th, 1962, Parliament began what would obviously be its pre-election session. Precisely a month later, Hazen Argue summoned the press and announced that he had quit the NDP. It was a free country and presumably he could support any party he liked. However, the Founding Convention had heard him pledge: "No matter what my role is in the years ahead, I shall speak for you, I shall work for you, I shall never let you down." Now, he insisted, his party had been captured by a clique of trade unionists. On the 21st, he repeated his charges in Parliament: "It would be most dangerous to the democratic process to have a party gain power, the effective control of which resided in a handful of labour leaders outside the House of Commons." In defecting to the Liberals, Argue had given respectability to what was becoming the most potent argument its opponents could offer against the NDP. Immediately, Argue's former colleagues picked H. W. Herridge as their parliamentary leader. An elderly and somewhat dogmatic socialist, he, at least, could be counted upon never to return to the party he had abandoned as a young man.

III. Setbacks

A political movement may survive for a time on its own dreams and self-approval. A political party must stand the test of competition. The New Democratic Party had been deliberately designed for that test but not for the non-stop electioneering of the mid-Sixties. There were four federal elections, interspersed by eight crucial provincial elections in the six years from 1962 to 1968.

In all but thirty or forty of approximately 265 federal constituencies, the CCF candidate had inevitably been a sacrificial lamb. Only the glow of spreading truth could compensate for the bruising humiliation of rejection. Underpinning the New Party movement had been the faith that, somehow, the Canadian Left could be made appealing to a host of people. At last the dreamed-of polarization would take place, leaving presumably the Liberals as a dwindling and irrelevant third party.

Illusions of early breakthrough had to ignore some discouraging evidence. The post-convention Gallup Poll indicated that only twelve per cent of the voters had rallied to the new party. Earlier that year, the Saskatchewan CCF had lost Turtleford to the Liberals and, after November 7th, when Douglas handed over his office to his Minister of Education, Woodrow Lloyd, attention shifted to the fate of his former riding of Weyburn. On the night of December 13th came the shocking news: its voters had also favoured the Liberals. In Ontario, there was a further test on January 18th, 1962, when five provincial by-elections took place. Only in Beaches, a Toronto constituency that had last voted CCF in 1948, the NDP seemed to have a chance. It ran third — though only 408 votes behind the Conservative winner.

By-elections, as those who lose them know, prove nothing. For the new party, the crucial test began on April 18th when John Diefenbaker dissolved Parliament. The NDP could hardly claim to be caught unawares. It had spent three years in an unprecedented dialogue with Canadians; the complacency of the Fifties had long since dissolved. For potential working class supporters, the NDP could offer a commitment to full employment and a national medicare plan; to middle class radicals, it promised a fervent opposition to the acquisition of nuclear weapons.

However, as Murray Beck observed, "policies and platforms had little to do with the electoral decisions of 1962." For voters then and for the next four years, the dominant issue seemed to be the contrasting personalities of John Diefenbaker and his Liberal opponent, Lester Pearson. In virtuoso performances which seemed to improve with time and opposition, Diefenbaker flayed the "socialist experimenters" and ivory tower dreamers who directed the Liberal Party (and presumably the NDP). He scourged bankers and advertising agencies too, rounding darkly on "sinister interests" which allegedly threatened both him and the common people. It was marvellous theatre and it hit home, for example, with those western farmers who had once seen the CCF as their guardian against "the interests." Diefenbaker, too, offered no troubling new ideas, no dangerous alliance with the urban workers. As for the cities, they responded better to a Liberal promise of prosperity and a return to that managerial efficiency Canadians had so peevishly cast off in 1957.

The NDP might willingly match the cocky, aggressive personality of its leader against his two rivals but image contests are extravagantly expensive. The CCF had financed its central campaign largely from grudging contributions from the stronger provincial sections; the NDP federal office had access to the major national union headquarters, leaving the provinces and constituency associations to approach individual members and affiliated local unions. As a result, its net expenditure in 1962, $116,332, was almost six times as large as the sum available to the CCF in 1958. Unfortunately, even this was meagre in what became the most expensive election campaign Canada had yet experienced. After paying for the leader's tour, for a supply of pamphlets and posters, and for organizers and deposits in the weaker provinces, only $50,000 remained to buy advertising space for the party's messages.

Even the leader's tour had to be done on the cheap. While Pearson and Diefenbaker traversed the country in chartered aircraft, surrounded by staff and reporters, Douglas and a couple of aides waited at airports for commercial flights or drove with local supporters, most of whom seemed to assume that the presence of a party leader gave immunity to speed limits and even minimal standards of safe driving. Douglas was the party's greatest asset. Diefenbaker's only equal as platform speaker, he combined homey wit with a vibrant passion, capable of bringing audiences roaring to their feet. Under a folksy geniality which could disarm doubtful supporters and antagonistic reporters, there a tough, demanding realism. A visionary could not have run Saskatchewan with brilliant success for almost eighteen years. However, there was a special worry that gnawed at Douglas as he jolted across Canada that spring. His own campaign to win Regina from the Conservatives was not going well.

Like almost everything else, that particular worry had to be left to Douglas's provincial section. Like the CCF, the NDP decentralized its campaign, leaving the critical tasks of finding candidates, organizing constituencies and distributing financial resources to each provincial NDP. Overall victory depended very largely on local efficiency, energy and experience. Obviously, Saskatchewan and British Columbia had to be equal to the task. Ontario, Manitoba, Alberta and Nova Scotia were all organizationally weaker but they could manage. Apart from Ontario, which missed four of its eighty-five seats, all of them fielded full slates of candidates. In the remaining provinces, a few organizers and the promise of deposit money helped provoke token campaigns in fifteen of the twenty-one seats in New Brunswick, Newfoundland and Prince Edward Island.

Quebec was more difficult. Despite its impressive victory at the Founding Convention, the Quebec delegaton had not returned to launch its own section of the NDP. Instead, it simply resumed its constitutional debate, discovering fresh demands and fresh discontents as its leaders struggled to remain on the leading edge of the growing nationalist and radical movement in French Canada. Despite formal support from the Quebec Federation of Labour, only a handful of local unions sought affiliation, most of them at the urging of their national offices. For all the exciting promise of August, 1961, Quebec was apparently still a desert for the new party. In a few English-speaking constituencies on the island of Montreal, NDP associations launched vigorous but lonely campaigns; elsewhere, there was little action. Douglas did his best. On May 20th, he descended on Quebec City, paid a ritual visit to Cardinal Roy and loyally endorsed co-operative federalism and the two-nation version of Canada. Meanwhile, a few devoted organizers scoured the province, searching for standard-bearers. By nomination day, they had found forty candidates for the province's seventy-five seats – compared to the CCF's twenty-nine in 1958.

Decentralized structure and leadership hiatus after the Founding Convention meant that there was little campaign strategy. Almost the only tactical decision, to be repeated in the two ensuing federal elections, was to reserve the final weeks for major rallies, beginning in Halifax and ending in Vancouver. Though the pundits insisted that television had ended the era of mass political meetings, party leaders believed that rallies were virtually the only way of penetrating the media blackout which would descend on the party during the final fortnight of the campaign. Moreover, organizing the rallies involved a special expertise which the labour movement could contribute.

Almost to the disbelief of the organizers, the strategy seemed to work. In Montreal, newspapers recorded that 1,500 cars had formed a Douglas cavalcade and thousands of supporters had cheered as he denounced nuclear weapons. On the following day, 6,000 people packed Toronto's O'Keefe Centre and hundreds milled outside as Douglas turned his wit on Tory millionaires. On June 13th, there were 9,500 people to hear him in Vancouver. As the campaign ended, New Democrats might once again believe that Canada was moving in their direction.

It was not. On June 18th, 1,036,853 Canadians marked ballots for NDP candidates but they represented only 13.5 per cent of the electorate – approximately the share the CCF had collected in 1949. The electoral system delivered nineteen seats to the party – one on Cape Breton Island, three in Toronto, three in northern Ontario, two in Winnipeg's north end and ten in British Columbia. In Saskatchewan, the party vote tumbled lower than in any election since 1935 and, as a supreme humiliation, Regina electors decisively rejected Tommy Douglas.

Save for a few decorous regrets about Douglas's defeat, the editorial writers were jubilant. The New Party experiment had failed. The NDP had lost the farmer's support without collecting the workers. A Gallup survey after the election reported that voters from trade union homes had split twenty-three percent for the NDP, twenty-five per cent for the Conservatives and an overwhelming thirty-eight per cent for the Liberals. On the other hand, party officials, scratching hard for a silver lining, found a few traces. Even if editors had not noticed, party members knew very well that farm support had been slipping for some years — long before the creation of the NDP or Argue's defection. If trade unionists had not switched massively to support their new party, it was also true that the CCF had never won as many as six federal seats in Ontario or ten in British Columbia.

If the 1962 election had settled anything, the NDP would probably have had the leisure for the potentially dangerous pastime of self-criticism. Instead, Canadians found that they had elected a minority government — only the fourth in their history. As well, a totally new phenomenon had appeared, twenty-six Créditistes from Quebec under the fiery Réal Caouette. With four conventional Social Creditors, they formed the third largest group in Parliament, reducing the NDP to a humiliating fourth position. There was a fresh excitement in politics when governments might be ejected for their sins, and the country began to adjust to a situation which would continue until June 25th, 1968.

Thanks to the election night generosity of Erhart

Regier, a successful British Columbia candidate, Douglas was given a vacancy to return to Parliament as M.P. for Burnaby-Coquitlam. By then, it was apparent that another general election would not be long postponed. The bubbling fiscal problems which had plagued the Conservatives during the 1962 campaign continued and politicians who had boasted of booming prosperity had to announce a sudden austerity in public spending and re-acquaint themselves with the mysteries of balances of payments. More serious for a government already condemned for apparent indecision was the bewildering confusion about whether or not Canada was formally committed to purchasing nuclear warheads for a new family of military weapons. Among political insiders, faith in the credibility of the government and its prime minister dwindled rapidly and the issue was highlighted after Mr. Pearson, freshly back from a trip to Washington, unilaterally reversed his party's stand and informed a Scarborough audience that a Liberal government was duty-bound to honour Canada's commitment to accept the deadly warheads. In Ottawa, exasperated Tory ministers began to hand in their resignations. The *Globe and Mail* reported a plot in the business community to dump Diefenbaker as Conservative leader. After defeat on a crucial supply motion on February 5th, the Prime Minister dissolved the House of Commons and led his divided and demoralized party out to meet the people he always claimed to understand.

The election result seemed to be a foregone conclusion. In October, 1962, the Liberals could claim forty-seven percent support in the Gallup poll and, if their strength had slipped a little since, it was still enough for a comfortable margin of victory. Almost every major Conservative newspaper in the country deserted to the Liberals and, to judge from their cacophonous outrage, it was easy to believe that the country would follow suit. Instead, the raging Diefenbaker offered an even finer one-man performance than the year before. If possible, as the sworn enemy of nuclear arms, Yankee imperialists and the eastern elite, he was even more effective in appealing to alienated CCF voters, than to traditional Conservatives. The speeches in which he had denounced opponents as soft on Communism and promised to roll back the Iron Curtain were forgotten now that the Prime Minister and his prairie lieutenant, Alvin Hamilton, were standing on guard against the Americans and their Liberal allies. However extraordinary such a posture might seem to close observers of politics, a great many ordinary voters found in Diefenbaker an effective evocation of their own frustrations and indignation. On the other hand, the Liberals appealed more effectively than ever to those who wanted to end the Diefenbaker political farce and who recalled the day when their country had apparently been prosperous at home and respected abroad.

For the NDP, caught between the smooth, self-confident Liberals and the embattled prairie populist, it was hard to find room. In 1962, the party had at least been a novelty; now it felt blanked out by the news media, apparently convinced that third parties were merely a nuisance. Almost instinctively reverting to a typical CCF response, the NDP could only offer the purity of its principles. On the nuclear issue, both the Liberals and the Conservatives had switched sides: the NDP had remained steadfastly and eloquently opposed. For many, nuclear disarmament had become a moral crusade — an affirmation of life against the cruelly anonymous forces of destruction — and, if it did no more, the issue persuaded candidates to stand in ridings where they now knew they had no chance while others opened their cheque books or agreed to knock on doors during bitter late-winter weather.

Financially, the election was a disaster for the party. Most provincial sections were still collecting membership dues and unions, which had spent prodigally by their own standards in 1962, had little left to spare. The NDP's central campaign had barely $70,000 to spend and even a meagre national advertising campaign was scrapped. There were a few compensating blessings. The earlier campaign had trained a small army of volunteers and the nine-month interval was not long enough to render the contact lists obsolete. With as much encouragement as the tiny federal office staff in Ottawa could provide, most of the provincial sections wearily got to work.

In one province, the nuclear issue seemed especially promising. In Quebec, the Conservatives were no longer an alternative. Intellectuals and labour leaders who could stomach neither the pro-nuclear Liberals nor the right-wing contortions of Réal Caouette, took a second look at the NDP. On February 25th, Gérard Picard, a diminutive labour leader who had transformed the Catholic syndicates into militant fighting organizations, became the NDP's Quebec leader. A number of Quebec intellectuals, among them Pierre Elliott Trudeau, editor of *Cité Libre*, endorsed NDP candidates. In *Le Devoir,* Jean Pellerin insisted that the election was a battle between "la grande bourgeoisie" and the ordinary people. By the end of the campaign, the NDP boasted a total of sixty candidates in the province. It had never seemed stronger.

More than ever, Tommy Douglas was his party's chief campaign weapon. Once again, he and a couple of advisers criss-crossed the country in the economy class cabin of airliners, occasionally being marooned by winter snow or fog. Though he protested that the issue of the election was not anti-Americanism, he obviously felt comfortable as he tied together the arms issue, the Liberals and the power of American-controlled businesses in Canada. If Liberals

Tommy Douglas at Maple Leaf Gardens, Toronto. During the first three general election campaigns, NDP strategy called for mass rallies in major cities, largely to compel the news media to pay attention to the new party.

wanted to refute charges of dependence on American corporate contributions, he told a Saskatoon audience on March 10th, let them open their books. With an apparent opportunity for gains in Quebec, Douglas offered a "council of confederation," with equal French and English-speaking membership, as a continuing forum for bicultural issues. A month later, he assured a Montreal audience that the NDP supported a tax-sharing formula which would give the provinces fifty per cent of direct tax receipts. Neither notion, incidentally, could be found in the party's programme.

Once again, the NDP campaign wound up with a nation-wide series of rallies. In Toronto, the local organization strained to top the previous year's O'Keefe Centre meeting by hiring the gigantic Maple Leaf Gardens and packing it with a precisely counted 15,842 people. Others were turned away. Not even a unanimously hostile local press could ignore that accomplishment but it responded with a drumfire emphasis on the need for stable government which, in the view of party organizers, began chopping into the NDP vote a week before election day. In most constituencies, there was little of the exhilaration of the previous year; the NDP was now an embattled minority and the members knew it.

So did the voters. On April 8th, the party won 1,037,857 of them, almost precisely the vote of the year before, but almost everywhere the NDP lost support, from a fraction of a point in British Columbia to a dismaying four per cent in Saskatchewan. The outpost in Cape Breton fell. So did Vancouver Burrard and the former CCF stronghold of York South, where David Lewis was abandoned by his more prosperous Forest Hill constituents. Across the country, the only consolations were a new seat in Hamilton and a tiny surge of support in Quebec — less than three per cent. If the "grande bourgeoisie" and the people had differed, the people had gone off with the Créditistes.

In fact no party could draw much pleasure from the 1963 election. If the Liberals had won, something in Mr. Pearson or his campaign helped the party to tumble a full six per cent in Gallup standing by election day. In Quebec the Liberals had not received a smaller share of the votes since 1882 and, across the prairies, they had elected a bare three members. If the Conservatives had been saved from disaster, it was because of the efforts of the man the party's eastern leaders now despised. Even Social Credit had lost six seats and tensions among the survivors were beginning to tear the group apart. Perhaps the NDP, like the CCF before it, would accustom itself to the small mercy of merely surviving.

Indeed, there was something of the mood of a CCF revival when the party gathered in Regina in August for its second national convention. The air was thick with memories of the famous Manifesto of thirty years earlier. It was this nostalgia, as much as the baking heat, which led Walter Young, a former New Party member of the NCNP, to warn that the city was a dangerous place for the Left in the summer time. If the Ottawa convention had been a triumph for the revisionists, it was now the turn of the fundamentalists. Though T. C. Douglas successfully inter-cepted an assault on NATO, other convention statements on planning, unemployment, native people and pensions hinted at a withdrawal from that "mere liberalism" which both left and right-wing opponents of the NDP had condemned in 1961. For two years, it had rankled with the fundamentalists that the word "socialist" had studi-ously been avoided in every official utterance of the party. Now they could take comfort from a statement of "Principles and Objectives" drafted by Charles Taylor, a McGill professor who was becoming the ranking intellectual of the party, and Colin Cameron, a robustly left-wing M.P. from Nanaimo. Little of the prose could have offended anyone to the left of the Chambers of Commerce but cautiously ensconced in the second sentence was the assurance that NDP principles were "the principles of democratic socialism applied to our time and situation."

If Canadians expected something new or different from the Regina meeting, they waited in vain. The chief excitement arose from some unfinished election business. Though only a corporal's guard of Quebeckers had travelled west to remind NDPers of their "breakthrough" in Quebec, Taylor and the party president, Michael Oliver, also of McGill, made sure that the Quebec issue did not lie dormant. On the July 1st week-end, a "conférence d'orientation" in Montreal, designed to plan a Quebec NDP, had split into tiny moderate and nationalist wings. If something was to be salvaged, Taylor and Oliver had to be able to bring back even more unequivocal commitments by the NDP to the "equal status of the French Canadian nation and the English Canadian nation" and a promise that the party would support Quebec's withdrawal from federal programmes without financial loss. Despite a little grumbling from western delegates, the convention overwhelmingly agreed to accept both positions and an equally firm stand in favour of bilingualism and biculturalism. There was a narrower margin of support for a further demand that the party allow its provincial organizations vastly greater programmatic and constitutional independence but again Taylor and Oliver prevailed.

Indeed, there was not much the NDP could have done about it. The nationalist group, led by the former Quebec CCF leader, Michel Chartrand, met in Quebec on November 16th-17th to proclaim a new Parti Socialiste du Québec. Denouncing even a modified federal system as intolerable for Quebec, the PSQ was prepared to concede that ten virtually sovereign states could associate in a Confederation. It also agreed to confine itself to the provincial sphere, vacating the federal field to the NDP. In fact, after the brief flurry of its creation, the PSQ soon vanished.

The NDP could be more tolerant than the CCF of extended provincial rights not only because of its desperate desire to make headway in Quebec but because it had learned in Saskatchewan that a province could be a satisfying base for socialist policies. It could also afford to be philosophical about federal election defeats because party strategists were convinced that the slower but more certain route to major party status was on the basis of provincial victories. That was the foundation for Laurier's victory in 1896 and Borden's in 1911, and the NDP could follow suit. The real short-range targets for the NDP were victories in British Columbia, Ontario and, in a slightly longer term, Manitoba.

The potential of provincial power had been vividly illustrated in the previous two years in Saskatchewan as the CCF had fought doctors, the press and their Liberal opponents to institute its medicare scheme. For the medical profession across North America, it had been the crucial test struggle against "socialized medicine" and never before had the CCF faced such a sustained onslaught. When the government rejected "compromises" which would have gutted the basic purposes of the scheme, it was denounced as tyrannical. A rising hysteria pervaded the province, deliberately fostered by the doctors and their political allies until, on July 1st, 1962, virtually all of Saskatchewan's physicians closed their offices. Replacement doctors, summoned from Britain, the United States and the rest of Canada, helped provide emergency services and a chorus of opprobrium from the rest of Canada helped bring the medical profession to a more flexible mood. Within a month, a settlement had been reached and, within a year, medicare was firmly established. The achievement undoubtedly gave pride and confidence to New Democrats across Canada but, together with by-election defeats and two disastrous federal campaigns, it debilitated the Saskatchewan party and solidified its opponents.

In Saskatchewan, the CCF had demonstrated since 1944 that it could create prosperity, begin to develop an industrial base, purify a notably corrupt political system and keep its promises — copybook virtues which so far not a single other province had chosen to adopt. In November of 1962, Manitoba's Premier Duff Roblin dissolved his legislature and presented the NDP with its first provincial election opportunity. When the polls closed on December 19th, not only was Roblin securely back in office but the NDP had lost two of the CCF's ten seats and watched its share of the vote plummet from twenty-two to fifteen per cent of the total. Most painful of all, both Liberals and Conservatives had made headway in the traditional social-ist and labour stronghold of North Winnipeg.

In the autumn of 1963, it was the turn of Ontario and British Columbia. Ontario's pre-election session saw its new premier, John Robarts, introduce an armload of legislation which just managed to undercut some of the NDP's chief election planks without actually completing them — partial medicare, partial portable pensions, partial redistribution. It was a further example of that busy but unadventurous reformism which Ontario premiers since Oliver Mowat have perfected. When Robarts called his election on August 16th, most Ontarians were enjoying the summer too much to notice and it remained as dull a campaign as the premier could manage. Liberal attempts to raise scandals fell on cotton wool. New Democrats, like most people in the province, were far more oriented to Ottawa than Toronto in their political interests and their leader, Donald MacDonald, had had to struggle desperately to switch their attention to the provincial contest. Almost penniless after the two previous federal elections, the party had to send its leader to rove the province in his own car, offering lifts to any reporter who cared to come along. An organization which had been badly stretched to cover eighty-five federal ridings had to be spread over 108 provincial constituencies and it buckled under the strain.

When the polls closed on September 25th, not even the party faithful could expect a triumph. In the final weeks of the campaign, even normally Liberal newspapers had repaid the favour of the previous April by beating their drums for the Conservatives and, while this embarrassed the official opposition more than the NDP, it presaged a Tory sweep. In the circumstances, with John Robarts's candidates collecting forty-eight per cent of the vote, perhaps the party was lucky to survive. The NDP dropped a percentage point in popular support and collected seven seats in an enlarged house. A weak incumbent lost what should have been a union stronghold in Oshawa but there was some compensation in an unexpected victory at Fort William, a blessing MacDonald greeted with all his renowned ability to discover triumph in adversity.

As Ontario voters went to the polls, British Columbians were in the final stages of their own campaign. Premier Bennett had called the election without even warning some of his colleagues. His haste was probably less motivated by NDP strength than by the advent of E. Davie Fulton, a former federal cabinet minister, as the province's Conservative leader. When Fulton failed even to collect a full slate of candidates, it was soon clear that the election would be fought as the traditional right-left confrontation. However, not only was the British Columbia party relatively well-financed and organized, it was newly committed to a New Party style of moderation. As the NDP unveiled detailed plans for a premium-free Medicare plan as well as its other planks, the emphasis was clearly on constructive debate rather than walloping the enemies of the common people. Even the conservative Vancouver *Province* felt constrained to congratulate the provincial NDP leader, Robert Strachan for "his frankness, dignity and statesmanlike approach to provincial problems." By election night, NDP candidates were so elated that they were discussing cabinet portfolios. The Conservatives had flopped, the Liberals were "me too" with all parties and the Social Credit campaign — "the construction gang versus the wrecking gang" was merely the same old stuff that had given Bennett victory in previous elections.

And on September 30th, it worked again. As Social Credit piled up a fresh majority, the NDP found that it had won two new seats but lost four incumbent MLAs. More painful, its popular vote had slipped a full five percentage points and, worst of all, the losses had been in the party's lower mainland working class fortresses.

The provincial setbacks were even more discouraging to the NDP than limited progress in two federal elections. In Saskatchewan, the Canadian democratic Left had shown that it could govern imaginatively and well. Some of the NDP's most popular programmes, including Medicare and government-run auto insurance, were provincial rather than federal and, for trade unionists, it was provincial even more than federal labour legislation which needed overhaul. Yet the NDP had so far failed even to match the CCF as a vote-getter. In all three provinces, trade union areas had actually defected from 'their' party. Perhaps it was time to abandon the entire New Party experiment.

At the British Columbia convention, barely six weeks after the electoral debacle, a Trotskyite-inspired "Socialist

Caucus" briefly took over the convention and persuaded delegates to endorse a sweeping programme of nationalization and government control. When discussion turned to the recent election, party leaders were roundly condemned for their attempt to remould the party and Strachan was even denounced for the dark suit he had worn for his campaign portrait. Nonetheless, he and the moderates on the executive were easily re-elected. In Ontario, revisionism moved in the other direction. There were complaints that the 1963 federal convention had turned its back on the "liberally-minded." Val Scott, a twice defeated federal candidate who had earlier appealed for greater commitment from party leaders, delivered a letter to the Toronto newspapers calling for an "Operation Candour" to discover what had gone wrong. Farmers, he insisted, were irredeemably conservative, French Canada was hopeless and the unions had brought neither votes nor money. On December 21st, a respected Toronto journalist, Mark Gayn, revealed, in expose fashion, that prominent NDPers and Liberals had met secretly to search out common ground. The report, which grossly exaggerated the importance and influence of the handful of individuals involved from the NDP side, nonetheless sent shivers of rage running through the party faithful and provoked resounding denials from both T. C. Douglas and the Ontario leader, Donald MacDonald.

Collaboration was harder to deny in the development of EPIC — "Exchange for Political Ideas in Canada" — a creation of the Woodsworth Foundation, an Ontario-based educational trust with links to the NDP. The latest brainchild of R. D. Sparham, the former director of New Party clubs, the organization featured intellectual collaboration between liberals and socialists, among them Douglas Fisher, the widely known maverick NDP member from Port Arthur and Pauline Jewett, a political scientist and

then a Liberal M.P. Financial backing from the Woodsworth Foundation suddenly vanished, for the highly
embarrassing reason that its president had embezzled its
funds, but EPIC staggered on to a founding convention in
Toronto on May 23-24th, 1964. With no regret from NDP
leaders, it then sank without trace.

The NDP might stagger, stumble and even split in the
rest of Canada — the Left had done so in the CCF era — but
always there was Saskatchewan — powerful, efficient,
perhaps a little smug but invariably generous and perennially willing to help beyond its own borders. In June of
1964, it was time for another of those quadrennial
elections in which Tommy Douglas had proved his mastery
over all comers. In 1963, the province had experienced a
boom and 1964 promised to be even better. Medicare was
working so well that, save for a few embittered doctors,
it was barely an issue. Certain as any politicians ever can be
of success, Woodrow Lloyd and his colleagues decided to
call the election a few months early. Moreover, to avoid
worrying voters who might well be satiated with political
turmoil, there were no fresh programmes of reform.

If the CCF planned a relaxed, quiet campaign, so too
did Ross Thatcher, the former CCF M.P. who led the
Liberals. For once, he and his colleagues abandoned their
slam-banging anti-socialist style, retired their amateur
spellbinders, hired professional entertainers and solemnly
took their advice from a shrewd Eastern advertising
agency. During the month-long campaign, Saskatchewan
discovered a new Thatcher, moderate, calm and occasionally swinging to the left of the government with promises
of reduced Medicare premiums and free school books. The
CCF was at first bewildered, and then amused, particularly
when Thatcher's overtures for an anti-CCF coalition were
rejected by the Conservatives. It was only a couple of
weeks before election day that the CCF's slightly parched

grassroots began to give frantic warnings. CCF canvassers were being shouldered aside on the doorsteps by a new, efficient Liberal machine. The young, unmindful of tedious depression recollections, were swinging behind the Liberals. In a few areas, government concessions to the separate schools had enraged Protestants without converting the normally Liberal Catholics. Still, it seemed impossible that the CCF could lose more than a few rural seats. Who would spit on prosperity?

On April 22nd, Saskatchewan voters did just that. Though the CCF lost less than a percentage point in its popular vote (the big fall had been in 1960), it could win only twenty-five of the fifty-nine seats in the Legislature. Except for a lone Conservative, the Liberals had the rest. After a couple of weeks' delay to see if recounts in a large number of narrowly lost seats might save him, Woodrow Lloyd resigned. The NDP was at its nadir.

IV. Elections

Riverdale was a small, downtown Toronto constituency, split between the working class East End and the slums of Cabbagetown. Twice in the Forties, it had elected a CCFer to the provincial legislature but it had become safely Conservative, the kind of seat cabinet ministers love. Federally, it had been home for George Hees; provincially, it elected Robert Macaulay, easily the ablest Ontario Tory. When Macaulay, disgusted with the triumph of lesser men, resigned in 1963, the succession was hardly in doubt. At worst, it would go to Charles Templeton, a handsome charismatic figure who had gone through a succession of careers, including a dramatically successful run at evangelism, and who now aspired to be Ontario Liberal leader.

The NDP had little hope of winning Riverdale but it did want to stop Templeton. His personality seemed to be precisely the tonic the lack-lustre Liberals might use to push their way into power, and the NDP could be badly trampled in the process. Ken Bryden, the NDP's member in neighbouring Woodbine riding, a former CCF provincial secretary and the shrewdest political mind in the party, had learned that you could find hidden votes by systematic repeated door-to-door canvassing. His colleague in the legislature, Stephen Lewis, and a party organizer, Marj

Pinney, had perfected "the system," as it was soon christened, and in Riverdale it was to be put to its most crucial test. While Templeton spent a small fortune on billboards and on radio and television time, the NDP summoned volunteers from as far away as Hamilton and Oshawa and sent them to knock on doors. When Templeton and his Tory rival spent more money, the NDP ordered additional canvasses. On September 10th, "the system" paid off. James Renwick, a radical corporation lawyer who had worked even harder than his canvassers, was the new member. A couple of weeks later, "the system" was tried again, this time in a federal by-election in the Tory constituency of Waterloo South, a mixed rural-industrial area sixty miles west of Toronto. Once again, canvassers were concentrated. Busloads of Riverdale veterans descended on the riding each week-end until, on November 9th, the NDP again pulled off a victory — this time for Max Saltsman, a Galt alderman and businessmen.

A little over a month later, in another by-election, Saskatchewan's former attorney general, Robert Walker, won back his Hanley constituency from the provincial Liberals. The province's honeymoon with Ross Thatcher had ended with remarkable speed. Apparently, all was not lost for socialism in what had once been its heartland.

There are times when one can learn a lot more from victory than defeat. During four years, the NDP could have compiled an interminable list of things it seemed to be doing wrong. It desperately needed to find that something worked. Whether or not "the system" had contributed to the by-election victories, it had not hurt. It had also given a lot of key party members a share in an experience they had rarely had before — success. Canvassing was less pleasant than discussing policy, less exhilarating than joining a demonstration. It could be disagreeably hard work but it was also politically valid and within the resources of the one element the NDP could not deny it had — people. It was probably healthy for the NDP to discover that its problems did not lie only in its programme, image or leadership but in its willingness to work.

If work was needed, the Ontario party was ready. For years, the CCF and NDP membership in the province had never pushed past 11,000. The party's 1964 convention set a target of 35,000 and endorsed a plan designed by Edward Phillips, a party vice president and a brilliant engineer, to help reach it. A year later, the party was a long way from its goal but it had met a more realistic objective of 18,000. Sustaining contributions from members, which normally totalled $40,000 or less, had more than doubled. With the extra money and with its mind set on organization, the party could launch some of the educational work it had hitherto only promised. A sprinkling of new pamphlets appeared, advising members how to cope with the rules of order or how to make silk-screen signs as well as the more predictable effusions on Medicare, the party's auto insurance scheme and the plight of Canada's native people. The party also began to expand its staff of organizers and to train its members in the techniques of Riverdale-style campaigning.

The NDP revival was not limited to Ontario. In Saskatchewan, the bitterness of the defeated CCF soon turned to fury. Thatcher's advertising advisers were barely back on the plane to Toronto before the new premier had reverted to type, swearing to carve twenty million dollars from provincial government spending and laying his axe to some of the most humane and forward-looking of the CCF achievements. Not only socialists were outraged; the Hanley by-election indicated that a good many voters shared their feelings. Farther west, the British Columbia party expelled its Trotskyites, paid off its debts and moved just far enough left to pacify its militants without alarming the middle class support which, it belatedly discovered, it had won in the 1963 fiasco. The party also seemed stronger at the centre. Its federal secretary, Terry Grier, was a cool young economist who had taken over his job just in time to bear the brunt of the two federal elections. Given even a brief breathing space, a more seasoned executive and some relief from the party's chronic poverty, Grier could begin to plan for a federal election which seemed inevitable in the spring or autumn of 1965.

Of course, the NDP revival was by no means only its own doing. Even the Riverdale victory owed something to voter reaction against the Robarts government's lop-sided majority. In Ottawa, the Pearson government's perform-ance dismayed its own followers. Instead of the crisp, managerial efficiency which Canadians had always associ-ated with the Liberals, the Pearson administration seemed to reel from crisis to crisis. The "Sixty Days of Decision" collapsed in a series of humiliating retreats. Throughout the spring and summer of 1964, Parliament wallowed in a debate on a new national flag which the government seemed unable to resolve. In the fall came rumblings and then eruptions of scandal, aggravated by the Prime Minister's apparent mishandling of affairs. Meanwhile, the Liberal tradition of strong central government dissolved as provincial premiers launched an extremely successful campaign to redistribute federal revenues and powers, presumably in the name of the slogan the Liberals had appropriated from the NDP – "co-operative federalism."

Quebec led the way, its demands enforced by the friendship owed to a fellow Liberal government and, even more, by the overdue realization that the province's discomfort in Confederation was real. Soon after the Liberal victory in 1963, bombs in Westmount mailboxes had claimed their first victims. When the government appointed a Royal Commission on Biculturalism and

Bilingualism, Quebec nationalists had promptly insisted that only a special associate status could possibly keep their province in Canada. The logic of the two-nation theory, first expounded to many English-speaking Canadians at the NDP's Founding Convention of 1961, was pushing closer to its only conclusion.

While other Canadians might react to Quebec demands with a mixture of uneasiness, sympathy and occasional resentment, New Democrats were more intimately involved. Electoral progress in Quebec was still a primary goal of the party, forcing it to listen to very unfamiliar sounds. To most New Democrats, French Canada's cultural demands had to be settled as fairly and fully as possible so that the entire country could cope with the shared economic problems which, to the NDP, seemed frankly far more salient. It was very difficult for New Democrats to realize that cultural issues could be involved in even such arid realms as economic planning or regional development, that Quebec's socialism had little in common with the NDP's populist Fabian tradition, that personal ambitions and careerism could be motives for professedly selfless radicals in either English or French Canada.

Plagued by ill health and unequal to the task of establishing the party in Quebec, Gérard Picard had never been more than a caretaker leader After a worried search, the NDP found his successor in early 1965. A lawyer from Quebec's rural Beauce region, Robert Cliche concealed a brilliant mind, cultural sophistication and a profound sense of his own heritage behind a bear-like exterior. A brilliant platform orator in French and English , he could not hide a warm humanity and a political acumen which had always been a rare combination in the Quebec Left. His was one of the finest and most frustrated talents made available to Canadian public life in the Sixties. In Cliche, the NDP had what the CCF had never possessed, a leader able to speak

Robert Cliche gave New Democrats what they had never had before: an authentic and powerful Quebec leader. His defeats in 1965 and 1968 had historic significance.

to rural and working class Quebec and to English-speaking audiences as well.

However, Cliche's presence meant that the party had to turn back to the complicated and perhaps insoluble problem of how its policies for an activist government in Ottawa could be reconciled with Quebec's insistence on political, social and economic as well as cultural autonomy. The problem was complicated by the party's constituency in Quebec. It is at least arguable that the workers who should have formed social democracy's electoral base had only a limited interest in constitutions. Certainly Réal Caouette rarely dwelt on such issues save to proclaim himself an unqualified federalist. Unfortunately, the people who tended to talk to the NDP in Quebec were not workers but, for the most part, intensely nationalist intellectuals and professionals, people for whom socialism might be an enchanting theory but to whom Quebec's constitutional grievances had become an incessant preoccupation. Through Cliche, the NDP might be able to reach a more natural milieu. First, he nonetheless needed a consistent constitutional position which would afford him credibility with Quebec political observers, to say nothing of the rest of the NDP.

The first attempt was not wholly successful. Finding a solution to constitutional problems tended to be the task the NDP assigned to Charles Taylor, and his bilingual philosophical brilliance was sternly tested. A federal council meeting on February 11th, 1965, agreed, on the one hand, that French Canada needed a strong provincial government and special consideration within Confederation but, on the other hand, that for the sake of the total Confederation, "certain basic matters had to be left to the jurisdiction of the federal government." The list, which included a dominant role in economic and social policies, was indispensable if the NDP was to promise full employment and nation-wide medicare in future elections, but there was some excuse for Paul Sauriol's complaint that, far from being decentralist, it was a major thrust toward a unitary state. And, as he reminded readers of *Le Devoir*, that was not how to win votes in Quebec.

The council statement, jointly presented by Cliche and Douglas, had been hurried before the public because, almost four years late, a Quebec NDP was actually to be formed on March 19th to 21st at Montreal. Reflecting criticism in *Le Devoir* and other nationalist organs about the NDP's constitutional stand, the 200 delegates insisted that the new group would set its own standard of autonomy, forming only an "associate" relationship and adopting its own platform plank of economic decentralization. Once again, the federal NDP faced an ultimatum from its fledgling Quebec wing that it adjust its own policy or live with the fact that Canadians would be hearing two messages from the party in the forthcoming campaign.

By July 12th-15th, when the NDP's third federal convention met in Toronto, a compromise had been worked out. Douglas and other leaders proclaimed that the party was now firmly allied with "new social forces" in Quebec. Western delegates bravely controlled their political qualms as the NDP pledged itself to work for the same rights for French-speaking minorities as the English-speaking minority enjoyed in Quebec. A complicated structure of joint federal-provincial consultation on economic planning was accepted, though Ottawa's power to initiate social programmes was justified on the grounds that some provinces might have reactionary governments. Plainly the delegates were eager to learn, to adjust their thinking and to sympathise and Cliche, who had charmed the convention, professed himself satisfied. The completeness of the educational process was, as usual, exaggerated. When delegates turned to more familiar issues — automation, consumer protection, foreign ownership, the conservation of resources — provincial rights were ignored in resolutions which essentially demanded all power for Ottawa. Perhaps the Quebec delegation was not listening or, perhaps, like other New Democrats, it was instinctively *centralisateur*.

The NDP's third convention was the prelude to its third election. On September 7th, when Mr. Pearson announced the dissolution of Parliament, even he seemed, in his television appearance, to be trying to persuade himself that it was necessary. To his advisers, Walter Gordon and Keith Davey, the reasons were quite straightforward: the country was prosperous, memories of scandal had faded, the polls were favourable. It was time for the Liberals to demand a majority. Besides, their Conservative opponents, bitterly at odds over the leadership of John Diefenbaker, were in worse disarray than ever and the NDP was no longer a threat.

Though Douglas, on the basis of the most recent Gallup poll, insisted that his party could just manage to form a government with the support of the undecideds, the Liberals had a point. In fact, the NDP had deliberately determined, with Grier's guidance, to concentrate its resources on sixty-odd priority ridings, stretching from Cape Breton to Nanaimo. In a compromise between the principle of concentration and a socialist concern for weaker brethren, organizational help, a limited national advertising campaign and the federal leader's tours would be designed to give the selected ridings as much help as possible. In another revelation which left party old-timers gasping, Douglas announced that the NDP would be spending an estimated million dollars in the campaign — a figure which was probably very close to the truth. To the party faithful and to hostile editorial writers alike, it seemed as though the party of Woodsworth and Coldwell had abandoned its virtue in a corrupt rush of affluence.

In fact, spread across Canada, distributed to printers and signpainters, landlords of committee rooms and merchants of advertising space, it was a meagre enough sum by Liberal and Conservative standards. In Ottawa, Grier had a budget of $200,000, substantially more than in 1962 or 1963, half of it earmarked for the leader's tour and to help the campaign in Quebec and the Maritimes. With a little extra help from the party's treasurer, Eamon Park, Grier found the money to run a modest four-city survey, an innovation which appalled veteran CCFers but which gave the campaign organizers greater confidence in their plans. Even more shocking to older socialists was the discovery that Grier has also retained an advertising agency to help with the campaign. The initiative had come from a bright, progressive little Montreal agency headed by Manny Dunsky. Why should the NDP be boycotted by the advertising profession, Dunsky argued, and at considerable risk to his own prospects, he took up his own challenge. The party was not an easy client. Amid suspicions from the NDP hierarchy, he and Grier helped put together a low-budget campaign designed to present a few carefully chosen messages with a mixture of bluntness and wit. To their own surprise, party regulars were delighted with the result and at least one slogan, "Let's give the two old parties a well-deserved rest — this country needs it," was regularly repeated on local party leaflets. A television commercial, attacking misleading advertising, was banned by the CTV network, owned by John Bassett, a prominent Conservative. For Douglas and other party speakers, no better illustration of corporate power could have been devised at short notice. In what, for all parties, proved a dull and issueless campaign, the NDP's advertising gave its own members an occasional badly-needed fillip.

In addition to a bolstered advertising campaign, the

federal party deployed its resources to hire full-time organizers, pay deposits for candidates in barren constituencies and to finance the federal leader's tour. One party representative toured the Atlantic provinces, ensuring that, in all but Newfoundland, a full slate was fielded. Another was assigned to the prairies. As usual, the party's research director compiled a set of "Speakers' Notes," a guide to current issues and the party response to them, together with sufficient statistics to bore any but an audience of economists.

Almost the only campaign item not prepared when Parliament dissolved was the party's official platform. Delayed by the convention, committees and the lassitude of August, it was apparent that an official version could not be prepared in time. Instead, virtually on his own initiative, the federal secretary produced a summary of party policies entitled, with the appropriate self-confidence of such documents, *The Way Ahead for Canada*. Avoiding some of the abrasive rhetoric and the formidable length of the party's official statements, it attempted to present NDP policy in a somewhat more readable form, with sections on the familiar topics of economic planning, foreign ownership, consumers' rights and the rest. However, its main attempt was to focus on the NDP's chief campaign issue − a sense of national purpose. An introduction from T. C. Douglas pleaded for new leadership to set the country moving while the final page featured a prose poem by the leader entitled "I Believe in Canada." The centre spread featured the party's approach to federalism and bilingualism, embellished with a photograph of Douglas and Cliche. Tucked into the statement was a cautious admission that Quebec was not a province like the others: in areas like education, town planning and rural development, it acknowledged, "Quebec must have the assurance that she can differ from the rest of Canada."

There was a reason. Except, perhaps, for York South, where David Lewis was collecting most of the spare resources of the Ontario party for his attempted come-back, the NDP's biggest hopes were for Cliche, running in his native Beauce and for C. G. Gifford and Charles Taylor, running in the Montreal seats of Notre Dame de Grace and Mount Royal. Apart from the two Montreal campaigns, money for the party's electoral activity in Quebec came from the federal office and from other provinces or, to an embarrassing degree, from Cliche's own pocket. Any enthusiasm for socialist politics did not extend to paying for it. Marc Boulard, the party's Quebec secretary, later reported: "If you had ever been with me on a door-to-door appeal for money for the NDP, and seen the expressions of disbelief or amazement on the average householder's face when I explained that I represented a party which financed itself from small individual donations you would know what I mean."

Fund-raising methods were only one of many ways in which the party was culturally alien to French Canada, and its apparent irrelevance as a vehicle for reform was pointedly demonstrated by the harshest blow the NDP suffered during the campaign. After persistent rumours, three prominent Quebeckers who might have been ex-pected to be disenchanted by the corrupt, bungling Liberals, Jean Marchand, head of the Confederation of National Trade Unions, Gerard Pelletier of *La Presse*, and Pierre Elliott Trudeau, all announced that they would be seeking Liberal nominations. After a search to find them safe constituencies, Trudeau found himself facing Taylor in Mount Royal. By helping to deny the NDP even a chance of electing a Quebec spokesman, the advent of the "Three Wise Men," as they were promptly nicknamed, was a serious setback. How serious would become even more apparent in 1968.

For the time being, however, it did not limit the NDP campaign. After a depressing start in the interior of British Columbia — making nationwide headlines only when he was bitten by a dog — Douglas soon caught his stride. If national purpose was the overall theme, there were many others — prominent among them, the virtues of minority government. To give the Liberals a majority would be to administer a tranquillizer he insisted. At evening rallies across the country, Douglas laid out aspects of the NDP programme, from an independent foreign policy to a natural resources inventory to free education so that brains, not money, would determine a student's progress. As before, the main theme was planning rather than control, and a concern — ill-requited in votes — for the poor and the elderly, abandoned in the era of affluence. In the final weeks, the pattern of huge rallies in major cities was repeated. In Montreal — where *Le Devoir* had conceded that it preferred the NDP programme to the others — Douglas insisted: "we are not one single nation, we are two. We have not one single language, we have two." In Toronto on the next night, November 5th, the party almost filled Maple Leaf Gardens to hear a warning that the Liberals were making secret plans for immediate harsh anti-inflationary measures if they won the election. In Vancouver on the following night, winding up his campaign in the crowded P.N.E. Coliseum, an exhausted Douglas repeated the charges. Then he went home to Burnaby to wait for the results.

More than ever, the experts were sure they knew what they would be. For all the gallant rearguard action of their leader, the Tories would be decimated. Pearson would have his majority and the NDP just might make small gains. After all, the pre-election Gallup poll showed the New Democrats hovering at eighteen per cent. It also suggested that the Liberals had tumbled from forty-seven to forty-four per cent in the course of the campaign, but that would be enough to hold the Conservatives, wavering between twenty-eight and thirty-two per cent.

The experts were utterly wrong. To the dismay of its operators, the Gallup reached to the limits of its built-in error. Pearson's candidates collected only forty per cent of the votes, lost all but one of their seats on the prairies, and emerged with a net gain of two. If the Liberals were victims of a lower-than-average turn-out, the NDP gained, collecting a new high – 1,381,047 votes or eighteen per cent of the total. The party lost Port Arthur (where Douglas Fisher had not stood again), but gained two seats in Toronto (including York South), another in northern Ontario's Nickel Belt and a fourth outside Winnipeg (captured by a youthful provincial member, Ed Schreyer). Bitterly, the party learned that, despite an unprecedented twelve per cent support in Quebec, it had not elected a single candidate.

Before the election, a popular Toronto columnist, Ron Haggart, had suggested that the ideal government for Canada would be a minority Liberal regime, obliged to justify its acts to a majority of opponents. Post-election pundits, full of anthropomorphic imagery, were prepared to suggest that an all-wise electorate had produced just that. It was, of course, nonsense. A voter is provided with precisely one ballot with which to express his preference for party, leader and candidate. If a voter sympathised with the Liberals, admired Diefenbaker and considered his local NDP candidate as the only fit representative, he made his choice or stayed home – a course a quarter of the eligible voters took in 1965. Obviously, disillusionment rather than conversion played a major part in the improved NDP totals but there was evidence – for example in York South – that a thorough, effective campaign could bring out votes.

Even more important for the party, in those areas where social democrats would normally expect to appeal – in heavily unionized and industrial constituencies – the NDP had finally become a force. In Saskatchewan, where the party had fallen to a miserable 18.6 per cent in 1963, it had started to climb again and, even if it failed to win a seat, it had pushed the federal Liberals back to third place.

Within a few months, the Twenty-Seventh Parliament had begun to look very much like its predecessor, with Gerda Munsinger playing the shadowy role of a Lucien Rivard and the NDP itself contributing the case of the unfortunate George Victor Spencer. It was time for the party activists to turn back to provincial politics. Unlike the Liberals and the Conservatives, the NDP organization served both levels of politics, with a basically provincial structure adapting itself to federal contests. That meant, of course, that the same members dug into the same pockets to pay for every election that came along – and in some areas, that had begun to include municipal campaigns. On the other hand, it gave local associations a continuous reason for existence and activity and it began to require a measure of inter-provincial co-operation. By 1966, a formula had been developed for the sharing of organizers and the expenses of volunteers to work in provincial elections. The originating province paid salaries of its loaned staff, the federal office paid for transportation and the host province paid expenses and made assignments. A form of cooperation which had been developing since the Saskatchewan Medicare crisis of 1962 and the ensuing campaign to develop community clinics was by now institutionalized. Ontario, with the largest permanent staff, was the chief contributor but other provinces did their best.

By 1966, a second cycle of provincial elections began. The results, like those of the 1965 election, were unsensational but encouraging.

The first province was again Manitoba. For months, Duff Roblin had been flexing his political muscles but denying that he would be a candidate to succeed John Diefenbaker when the Chief's clutch on the leadership was finally loosened. However, a fresh mandate from Manitobans would be a convenience. On May 18th, the contest began. After so many victories, no-one now believed that Roblin could be defeated — certainly not by the NDP or its ailing leader Russell Paulley. Perhaps that impression helped. When the votes were counted on June 23rd, Roblin's support had dropped from forty-five to forty per cent of the electorate, the Liberals had fallen to thirty-three per cent and the NDP was back at its pre-1962 level of twenty-three per cent. Moreover, the party had added four seats to its caucus and dropped several years from its average age. A party which had suffered from advanced years, feeble membership, chronic deficits and a fixation on 1919, began to look surprisingly young. Later that year, when Roblin gave himself and his ministers a substantial raise, Manitoba acquired a new political personality. An ex-miner and merchant from Thompson named Joe Borowski decided to camp in protest on the steps of the Legislature for two months of media coverage, official harassment and public attention before his sick wife summoned him home.

On August 6th, 1966, it was British Columbia's turn. Shrewdly, Bennett calculated that his opponents would find great difficulty in rousing voters from mid-summer torpor and he was right. However, when he began to denounce his understrength opposition for "obstructionism," he began to sound too much like a ranting dictator even for easy-going British Columbians. A Social Credit victory might be a foregone conclusion but fair play demanded at least a bit of criticism. Robert Strachan and

Tommy Douglas, their Liberal rivals and even the veteran newspaper editor, "Ma" Murray from Lilooet, roared into action against the arrogant premier and his "steamroller." Their protests came late — perhaps too late for any but the media-sensitive lower mainland to be affected — but they gave added push to a number of constituency campaigns. On September 12th, the NDP lost a few seats in the hinterland but more than made up for them in the Vancouver area and collected thirty-four per cent of the popular vote, about as much as the CCF had ever won. Among the members of the enlarged caucus was Tom Berger, an able young lawyer who had briefly represented Vancouver-Burrard in Ottawa in 1962-63.

In neighbouring Alberta, the NDP had been shut out federally and provincially since its foundation. Even there the party experienced a brief triumph. In a by-election on October 6th in the coal-mining constituency of Pincher Creek-Crowsnest, Garth Turcott, a local lawyer, unexpectedly won a seat for the party. In the provincial legislature, however, he abruptly broke the clubhouse rules by demanding that two prominent Social Credit ministers, E. W. Hinman and A. J. Hooke, answer charges already published in a Calgary newspaper. Even the vestigial Liberal and Conservative opposition rose in outrage. In the ensuing general election, Turcott found his margin erased and both he and his party were pursued through the courts for their temerity.

Though Manitoba and British Columbia were important and even a small victory in Alberta was delightful, the main contests of the second round were in Saskatchewan and Ontario. Normally, Saskatchewan would have waited until the spring of 1968 but Ross Thatcher discovered that, while the current crops were far better than expected, the economic prospects were discouraging. It was election weather. Accordingly, on September 8th, 1967, he announced that he needed a mandate to prove to investors that socialism had been banished forever. For its part, the CCF-NDP announced that it would fight the election on the sell-out of natural resources, on its policies of a new, citizen-owned development corporation and of the gradual elimination of university tuition fees.

Whatever their proposals, both parties were essentially fighting on their record and, as Dalton Camp has pointed out, a party in its first term is remarkably hard to defeat. Its predecessor's sins are not forgotten; its own novelty has not worn off. Woodrow Lloyd's denunciation of a resource sellout, however amply backed by statistics, found little favour among those who had found new jobs in the potash and oil industry or among those who were now persuaded that Saskatchewan could at last share the wealth of neighbouring Alberta. Moreover, in opposition, the CCF-NDP had behaved too much like the father of the prodigal son, prepared to welcome voters back to the same old leaders and the same old policies as soon as they had repented of their three-year folly.

In fact, the results were very close. On October 11th, the CCF-NDP collected 44.4 per cent of the vote, a better share than in any election since 1956 but, thanks to the near-disappearance of Conservative candidates, the Liberal vote rose to 45.6 per cent. Because of the province's custom of politically motivated redistribution, a sin shared by CCF and Liberal governments alike, the Liberals took thirty-five seats to the CCF-NDP's twenty-four – an election night survey suggested that it took 800 more votes to elect a CCF candidate than a Liberal and in Saskatoon, where the CCF had a city-wide majority of 1000, the Liberals took three of the five seats.

Post-election calculations and rationalizations do not win governments. True to custom, the party's ensuing convention blamed opponents and the media for the setback; it also reconfirmed Lloyd as its leader. There was only one permanent casualty – the letters CCF. Henceforth, the convention decided, the democratic Left in Saskatchewan would campaign as the New Democratic Party.

There were rumours that Thatcher had timed his election to prevent intervention by the NDP's travelling corps of organizers. During his election, they were fully engaged in Ontario. There, a new zeal for organization had produced almost 25,000 members and an annual income of $125,000 by the eve of the 1967 election. With help from unions and individuals, the organization staff had grown to thirteen and the provincial office had three full-time officers. The party's federal secretary, Terry Grier, had resigned to work with the Ontario leader, Donald MacDonald. The new provincial secretary, John Harney, a former university professor and Trevor Lloyd, a University of Toronto historian, had helped develop a party programme which stressed what they called "pragmatic radicalism." Though nominalists had been delighted by occasional references to "socialism," the *Globe and Mail* commented that the programme's emphasis on the protection of the individual from the abuses of government and corporate power might make it welcome to many conservatives. Certainly it helped attract the most impressive slate of provincial candidates the party had ever offered.

Some of the political sophistication which Grier had pioneered in the federal party came with him to Ontario. Following the federal NDP example, the party commissioned a pre-election survey – though it economized by having the analysis performed by sympathetic academics. It showed the NDP running third, but indicated that there was a significant target group of potential supporters who wanted to hear the party talk about bread and butter issues like housing and taxes rather than more esoteric interests like pollution and foreign ownership. Though MacDonald and the party leaders used the slogan "67 seats in '67," the party had, in fact, selected thirty-five constituencies for priority campaigning, doing its best to develop Riverdale-style organizations in each of them. To run the campaign, the party budgeted an unprecedented $90,000 for its central campaign, including $50,000 for an advertising campaign to be run by the Dunsky agency.

The campaign was closely related to the available political pressures. On the whole, Ontario seemed remarkably content in 1967, its only visible diseases the consequences of unplanned prosperity. However, the province's trade unionists were increasingly indignant about the use of injunctions to break strikes. After a series of defiances which left twenty-six of its members facing jail sentences, the labour movement was even more eager to attempt political action. In Sudbury, the end of inter-union battling allowed the huge Inco local, now a part of the Steelworkers, to affiliate most of its 15,000 members. In June of 1967, the NDP demonstrated the power of its new alliance by taking Sudbury from the Liberals in a bitterly-fought federal by-election. Closer to provincial concerns, the Robarts government fired its outspoken chief coroner for Toronto, Dr. Morton Shulman, and turned him into an NDP candidate.

These were not, of course, the issues which could defeat a well-established government, full of the good works and the euphoria of Centennial year, generous with promised bounty and well-supplied with money to pay for it. The Ontario Liberals, under their fourth leader since 1963, plagued by defeatism and the blunders of their federal government colleagues, were no threat. The NDP, with only eight seats as a base, could hardly dream of becoming the government. Nor did it expect to. Travelling in the unaccustomed comfort of a campaign bus, Donald Mac-

Donald made his impact on the party's chosen areas of concentration, the north and the south-west, sticking doggedly to his pre-selected themes. If electioneering can ever be a rational business, the NDP had left little to chance.

Of course, electioneering can only be as rational as the electorate. Against the political skill of John Robarts and the smooth self-confidence of the Conservative machine, the opposition parties did not seem likely to make much headway. On October 17th, the NDP did not capture its thirty-five concentration ridings or even achieve its private goal of becoming Official Opposition, but its supporters still had a lot to cheer about. The only political group to gain both seats and votes, the NDP moved from sixteen to twenty-five per cent of popular support and from eight to twenty seats in a somewhat enlarged legislature. Except for those who had believed the party's own propaganda about its prospects, it was an impressive advance.

In Manitoba, British Columbia and Ontario, the second provincial round had strengthened the NDP caucuses, rejuvenated its leadership and established the party as a credible contender for provincial power. By the end of 1967, the New Democrats could afford to be in a bullish mood.

In the CCF, the standing rule was "Clear it with David." In the NDP, David Lewis was even more dominant as the architect of the labour-political alliance.

V. Conflict

The fourth biennial convention of the NDP met in the Royal York Hotel in Toronto from July 3rd to 6th, 1967. Original plans to go to Montreal were scrapped when Expo 67 proved too expensive a competitor for hotel rooms, and there was an air of tired ritual as delegates assembled in the big, familiar, slightly shabby hotel. Perhaps in an attempt to give the gathering added excitement, Stephen Lewis, an Ontario provincial member and the eldest son of David Lewis, proclaimed that it would be a watershed for the NDP, witnessing "the emergence of a new generation socialist who is beginning to say things that people in this society are very much looking for."

That year, as both Liberals and Tories got ready to change leaders, youth was very much in fashion in Canadian politics but, if a new generation was present at the Toronto convention, it was more seen than heard. Its only coup, organized largely by the former federal secretary, Terry Grier, Grant Notley, a future Alberta leader, John Brewin, the son of a veteran M.P., John Harney, the Ontario secretary and John Penner, a prominent Montreal New Democrat, was to topple the federal officers' chosen candidate for party president. A respected ex-cabinet minister from Saskatchewan, J. H. Brockelbank's only fault was his age. Aware that the NDP would soon have the oldest leader in federal politics, the so-called "young Turks" were determined to add at least one younger face to the party hierarchy. Rebuffed by Robert Cliche and Charles Taylor, they turned to James Renwick, the victor of Riverdale. By dint of feverish canvassing, they won.

A much more important convention decision was the adoption of an extensive statement on economic planning and foreign ownership, the joint work of Max Saltsman, the M.P. from Waterloo South, and Colin Cameron, the veteran socialist M.P. from Nanaimo. The product of lengthy study, the document eschewed much of the anti-Americanism of the party's earlier (and subsequent) declarations — why blame the Americans, demanded Saltsman, "for what is essentially our own fault?" — and offered a detailed, comprehensive and wide-ranging review of what Canadians could do about their branch plant economy. In summary, it proposed mechanisms to generate domestic capital, to organize Canada's own capacity for technological innovation and to ensure that both domestic and foreign-controlled corporations served the national interest.

Of course, the 861 delegates had other interests — from passing the usual statements of concern about agriculture, women, consumers, labour and Vietnam, to listening to guest speakers. Among them was Claude Ryan, the editor of *Le Devoir*, and he brought solemn advice. Already, he claimed, the NDP had support from French Canadian union leaders and academics. Now it must turn to middle class nationalists and to the under-privileged. "Offer specific, practical solutions and Quebec will listen."

Although Ryan made no acknowledgement, the convention had already endorsed a specific constitutional solution which his own newspaper was currently urging:

"special status." It was the logical outcome of six years of resolutions and it had already been expressed in the NDP's 1965 election platform. If the party believed that the other nine provinces neither wanted nor deserved the kind of autonomy Quebec increasingly demanded, why not recognize the historical fact that she was "not a province like the others." Already the federal Liberals had offered a specific example by allowing both a Canada and a Quebec Pension Plan. As usual, it was Charles Taylor, after interminable drafting sessions, who put the words together: "In fields of government which touch a community's way of life – fields such as social security, town planning, education and community development – Quebec must have the right and the fiscal resources to adopt its own programmes and policies in place of those designed by and financed by the federal government. At the same time, the federal government must be able to play an increased role in these fields where this is desired by the people of other provinces." Once Taylor had described the formula, an even more persuasive figure, Laurier LaPierre, a McGill University historian and former popular co-host of a CBC television programme, was available to sell it to the delegates. With a little outspoken grumbling from Robert Strachan, the British Columbia leader, LaPierre, Cliche and Taylor won an overwhelming vote of support.

As a whole, the convention brought little enthusiasm from the press or the delegates. The *Financial Times* noted acidly that while the party had "peeled off yards of discarded socialist dogma," it had left "a figure as emaciated and indeterminate as Twiggy." However, on its "special status" proposal, there was a sudden, strong and, to most New Democrats, a surprisingly hostile reaction. So far, apart from some academic grumbles and the resignation of Dr. Eugene Forsey because of the "two nations" position, the NDP had suffered very little for its attempt to respond to Quebec nationalist demands. In the summer of 1967, that immunity ended. Perhaps it was President de Gaulle's outburst in Montreal, perhaps it was the uproar over the Conservatives' flirting with their own "two-nations" policy, perhaps it was a belated realization, particularly in academic circles, that separatism had become a serious force in Quebec, but suddenly it was no longer possible for the NDP to continue its good-natured attempts to find out what French Canada wanted. Ramsay Cook, a well-known historian and former NDP sympathiser, broke openly with the party on "special status," insisting that it not only opened the way to national dissolution, it also would rob English-speaking provinces of their rights. His criticisms were echoed by Kenneth McNaught, the biographer of J. S. Woodsworth. Donald Smiley, a prominent political scientist at the University of British Columbia, insisted that the NDP had practically destroyed its usefulness even by espousing the "two nations" position, "a formulation which is inherently destructive of Confederation and which is neither understood nor accepted among those groups or in most of those areas who have for a generation supported the democratic left."

Perhaps surprisingly, the party did not really answer these criticisms by pointing to the impressive historical precedents for treating Quebec differently, or emphasizing the limited realm in which the doctrine would operate. The NDP might have mobilized the frustration of Canada by arguing that the federal role throughout the country dwindled at the behest of a single region, and that a potentially far more destructive regionalism was fostered by the status quo. Instead, the party's academics retired to their studies and its parliamentary spokesmen returned to the economic and social issues which were their natural preoccupations. The party's administrators had their own problems. The new federal secretary, Clifford Scotton, transferred from the Canadian Labour Congress where he had edited its prize-winning magazine, discovered that he had acquired a substantial debt and a budget which stubbornly refused to balance. The party's financial dependence on its provincial sections meant troubles when those provinces were preoccupied with their own contests and paying the resulting debts. Even with 70,000 regular members and 245,000 more in affiliated organizations, a new record, the NDP had not escaped chronic poverty. The result was elimination of an apparently ineffective women's department and of the federal party's organization staff. Both responsibilities would fall directly on the provinces. After two years of supporting the minority Pearson government, constantly worrying about impending elections and its own financial and policy problems, the NDP was in the psychological doldrums. Perhaps in desperation, the party's federal council accepted a scheme from Laurier LaPierrre, its newest vice-president, for an "Operation New Canada — Refaire le Canada." Instead of churning its own soul for answers, the party would send out its renowned army of canvassers door-to-door "to establish the real problems Canadians have in common as well as those reflected by regional factors." The scheme never got off the ground.

Few politically-minded Canadians would have much attention to spare for the NDP and its canvassers that year. Amidst the excitement of Centennial celebrations and Expo '67 came the agony of the Conservative party's struggle to replace John Diefenbaker. By March 1967, the party's public esteem had fallen so low that the NDP actually pulled ahead of it in the Gallup polls: twenty-eight per cent to twenty-five. However, once the Tories had chosen Robert Stanfield, the tall, craggy, cautious premier of Nova Scotia, their fortunes bounded. Freshly transfixed by issues of political leadership and personality, Canadians greeted the new Conservative leader by indicating forty-two per cent support in October, enough to give the Tories a comfortable majority if Mr. Pearson had generously called an election. Instead, on December 14th, the Liberal leader announced his own impending retirement. By April, 1968, not only were there nine candidates in the race for the succession but the Liberals had recovered their commanding lead in the opinion polls. In the home stretch of the leadership race, veteran politicians were outpaced by the political novice who had voted NDP in 1963 and who had only entered Parliament in 1965. Within three weeks of his April 6th convention victory, Pierre Elliott Trudeau dissolved parliament and presented Canadians with their twenty-eighth and, in some respects, their most extraordinary federal general election.

If Mr. Trudeau had been a more conventional as well as perhaps a more sincere reformer, he might have used his initial months in power to cleanse the party he had so often condemned, reinforcing the progressive wing in his cabinet and using his new prestige to pass a raft of overdue measures of social justice which voters could have judged in the autumn. Instead, he presented himself to the voters before the momentum and glamour of his leadership victory had been exhausted. To Conservatives, he might be the crypto-communist who had visited Cuba and Red China; to New Democrats, he was the man who had let them down in 1965 and who had emerged as an arrogant intellectual whose attitude to welfare reforms had been summed up as "no more free stuff." To most Canadians, he was virtually unknown save as the French Canadian who had successfully bullied Quebec's Premier Daniel Johnson at a televised constitutional conference. To radical liberals, he was the man who had legalized homosexuality and reportedly wished to chase the state from the bedrooms of the nation. In an extended period in Parliament, the opposition parties might have had a chance to compel the new prime minister to reveal himself and his ideas; in an election campaign, inter-party confrontation virtually ceases or is reduced to the almost meaningless and monotonous formula of a television debate or an all-candidates' meeting. The task of probing a politician falls to the news media and, in 1968, with few exceptions, its leading figures were enjoying a love affair with the new Liberal leader. Only by the end of the campaign did a few of the more perceptive of them conclude that they had been victims of a confidence trick and, even then, like most such victims, they grimaced at their own naiveté and passed on.

Though the NDP had been sending itself readiness warnings since the day after the 1965 election, and though it had momentarily expected an election in February when the Liberal government was defeated in Parliament, it was by no means anticipating the kind of campaign it faced in the spring of 1968. In some respects, of course, it was ready. Two and a half years had been time to collect an array of attractive new candidates and the prospect of a post-election leadership change drew others into the race. Douglas Fisher chose to run in Toronto's sprawling York Centre; John Harney, the Ontario NDP secretary, ran in a new riding of Scarborough West; Bruce Rogers, a widely-known CBC announcer, was nominated in Toronto-Parkdale. In Montreal, Laurier LaPierre was the candidate in suburban Lachine. Already, *Maclean's Magazine* had tipped him as the first socialist prime minister of Canada. In Dollard, Charles Taylor had built an organization and, at Quebec NDP insistence, Robert Cliche had retreated from Beauce to find a seat in working class Duvernay, an area which had done well for the party in 1965. In other respects, the party was caught at a disadvantage. Money was short. Party prospects, bright in 1967 and even in early 1968, had sagged. Party leaders were exhausted and the party's message, fundamentally unchanged since 1961, seemed tiresomely familiar. Advertising arrangements already made with the Dunsky agency were recalled, amended and re-established with little alteration after the campaign had started, involving a significant loss of time and money.

The party's approach to the election conveyed honesty or lack of confidence according to viewpoint. In earlier campaigns, Douglas felt that he had damaged his credibility by telling the truth about everything but the party's prospects which, true to established custom, he wildly exaggerated. In 1968, he began by confessing that the party could not win but that it had designs on capturing fifty seats. It happened to be the truth but there was a chorus of anguish from party regulars and of ridicule from the news media. By the end of the campaign, buoyed up by evidence that the party was fighting a more effective and well-organized campaign than even it had expected, Douglas was willing to increase his estimate from 50 to 132 seats. The party's campaign slogan, "You win when you vote NDP," also reflected realism (or defeatism) with its argument against those who complained about "losing their votes" by backing candidates who could not win or form part of a government. In the NDP view, you lost your vote only when you voted against your own interests, and for ordinary working people, concerned about issues which the NDP saw as important, like jobs, homes, taxes and the cost of living, that meant voting Liberal or Conservative.

Douglas's own campaign was based on the need to bring the dashing, romantic Liberal leader to bay on crucial economic issues. Of these, the most important had become foreign ownership, reflected in the report of the Watkins task force, and tax reform, advocated by the massive report of the Carter Royal Commission. The NDP had extensive policies to capture any interest in economic nationalism, and Douglas propounded them from coast to coast, including branch-plant centres like Windsor and Toronto. Constantly, he hammered Trudeau, the professed anti-nationalist, and his party, as committed to a policy of continentalism. Except in a national television debate between the three English-speaking leaders, in which Douglas scored so heavily that the media began again to take the NDP seriously, the party had simply no means of forcing the Liberals to their ground.

Only on one issue did the two parties meet head-on: Quebec. If Trudeau promised anything beyond charisma and what Britain's Harold Wilson had called "the smack of firm government," it was an end of concessions to Quebec nationalists. For the first time, NDP candidates began to be confronted with the issue in the rest of Canada. In Douglas's new riding (redistribution had disintegrated the faithful Burnaby-Coquitlam), his opponent was the former provincial Liberal leader, an able campaigner who portrayed the NDP leader as the spokesman for a remote, alien and aggressive Quebec. Ramsay Cook, the former NDP supporter, rode prominently in Trudeau's entourage. In Quebec, hopes were high. The new prime minister's defiance of the nationalists brought the NDP support from unfamiliar places, including two ministers in the Union Nationale government, Gabriel Loubier and Paul Allard. Organizers, including two of Ontario's ablest constituency specialists, Stephen Lewis and Gerald Caplan, were sent to help Taylor, Cliche and other key candidates. However, the seemingly fatal misfortunes which beset the NDP's ventures in French Canada struck again. While the press made what they could of alleged differences between Douglas and Cliche, the Liberals persuaded Eric Kierans, a respected and progressive Montreal Liberal and an unsuccessful rival of Trudeau for his party's leadership, to run for Duvernay.

NDP campaign lore suggests that Conservative voters are usually visible and audible; it is Liberals at the doorstep who are smilingly noncommittal. By the eve of June 25th, one could build high hopes on the basis of apparent NDP support but veteran campaigners counted the uncommitted and worried. Then came St-Jean Baptiste day. The eve-of-election broadcasts of the prime minister calmly defying separatist rioters helped spur weakly motivated Liberal voters to the polls, saving their party from most of the customary slump between final Gallup estimates and the real thing. It certainly did no harm. The Trudeau campaign took 45.2 per cent of the popular vote and an eventual 155 seats, more than enough for a comfortable majority. For the NDP, spirits belatedly raised by a surge of volunteers, apparent support and Douglas's performance, it was a bitter defeat. Every one of the apparently potential national leaders – Taylor, LaPierre, Harney, Fisher – was defeated. Across northern Ontario, the NDP lost three of its four seats as Franco-Ontarian voters swung back to Liberalism. It was even worse in British Columbia where the party's vote slumped below the Liberals for the first time since 1963. With redistribution, the party should have taken eleven seats; it lost four of them and, worst of all, one of them belonged to Tommy Douglas. In Montreal, where Duvernay was almost the only serious contest, Robert Cliche joined him in defeat.

For those who sought comfort from the NDP result, it could be found. Losses in Ontario and British Columbia had been handsomely compensated by gains in Saskatchewan where the party had gained thousands of voters who had stayed with Diefenbaker since 1957 or 1958. For the first time since Argue's defection, the party had representation in the prairie province — six M.P.s and a by-election would eventually add a seventh. Across Canada, the party's total vote was 1,390,221, 17.4 per cent of the total and an answer to those who had claimed in 1965 that the party's support was merely a protest vote. In the industrial areas and in most of the major cities, the NDP had lost ground but it had kept its position as the alternative.

If the new parliament had been one of minorities, faced with yet another imminent election, the NDP would doubtless have pulled itself together, counted its blessings, exaggerated them a little, and soldiered on. With the new House of Commons firmly in place until 1972 or even later, there was no need. The party could abandon itself to its sorrows. Deprived of many of its leaders, bruisingly reminded that it had again been brought to an electoral standstill, the party found that it had accumulated a debt of over a hundred thousand dollars. By the end of 1968, its central newspaper had been scrapped and its research department dissolved — to be re-established under federal caucus control as a result of sudden new government benevolence to opposition parties. It was a more serious loss than the party could immediately realize for it was a sacrifice of its only internal mechanism for policy generation and innovation. Henceforth, caucus research directors were to play a part in NDP policy review but their primary focus would inevitably be on the day-to-day preoccupations of Parliament. As the party turned to self-examination in the months and years after the 1968 election, the absence of a clear, uncluttered lead from the party's own internal resources would leave an intellectual vacuum.

In the immediate aftermath of the 1968 election, leadership seemed a more salient question than policy. For years, the Canadian news media had had a fixation about political leadership, first in the controversial figure of John Diefenbaker, now in the person of Pierre-Elliott Trudeau. The NDP had not been immune. Immediately before the 1968 campaign was launched, Stephen Lewis had flown to Vancouver to persuade Tommy Douglas that he should clear the way for a new leader. Certainly, responded Douglas, he was no Diefenbaker. He would stay no longer than his party wished, but he also felt that the replacement must come from a new generation. Lewis's father, narrowly re-elected in York South and soon to be chosen as NDP house leader, would hardly qualify. Who would? Ed Schreyer, the thirty-two year old M.P. from Selkirk, apparently yearned to return to Manitoba politics. Winnipeg's Stanley Knowles and Andrew Brewin, the M.P. for Toronto-Greenwood and NDP foreign affairs critic, were both veteran CCFers. Taylor, LaPierre, Harney, Fisher and other hopefuls had all been defeated and Ed Broadbent, a young York University political scientist who had just been elected from Oshawa-Whitby, was utterly untried. Taylor, young, bilingual, attractive and articulate in a slightly academic way, was the favourite of the party leaders, but he was reluctant to consider himself a candidate and adamant that he would not seek a seat outside Quebec. At an executive meeting immediately after the 1968 election, Douglas announced his intention to step down at the 1969 convention, and repeated this to press reporters. A statement was issued from the meeting to this effect. Then, at the urging of the party council, Douglas remained, accepting an assignment to study the NDP's electoral methods. That chore was promptly forgotten when Colin Cameron, re-elected for Nanaimo-Cowichan-The Islands, suddenly died. His seat, by no means safe but among the best at the party's disposal, was available and Douglas headed west for his sixth personal battle for a place in Parliament since he had come back to federal politics.

The problem of leadership was not merely federal. In 1968, most of the party's provincial leaders – Strachan in British Columbia, Lloyd in Saskatchewan, Paulley in Manitoba and MacDonald in Ontario – had also been CCF leaders. Of course, as the NDP had boasted during the Diefenbaker shambles, their leaders had to win approval at every party convention but, as Robert Michels pointed out in his classic study of the German Social Democrats, left-wing parties are more prone to criticize their leaders than replace them. To them, ideology rather than personality should be the salient feature of political decision-making. It had always seemed unfair to blame a leader when it was the party's policies and image which clearly barred it at the polls. Moreover, both the CCF and the NDP made such extortionate demands on the time, energy and financial security of their leaders that it seemed common decency to leave them in the quiet enjoyment of whatever meagre pleasures the office afforded. Except for Argue, the CCF leadership had been held by only Woodsworth and Coldwell. In Ontario, MacDonald was only the second person to hold the CCF or NDP leadership.

That era of tolerance was fading. In 1967, Tom Berger, elected to the British Columbia legislature only a year before, challenged Robert Strachan. The result was a bruising contest which pitted the party's provincial office against the majority of the caucus and split the party into a more radical old guard and a more pragmatic group of "young Turks." Strachan won but the bitterness was sufficiently sustained that the party found it prudent to bring organizers from Ontario to help run Douglas's Nanaimo by-election campaign and to share in the victory.

A year later, both Paulley and MacDonald faced similar

tests. The Manitoba leader's ill-health and his limited appeal to ethnic and middle-class voters persuaded another relative newcomer, Sidney Green, a Winnipeg lawyer and former municipal councillor, to make his bid. By making it clear that he was simply keeping his seat warm for the popular Ed Schreyer, Paulley kept his job but only by 213 votes to 168. In Ontario, where Donald MacDonald had been shepherding the CCF-NDP back from near anni- hilation since 1953, there could be no question of strength and ability, only a claim that he had acquired a "loser's image." The challenge came from James Renwick, the party's federal president, with the argument that the party's significant advance in the 1967 election was a setback, not a triumph, and that MacDonald had to bear the responsibility. Backed by Stephen Lewis and a minority in the provincial caucus, Renwick began his campaign by insisting that his cool image would attract more of Ontario's traditionally conservative voters than MacDonald's. At the convention, he switched images, with an appeal to the party's radical wing. With almost thirteen hundred delegates attracted to Kitchener for the unwonted excitement, MacDonald won by a margin of 859 to 370.

At the federal level, too, change of leadership was postponed, not least by the conclusion that it would be too expensive. To make a leadership convention suf- ficiently democratic, the party would have to help delegates from more remote provinces with their travel expenses and that, the heavily indebted party was not in a position to do. Instead, the party announced that its 1969 convention in Winnipeg would concentrate on policy. "In our preoccupation with the mechanisms of elections," a party newsletter observed, "we have had to forego the thorough and continuing review of philosophy and pro- gram which should characterize democratic socialist parties."

Constitutionally, policy-making in the NDP starts with the resolutions which constituency associations and affiliated organizations submit to conventions and councils. These are solemnly translated, printed and distributed in their hundreds to delegates. Unfortunately, it is rare to find among the submitted resolutions any which sufficiently encapsulate a party stand on the more complex and current of political issues. In some cases, a workable composite could be assembled from a number of grassroots resolutions; more often, in the CCF and the NDP, it was customary for the party's research or policy review committee or even a convention resolutions committee to draft a statement for submission under the auspices of the party's council. That was how the NDP had evolved its policies on federalism, foreign ownership and a host of more mundane matters. It was a process which depended on a fair degree of consensus within the party about its policies and a reasonable degree of confidence in its leaders. During the Sixties, much of the work was done by Taylor, George Cadbury, the party's treasurer and a committed British socialist, Marion Bryden, the Ontario party's research director, and J. C. Weldon, an economist at McGill, together with a succession of federal party research directors.

In the aftermath of the 1968 election, by its own definition of the term, the NDP turned "left." In part, this was because of a premature judgement that Trudeau, himself, represented a leftward lunge by the Liberal party. Certainly middle class radicals had been enchanted by what seemed to be his view of external affairs, private morality and "participatory democracy." To a degree the NDP was slow to appreciate, its own working class base had been remarkably immune from Trudeaumania but the party's middle class supporters had been badly singed by it. Outside Canada, there were other pressures. United

States involvement in Vietnam seemed a travesty of the ideals of liberal internationalism and produced, particularly among American intellectual opinion leaders, a remorseless critique of their own flawed society. In Britain, the failure of Harold Wilson's Labour government to solve the country's economic problems devalued the most important single source of NDP ideas and political philosophy. Within Canadian politics, most of the content of the NDP's faded green programme book seemed to have been expended. National medicare was due on July 1st, 1969. Canada had a national portable pension plan, departments for regional development and manpower planning and, under Trudeau, she would soon even recognize the People's Republic of China. Certainly the NDP could insist that all could have been done better and sooner and, more to the point, that critical elements remained in the party programme, almost untouched. But it was getting more difficult to claim to the party's own radicals that the sum of all of the NDP's social democratic measures added up to their vision of a socialist society.

By the late Sixties, it was increasingly fashionable to talk of a rejection of established politics, particularly by the young. Editorial writers expended quantities of their own wisdom and of their publishers' ink on the prospect. In May of 1968, Paris had been paralyzed by student riots and in the United States and Canada, civil rights, student and Quebec nationalist demonstrators began to abandon non-violence in an almost atavistic enthusiasm for destruction. Everywhere these outbursts were the work of small minorities; almost everywhere they were ineffectual. The French government went on much as before. In Canada, the young flocked to Trudeau as they would four years later. Revolutionary protest produced a flow of comfortable jobs for the children of the middle class and radical chic became an aphrodisiac for their elders. The NDP could not possibly have remained immune. For a party which had not been dramatically successful at the ballot box, there were many who now insisted that the choice was either oblivion or surging into the streets.

Pressures for a more radical NDP began at the top. In December, 1968, David Lewis persuaded most of the federal caucus to spend a week-end at Wakefield in the Gatineau hills, listening to papers by Charles Taylor, exploring the extent of corporate power, and Kari Levitt, a radical McGill economist, analyzing the implications of the branch-plant economy on Canadian economic and even political independence. Later that winter, amidst obvious uneasiness from the party's leading trade unionists, Ed Broadbent started an enthusiastic study of industrial democracy. In a process launched by Lewis, Taylor and the party's latest research director, Marc Eliesen, a substantial number of papers were soon circulating on topics ranging from guaranteed annual income and urbanization to science policy and sports. To ensure that party members and the public had some inkling of the development, the Ontario party published a thirty-page booklet, entitled *Socialism Canada Seventies*, summarising the papers and their general direction. "A union of awareness and experience," claimed the introduction, "has brought a radicalism to the re-definition of the New Democratic Party in the Seventies which may astonish those who believed that we were drifting into the comfortable consensus."

The public reaction, to judge from the press, was cool, if not splenetic. In two furious editorials, the Toronto *Globe & Mail* condemned the booklet and its ideas as simutaneously anti-American and anti-Canadian while Douglas Fisher, once again a columnist for the Toronto *Telegram*, suggested that its authors were the sort of theoreticians that a wise party hid at the back of the committee rooms, folding leaflets. Within the party, reaction had already been overtaken by the emergence of a group which, for the most part, had little to do with either leading party members or the traditional, Trotskyist-infiltrated Socialist Caucus. The inspiration came from James Laxer, a big, attractive and highly articulate graduate student who had inherited his politics from his father, formerly a leading Communist, and his experience from the Canadian student movement in the Sixties. He was joined by Gerald Caplan, who had run campaigns for David Lewis in the early Sixties while still a student, by Ed Broadbent, the only academic radical in the NDP federal caucus and by Mel Watkins, the University of Toronto economist whose report had been a handbook for Douglas in the 1968 campaign, but who had now moved through continentalism and liberal nationalism into a full-scale, doctrinaire socialism. In the spring of 1969, this group and others attracted to it drafted a "Manifesto for an Independent Socialist Canada." The chief authors, so far as a collective enterprise could have them, were Laxer, Broadbent and Caplan. In a phrase apparently coined by Broadbent, the document deliberately rejected concessions to consensus radicalism: if it waffled, it would "waffle to the left." Tactically, it was loaded with the rhetorical symbols which could crystallize the "left" in a party where it was increasingly wrong to be "right." Emotionally, it was a catharsis for younger, radical academics, fed up with catering to the presumed tastes of the mass electorate and eager to challenge a party leadership which had delivered neither electoral victory nor spiritual gratification.

In a paper prepared for the party's policy review committee and summarised in *Socialism Canada Seventies*, Watkins had presented part of the reasoning which lay behind the Manifesto: "On the road to socialism, aspirations for independence or feelings of nationalism and particularly anti-imperialism, should be taken into account in their own right. For to pursue independence in a serious way in Canada is to make visible the necessity and desirability of socialism." In short, an appeal to the cyclical mood of Canadian nationalism was a convenient way to recruit mass support for socialism. Although the Manifesto ranged across a broad spectrum of left-wing concerns, from women's liberation to industrial democracy, its two chief themes were a fervid anti-Americanism (the attributes of American society were characterized as "militarism abroad and racism at home") and a harkening back to the certitudes of the Regina Manifesto ("Capitalism must be replaced by socialism, by national planning of investment and by public ownership of the means of production in the interests of the Canadian people as a whole.").

The argument was not universally accepted. Although Donald Creighton, Canada's most Tory historian, allegedly gave his blessing to the Waffle cause, George Bain, then the *Globe and Mail's* perceptive Ottawa columnist, wondered whether, if socialism was the price of independence, Canadians might not reject both. A colleague of Watkins, Abraham Rotstein, who had exercised a powerful influence on both the NDP and Watkins in the direction of economic nationalism, was obviously dismayed that his views had been trapped in an out-dated brand of socialism. Like Cameron and Saltsman in their 1967 paper, which Rotstein had certainly influenced, he insisted that the NDP had a wide range of mechanisms to counter the effects of external economic domination. However, neither these nor other criticisms of style or text could persuade the authors to modify their Manifesto. Intransigence cost them the support of Charles Taylor and of Ed Broadbent, their only M.P. and a part-author, but it did not deter a total of ninety-four signatories, most of them academics, and including Laurier LaPierre, Cy Gonick, the Winnipeg editor and publisher of *Canadian Dimension*, and Dave Barrett, a British Columbia M.L.A. and a recent leadership aspirant.

Ostensibly, New Democrats possess great enthusiasm for policy discussion; in fact, it is a minority taste. Robbed of the excitement of a leadership contest, the Winnipeg convention had few charms and registrations lagged until the emergence of the Manifesto brought promise of a major battle. In retrospect, the party leaders might have been wiser to accept the Manifesto, grit their teeth during the ensuing storm and trust that it would fall into the capacious oblivion reserved for the party's prose. But like most outsiders, including columnists Doug Fisher and Harry Crowe, they under-estimated the support the Manifesto would draw and, like Broadbent and Taylor, they soon discovered the utter inflexibility of its architects. Hurriedly, David Lewis and Taylor drafted an alternative statement, "For a United and Independent Canada," restating the theme of economic and political nationalism in more familiar NDP language, and won endorsement by the party's federal council prior to the convention on October 25th.

The ensuing four days were a nightmare for party regulars. To democratise procedures, the party had adopted a "panel" structure for the convention, allowing simultaneous debate on resolutions, more participation and greater productivity than in the more familiar plenary sessions. A procedural loophole allowed the Left to rush its forces from panel to panel for crucial votes. It took a couple of days before the moderates were sufficiently organized to counter-attack but soon rival clutches of delegates were sent panting through the corridors of Winnipeg's vast Civic Auditorium. Next, the Left cried foul play when the majority overthrew most of their victories during the ratifying plenary sessions. The Left's chief triumph was the NDP's final abandonment of support for NATO. The convention highlight was an hour-long, nationally-televised debate between supporters of the rival manifestos. Teams of speakers, including most of the potential federal leadership aspirants, followed Watkins and Lewis to separate microphones. When the television coverage and a good many more pedestrian speeches had ended, a fair number of the delegates had departed, but enough remained to endorse the Lewis-Taylor document by 499 votes to 268.

The critical moment of the Waffle movement came not with the production of the manifesto but at the end of the convention. Collectively, the NDP had responded to the left-wing pressure as any party would, by co-option and concession. Watkins was elected a party vice-president; seven of the twenty party councillors elected by the convention were prominent Waffle backers. The "United Canada" statement, while closer to the NDP mainstream, had swung considerably to the left of previous party policy. The articulate, youthful leaders of the Waffle had acquired considerable respect from the party and a good many voted against their document less from conviction than because it was "bad politics." In the convention aftermath, the Wafflers were in an influential position to contribute their own current to the party's mainstream.

That was not the New Left style. In the jargon of the student movement, in which some of its leaders had learned their politics, Waffle demands on the NDP were "non-negotiable." They were also automatically escalating. Later, both Watkins and Laxer confessed astonishment at the level of support they obtained at Winnipeg. After four days of meeting, plotting, mutual congratulation and media attention, what was the point of stopping? Youthful adherents, assured by the media that their role was confrontation with their elders, decided to act out their parts. Veteran CCFers, unreconciled to the New Party broadening out, sensed that the party might be shoved back to its old moorings. Even NDP activists could escape from the frustrations of a near-decade of electoral politics by becoming part of a morally fulfilling movement.

In a paradox Wafflers could hardly appreciate, because of a cultural and intellectual continentalism few of them could even perceive, the Waffle was pressing the NDP to follow the route of the American Left. In the late 1960s, with ghetto and university riots, Vietnam demonstrations and an entire country in a state of turbulence, it seemed a fashionable and widely publicised route. Radical chic obscured the fact that taking to the streets is a tactic of the weak. The Waffle demands on the NDP echoed, almost unconsciously, those of the American New Left, from the rhetoric of "American imperialism" to appeals for sexual freedom and for the tactics of extra-parliamentary protest. To a degree, the NDP responded. A federal party committee, with Karl Jaffary, a Toronto alderman, and James Laxer as co-chairmen, was appointed to explore tactics of community organization. The Ontario party actually approved financial aid for a community action experiment in Kitchener.

To confront the NDP rather than work entirely within it required a separate organization. A newsletter was prepared, a network of "steering committees" was established, based in Toronto, and, to avoid charges of a separate membership, individuals indicated their support by joining a "mailing list." Funds were collected and, at its height, the Waffle hired organizers for its activities, maintained an office and issued statements to the press. With the news media increasingly tuned in to Canadian nationalism and naturally eager for news of intra-party dissension, Waffle leaders like Watkins and Laxer were frequent performers and their differences with the NDP leadership got regular, if *ex parte*, airing.

For party leaders, the challenge of the Waffle posed a difficult and increasingly exasperating dilemma. On the one hand, the group included able, personable individuals, potential recruits for the next generation of party leaders. The Waffle had tapped a genuine need among many constituency members. It could shelter behind the party's respect for democratic dissent and its inherent anti-authoritarianism. On the other hand, particularly in the middle-class milieu where both the Waffle and the party's leadership operated, it was apparent that the NDP's position was being steadily obscured. The party's disunity was exploited in the media and by those, particularly the Conservatives, who had their own problems in that area. Most offensive to party leaders, especially in Ontario and Manitoba, was the increasing tendency by Waffle spokesmen to attack trade union leaders and, particularly, international unions. Even the original Manifesto had been restrained in that area, but Wafflers soon discovered and exploited the deep well of anti-union sentiment among both old CCFers and the young. By and large, the NDP leadership had remained restlessly quiet under attack; pro-NDP union leaders like Larry Sefton of the Steelworkers and Dennis McDermott, the new Canadian director of the United Autoworkers, were not so tolerant. Veterans of fighting both Liberals and Communists in their own unions, they detected identical kinds of abuse from Waffle spokesmen.

Perhaps the chief problem for the NDP leadership and for many of their rank-and-file supporters in meeting the challenge was that they were too busy with the routine but unavoidable chores of running a political party between elections. Debts had to be paid off, conferences organized, government policies criticized. When neither a provincial nor a federal election loomed, there was usually a by-election campaign to be conducted. An exhausted cadre of leaders and workers had little time to spare to meet Waffle criticisms or to expound a clearer definition of the responsibilities and limitations of the New Democratic Party as an instrument for political change. A handful of pamphlets and occasional sessions at schools for election workers were insufficient to explain that the NDP did not have to follow the path of branch-plant radicalism, that it had a tradition of its own and a goal — to become a majority party of the democratic left. It was the Americans, after all, who had allowed their own socialist party to die.

VI. Progress

"While we have a responsibility as politicians to provide the public with leadership on social concerns, we're being ineffective politicians if we are so far out in front the public can't even see us."

The sentiments may have jarred on Waffle sympathisers at the 1969 convention but they came from a man most delegates had never expected to see at an NDP meeting: a New Democratic premier of Manitoba.

In 1966, when the party garnered twenty-three per cent of the provincial vote, it had reached the limits of its traditional Manitoba support. Where could it go next? A very few people thought it might try for power. Three years later, most of the familiar faces in Manitoba politics were gone. Defeated in a bid for the Tory national leadership and again in the 1968 election, Duff Roblin had retired to a Montreal boardroom. His successor, a Minnedosa funeral director named Walter Weir, scrapped Roblin's mild progressivism and returned to a familiar Manitoba preoccupation — cutting taxes. The leaderless Liberals turned to a veteran of the Fifties named Bobby Bend, whose only detectable policy was to out-Weir Weir. By 1969, the provincial government faced a number of troubles. The noisiest was Indian and environmentalist protest against a hydro development which would drown South Indian Lake; the quietest was the disturbing state of Churchill Forest Industries, a complex scheme of public and private co-operation at The Pas, launched by Roblin in 1966. Weir saw his chance. If Trudeau could win in 1968 by being rude at a federal-provincial conference, so could he. Accordingly, he went to Ottawa, pounded the table against bilingualism for the sake of the television cameras, and returned to announce a provincial election for June 25th, 1969.

Weir expected to catch the NDP leaderless. Russ Paulley had resigned at the beginning of the year and a convention was scheduled for the end of June. Instead, the date was shifted to June 7th and nominating meetings provided a setting for debates between the two contenders, Sid Green and Ed Schreyer, the thirty-three year old M.P. for Selkirk, political science lecturer and the former CCF boy wonder who had captured Brokenhead riding at the age of twenty-two. With lengthy television coverage as a bonus, Schreyer swept the convention by 506 votes to 177, leaving the impression of a cool, unflappable moderate. While Weir left his campaign to an advertising agency and the Liberals tried to pretend that the unfortunate Bend was Trudeau, Schreyer whirled through the ethnic areas of northern and eastern Manitoba, switching to German, French and Ukrainian to persuade his listeners to ignore directives from traditional leaders to stick by the Conservatives. When Weir and Bend denounced socialism, Schreyer insisted that he was a social democrat with a list of specifics: premium-free Medicare, government-run auto insurance, consolidation of Winnipeg's municipal governments, better roads for the North, more public housing. When Weir defended the South Indian Lake diversion and Bend promised to stop it, Schreyer cautiously offered a fresh study. On an even more sensitive issue in Manitoba politics, the federal government's Official Languages Act, he was unequivocal: acceptance of the Act was NDP policy.

To some ethnic leaders, that was more ammunition against the NDP; to their followers, it made less difference. Schreyer was the first non-Anglo-Saxon party leader since John Norquay in a province where other groups now totalled a significant majority. Almost imperceptibly, the NDP had broadened its ethnic representation; the others, particularly the ruling Conservatives, had not. Perhaps too, as Tom Peterson has suggested, the Schreyer campaign transcended traditional ethnic voting patterns; Manitobans stopped voting because they were French or German or Jewish and began picking parties because they favoured the rich or the poor. Meanwhile, the Manitoba party benefited from an impressive influx of organizers, among them Ontario's Terry Grier.

It may have helped a little that the experts were so unanimous. Weir would win, they promised. If there was any change, Bend might be beaten and Schreyer would lead a strong opposition. On that assumption, almost fifty years to the day after the Winnipeg General Strike collapsed, Manitobans voted. By a narrow margin, they elected the first actual New Democratic Party government in Canada. When the recounts were over, Schreyer and his candidates had collected 38.1 per cent of the votes and twenty-eight New Democrats were elected. The Conservatives, at 35.5 per cent, had elected twenty-five and the Liberals, at 23.9 per cent, had five. To complicate matters there was an Independent and a Social Crediter. Despite frenzied efforts to manufacture a "stop-the-Socialists" coalition, one Liberal, Larry Desjardins, announced that he would sit with the NDP. Schreyer's vote-losing defence of French-Canadian rights had ironically given the NDP

Ed Schreyer. The election of the NDP in Manitoba in 1969 was the first major breakthrough for the party since its formation. Schreyer's firm allegiance to "social democracy" offended some of the party faithful but reassured Manitoba voters.

power. Three weeks after the election, a bitter and bewildered Weir made way for the new government.

Schreyer had inherited no prize. His majority was shaky, his caucus inexperienced and by no means dependable. It spanned the spectrum from Desjardins to Cy Gonick and back again to the unpredictable, explosive tribune of the people, Joe Borowski. Even more serious was the absence of the trained, venturesome bureaucracy which had made so many of the triumphs of the Saskatchewan CCF possible. In 1944, T. C. Douglas had been able to recruit brilliantly talented people from across Canada and in the United States and Great Britain to share the challenge of running North America's first socialist government. Who, in the summer of 1969, would abandon a well-paid career to work for a government whose life expectancy had to be counted in weeks, not months? The available civil service machinery was the product of generations of some of the most conservative and penny-pinching regimes in Canada.

In spite of the difficulties, in spite of orders from Winnipeg newspapers to consider himself merely a caretaker premier, in spite of predictions from *Canadian Dimension* that he would betray the socialist revolution he had never promised, Schreyer announced that his government would run its full term, there would be no snap election and that he would do what he had promised during the campaign. And he did. An August session of the Legislature strengthened the power of the province's proposed ombudsman, imposed a four-day cooling-off period on door-to-door sales, cut the voting age to eighteen, raised welfare allowances by ten per cent and started a series of increases in the province's minimum wage. Medicare premiums were slashed by eighty-eight per cent and the cost was transferred to income and corporation taxes. Expostulating opposition politicians struggled to find reasons to object, failed and went along.

When, in December, the government started to face trouble, it was for a major element in its election platform – government-run, universal, no-fault auto insurance. Since 1946, Saskatchewan motorists had been saving money from a government plan and not even the Thatcher government had dared to cancel it. Both the CCF and the NDP had argued that universal coverage from a single carrier, the government, meant protection for everyone, lower premiums and a great reduction in litigation. The Saskatchewan plan annually proved the point. Even private insurance agents sometimes complained that their automobile business was a source of trouble but, when threatened by its loss, they rallied with all the impressive power of the North American insurance industry behind them. Schreyer and his colleagues found themselves at the centre of the kind of barrage the Saskatchewan government had experienced during the medicare debate. Public relations firms deployed their genius in letter-writing campaigns, full-page newspaper advertisements and a number of "spontaneous" demonstrations of public wrath. Bumper stickers blossomed and the opposition joined the fight.

In the Legislature, the government staggered. Desjardins and some elected New Democrats began to shift under the pressure. On April 22nd, when a government minister announced details of the plan, the opposition pressure built fast. A crowd of 7,000 gathered outside the Legislature to condemn the government; in the chamber itself, scenes verged on bedlam. The provincial NDP, by no means strong in members or money, summoned help from other provincial sections to produce a grassroots campaign to counter the insurance lobby. By the end of July, when Desjardins announced that he could not support the bill, an election suddenly became imminent. Then, with astonishing suddenness, the storm subsided. The Winnipeg newspapers, vitriolic against the socialists, proclaimed that an election would be unwise and unnecessary. The clamor died away like magic. Schreyer, who almost alone had remained calm in the turmoil, announced a handful of concessions to individual agents who might be hurt by the government scheme. Desjardins and even an independent switched back and the bill became law.

The car insurance battle gave Manitoba almost its first political excitement in generations. It also demonstrated that the NDP government was no mere electoral accident. When the legislative session finally adjourned, even the Conservative-leaning Winnipeg *Tribune* confessed that it had been "the longest and most productive of new legislation in the history of Manitoba." Wiretapping was outlawed, hospital insurance coverage was extended to nursing homes for the elderly, and the most thorough landlord and tenant legislation in Canada was adopted, including the appointment of a "rentalsman" to help settle disputes. An election act limited campaign spending, compelled reporting of contributions and abolished the candidate deposit. Over noisy opposition from mining interests, the government forced through taxes and royalty agreements which more than doubled provincial income from mineral resources.

While Ed Schreyer wrestled with the unfamiliar problems of power, his June victory sent hopes soaring in British Columbia. There, too, the NDP found itself with a cool, moderate new leader. At the beginning of 1969, Robert Strachan had announced that he would not stand again for the leadership. A tall, dignified and eloquent carpenter from Nanaimo, he had too little appeal and too many defeats to his record for the party's middle-class backers. The organizationally-inclined complained that he limited his role to the province's brief legislative session. The struggle for the succession brought four candidates to the convention but only two, Tom Berger and Dave Barrett, an exuberant former social worker, possessed widespread support. Of the two, sober, intellectual, politically moderate Tom Berger claimed the support of union leaders, party executive, most caucus members and, by a narrow thirty-six votes, the convention.

Berger's personality and the apparent lessons of Schreyer's victory determined the campaign. If British Columbians could ever be persuaded to trust the NDP, the earnest, slightly solemn Vancouver lawyer and his slate of businessmen and professionals could surely do it. With Wally Ross and Michael Lewis, another son of David, to organize the campaign, an Ontario-style canvassing approach was attempted in constituencies where the NDP had barely ever knocked on a door. Priority ridings were selected, organizers assigned and money spent in a "now or never" mood. Berger's tour, carefully tailored to cover the party's priority areas, allowed him to lay out his programme and to insist that the party's plans for public ownership began and ended with car insurance and the British Columbia Telephone Company.

Moderation cut no ice with W. A. C. Bennett. He and his followers were as aware of the Manitoba upset as the NDP and his province would not be caught napping. When he announced the election on July 21st, taking full advantage of the summer doldrums, Bennett proclaimed that it was to meet the menace of "Marxist Socialism." The usual flood of public works was mixed with florid denunciations of Berger as "the city slicker labour lawyer" and his party as the "New Depression Party." It was a battle, insisted Bennett, between "those who seek a responsible, developing private enterprise economy and those who would impose on you the heavy hand of socialism." As usual, the message was not limited to the premier's booming voice but echoed across billboards, full-page advertisements, a crescendo of television spots and even a government-financed film. On August 27th, the Berger approach was tested — and it failed. The NDP vote, 33.9 per cent, was almost as high a share as the Left had known in the province but Social Credit support reached a new record, 46.8 per cent. The Liberals, safe in their middle-class strongholds, were untouched but the NDP lost five seats, including Berger's own. "The people of British Columbia have stopped the Socialists in their tracks," exulted Bennett, adding the somewhat Delphic comment that, perhaps, there would not need to be any more elections. He was, he explained to reporters, "plugged into God."

Berger, obviously, was not. Within weeks, he had abandoned the NDP leadership and returned to his neglected law practice. Whatever his political resemblance to Schreyer, British Columbia was not Manitoba and Bennett was distinctly not Walter Weir. Berger's inevitable successor was Dave Barrett. Flamboyant, rhetorically radical, extroverted, he made few efforts to conciliate traditional factions in the party and almost no overtures to the province's trade union leaders. Laden with debt and damaged by the failure of a campaign on which it had staked so much, the provincial organization sagged close to collapse. The party's office in Vancouver was almost closed for lack of funds. In the circumstances, it hardly seemed to matter who led the British Columbia NDP.

That was not true in Ontario or Saskatchewan and in 1970 both provincial sections changed leader. After the Winnipeg convention, the left wing had returned to Saskatchewan with sufficient momentum to dominate the provincial convention and sweep most of the executive positions. To the dismay of Woodrow Lloyd, the most prominent party leader to support the Waffle Manifesto, members of his provincial caucus and moderate leaders set to work to regain control. Combined with growing doubts of his ability to lead the party back to power and his own deteriorating health, this was enough to persuade the provincial leader to announce that he would not seek re-election in 1970. After efforts to persuade him to reconsider failed, by mid-April a first candidate was in the field; Allan Blakeney, a fortyish Regina lawyer, former Rhodes Scholar from Nova Scotia and a respected minister in the CCF-NDP governments. By July 2nd, when the convention opened in the Regina Armouries, there were three more — Roy Romanow, a Saskatoon lawyer and MLA, clearly on the right; Don Mitchell, the Waffle nominee, and George Taylor, a Saskatoon lawyer and alderman whose ideological position lay somewhere between those of Mitchell and Blakeney. With candidates and their supporters scrambling for votes, both moderates and Wafflers scored victories in the policy debates and the word "socialism" was flourished with uninhibited abandon. On the key issue of leadership, the strength of the moderates was apparent. Romanow retained a narrow lead for two ballots until Mitchell's retirement released a hundred ballots to elect Blakeney. Close to another hundred refused to vote. Hard-core Wafflers, they insisted that there really was no choice.

In Ontario, the leadership question had apparently been settled in 1968 when Donald MacDonald had decisively beaten James Renwick. However, by early 1970, it was obvious that Stephen Lewis, a former Renwick backer, was manoeuvring for a challenge of his own, building alliances within the provincial caucus and serving as party labour critic in an attempt to win union support. For MacDonald, it was a bitter discovery. His own prestige in the province at large was rising, confirmed by a by-election victory in Middlesex South in the autumn of 1969. A second leadership challenge would be fatal blow to his own standing and to party unity. After attempts by senior labour leaders and the Ontario party executive to discourage Lewis had failed, MacDonald weighed the consequences for his party against his own long years of struggle and calmly announced his intention to resign.

Until the end of July, Lewis was the uncontested heir-apparent. Senior union leaders had discovered, somewhat to their chagrin, that he had quietly lined up many of the second-level leaders in their organizations as well as Dennis McDermott, the aggressive new leader of the United Autoworkers in Canada. Accepting MacDonald's obvious hint that a uncontested succession would do the least harm to the party, most of the senior union officials joined the Lewis camp. Only a few remained to give private support when Walter Pitman, the former New Party M.P. and currently the provincial member for Peterborough, was persuaded to enter the contest. For some of his backers, he was a rallying point in their bitterness at the treatment of MacDonald; for many he seemed a more likely figure to attract Ontario voters. According to Professor John Wilson, a supporter, Pitman was "the personification both of progressive change and of cautious common sense" which Ontarians wanted in a political leader. The Lewis campaign, headed by Gerald Caplan, answered that Ontarians really wanted a radical alternative for their discontents. Whatever the provinces's electorate felt, Lewis plainly reflected the wishes of a large, ebullient convention by a margin of 1,188 votes to 642.

Though the Waffle had run a leadership candidate in Saskatchewan, the more sophisticated Ontario branch chose different tactics. A pre-convention Waffle meeting heard both candidates, proclaimed that neither was a "socialist," and proceeded to concentrate on achieving policy victories and winning control of the party executive. As the badly divided party leadership threw itself into the Lewis-Pitman race, Waffle spokesmen dominated the convention microphones and committees, delighting delegates with roundhouse assaults on American corporations, resource barons and "right-wingers" in the party leadership. By the time the moderates realized what was happening, the convention had endorsed Waffle-inspired resolutions calling, among other things, for nationalization of energy resource industries and abortion on demand. Delegates were even within an ace of adopting an Ontario version of the Waffle manifesto as a statement of party goals. A last-minute salvage operation reversed the tide but could not undo some of the Waffle triumphs.

From the moderate standpoint, forcing a contest had probably been a mistake. The chances of beating Lewis, even for a contender as respected as Pitman, were slim. Campaigning as "Pitman for Premier," the challenger and his team used their opportunity for public attention to speak to Ontario voters while Lewis concentrated on the short-range need to arouse the emotions of party members. Not only did the contest allow the Waffle considerable freedom to control the convention, it presented Lewis, the quintessential "party" man, as the rhetorician of a socialist "movement." Far from moderating his public image as some Pitman supporters had hoped, Lewis played to the version of the Ontario electorate his advisers had concocted for him.

While Lewis and Blakeney prepared to test their appeal with a wider public than NDP convention delegates, there were faint signs of life from the Atlantic provinces where the party, like the CCF, had so far achieved little more than a holding operation. In the autumn of 1969, an erratic and not notably temperate member of the New Brunswick legislature had abandoned the Liberal government to sit as a New Democrat. There was no great regret when he returned to his own party in the spring. In Newfoundland, the NDP had made virtually no headway since the disintegration of Ed Finn's Newfoundland Democratic Party. From a tiny bridgehead at Memorial University, the party reached unavailingly to find some new indigenous roots. Negotiations with Tom Burgess, future leader of the New Labrador Party, foundered on his desire to have a paid position on the Steelworkers' staff. Approaches to Richard Cashin, a former Liberal M.P., were momentarily more promising but he turned his energies to the more immediate task of organizing fishermen.

Only in Nova Scotia was there discernible progress. Throughout the Sixties, the NDP had consisted of a small but valiant outpost of supporters in Halifax and a slightly larger but ageing group on Cape Breton Island, reproducing in miniature most of the strains and jealousies which traditionally divide the island and the mainland. The leader, Professor James Aitchison, was a respected and selfless worker for the party, with little prospect or expectation of leading it to a position of influence or power. In 1969, the dominance of the Halifax group was challenged by two abrasive young men, Jeremy Akerman, a former radio announcer, and Paul MacEwan, a teacher, who set themsleves the task of organizing for victory in Cape Breton. Amidst general scepticism and with what meagre finances the federal party could spare and their own supporters could collect, Akerman and MacEwan were rewarded for their labours by election to the Nova Scotia legislature on October 13th, 1970.

In 1971, elections were due in Saskatchewan, Alberta and Ontario. Camp's law of political longevity may allow a provincial government a good second chance but it does not promise a third. By May 25th, 1971, when Ross Thatcher declared an election on June 23rd, his confidence in success had to depend more on his opponents' weakness than his own strength. If there was any group Thatcher had not alienated, complained his lieutenant, Dave Steuart,

Allan Blakeney. Saskatchewan's return to a left-wing government in 1971 demonstrated that the farmer-labour alliance was politically possible. Blakeney, himself, was a former federal NDP president and a CCF cabinet minister.

it was because the premier had not yet met it. In fact, the Liberal leader campaigned as though he was trying to topple a government, not retain it, flailing the NDP and the Trudeau regime with equal vehemence, demanding labour courts as a weapon against the province's tiny labour movement, and promising a second pulp mill for the province at a time when the NDP was getting growing support for its opposition to fast sale of Saskatchewan resources.

While Thatcher flew over the province in a chartered airplane, Blakeney rode from hamlet to farmyard in a chartered bus, focussing on nagging issues like the Thatcher government's deterrent fees for Medicare users or a ruthlessly gerrymandered election map. When the Liberal slogan boasted "They can do more for Saskatchewan," Blakeney suggested that perhaps they had done enough already, with low farm prices, unemployment and inflation. Instead, re-defining its initials as "New Deal for People," the NDP stressed land bank and credit legislation to save the family farm, reduction in property taxes, help for small businesses and a determination to get a better return from the province's oil and mining industries. The Liberal appeal for "growth" was answered by an NDP emphasis on "quality of life." Thatcher, who had begun the campaigning by patronising Blakeney as "little Allan," woke up to his danger with a last-minute refrain of a familiar campaign song, "socialism versus free enterprise." It was too late. On June 23rd, Saskatchewan voters gave the NDP 55.2 per cent of their support and forty-five seats in the most one-sided victory for the Canadian Left since the 1940s. A shattered, demoralized Liberal party could not even muster the courtesy to thank its defeated premier; it was the NDP rally in Regina which turned from its celebration to cheer Ross Thatcher as a worthy opponent. Less than a month later, he was dead.

Blakeney took office with the smoothness and assurance of experience. A cabinet drawn from the moderate majority (only one had endorsed the Waffle manifesto) started to turn the province around. Contracts for the controversial pulp mill and a Liberal-sponsored iron mine were cancelled for re-negotiation, a Family Farm Protection Act relieved small farmers of impossible debt burdens, Thatcher's anti-union legislation was repealed, deterrent fees for visits to doctors and hospitals were cancelled and all fees for patients over sixty-five were abolished. There was more to come as the new government went on to tackle more complex problems like its land bank proposals and the foreign ownership of the province's farm land.

Just as the Manitoba victory had influenced the British Columbia election in 1969, the second NDP electoral success fuelled the already surging expectations of the Ontario party. At the end of 1970, the dull grey John Robarts announced his forthcoming retirement. His heir would be William Davis, the Minister of Education who had floated almost unscathed by criticism through the buoyant Sixties. However, at the convention, the certainty faded. Allan Lawrence, a mildly maverick cabinet minister with backing from rich Torontonians and the party's middle class youth, chased Davis through five ballots before allowing him the prize. To an outsider, the Tories appeared deeply divided, with a leader who barely commanded the support of half his party.

Ontario Tories would not have lasted in office since 1943 without a powerful sense of survival. Davis co-opted the Lawrence organizers to his own team. He also turned to his American political kinfolk, employing Market Opinion Research, a Detroit firm which had worked for the Republicans, to programme his campaign. MOR gave Davis his strategy. A survey showed that Ontario voters liked Davis but considered his NDP opponent "the least competent, the least trustworthy and the least sociable of the three party leaders." Unemployment was the chief issue; economic nationalism issues were only mentioned by 8.8 per cent of those polled. On a subsidiary but troublesome issue, MOR found that a big majority of voters opposed giving more money to Catholic schools, a policy favoured by Liberals and New Democrats. Shortly before the writs were issued, proclaiming that it should not become an election issue, Davis announced his own stand: no money. His support among middle-class Torontonians also jumped when he stopped the city's controversial Spadina Expressway. Both acts boosted the premier's "decisiveness" quotient; both were pre-planned to be popular. By September, when the campaign officially began, the Conservatives had built themselves into enviable strength.

Even Liberals wrote off their own party as a threat in the 1971 elections and conceded that the main opposition would come from the NDP. Davis had helped give that impression in the spring when he ran his own "socialism versus free enterprise" campaign to load up the Conservative campaign coffers for a special effort. The NDP itself felt more confident than usual. It was well prepared, well organized and, by its own modest standards, well financed. Province-wide expenditures eventually totalled $197,000 (half from constituency association quotas, a quarter from unions, the rest from fund-raising efforts like the sale of campaign buttons). At least $300,000 was spent by local campaigns. More than fourteen organizers had worked for a year to develop canvassing organizations and more were available from sympathetic unions and other provincial sections of the party as soon as the campaign started.

There was only one major economy. Unlike their

opponents, the NDP had no survey to guide the campaign or the intuition of Lewis and his advisers. Instead, working on their own conception of Davis, the issues and the electorate, the NDP campaign committee offered Lewis as "a fully accredited moderate," stressed the party's forthright enthusiasm for economic independence and avoided the monotonous reiteration of basic issues like taxes and housing which had been a feature of MacDonald's 1967 campaign. Instead, more exciting items from the party platform were featured: a guaranteed annual income, free tuition, salaries for housewives, the extension of medicare to cover drugs and dental treatment. To help display its new leader, the party supplemented the usual campaign bus with an elderly airplane chartered for long northern hauls.

If the Conservative party's surveys were accurate, the NDP could hardly have done better if the Tories themselves had given the orders. As for their own campaign, the Conservatives emphasized job creation and a sense of economic purpose ideally suited to match the sudden chill after the proclamation of American economic countermeasures in August, 1971. While the NDP leader challenged Ontario voters, the Conservatives, with their anodyne "Call me Bill" image of the premier, sought to reassure them. The result, on October 21st, was derived from the highest turn-out of the provincial voters since 1898. The Davis campaign netted 44.5 per cent of the vote and seventy-eight seats; the Liberals won 27.8 per cent of the vote and twenty seats and the NDP stayed almost where it had been in 1967, with 27.2 per cent and nineteen seats.

For Lewis, it was a bitter evening after a year and a half of virtually non-stop campaigning. As newspapers boasted of a Tory landslide, he discovered that he had barely held his own seat. There were five NDP victories over incumbent Liberals or Conservatives but seven other sitting members, among them Walter Pitman, had been beaten. The party had even been narrowly edged out of its minimum goal of replacing the Liberals as official opposition. The Liberals had fallen, but not far enough. There were NDP gains in the north and in normally barren eastern Ontario but in industrial cities like Hamilton, Oshawa and in the outskirts of Toronto, Conservative talk of jobs and security obviously meant more than the challenge of economic nationalism. Once again, the NDP had failed to connect with masses of potential working-class supporters. For a leader who had staked so much on his own capacity to articulate a political mood and to sense the barometer of public feeling, it was a double disillusionment.

Not all provincial governments held the secret of eternal life. On August 31st, 1971, Peter Lougheed and the Conservatives ended the thirty-five year regime of Alberta's Social Credit League. Alberta New Democrats, long hardened to disappointment, could take comfort in the election of their provincial leader, Grant Notley, in a Peace River constituency.

David Lewis during the 1972 election campaign. With the brilliantly orchestrated denunciation of the "Corporate Welfare Bums," thousands of party members who had forgotten why they belonged suddenly remembered.

VII. Clarification

The newspapers which recorded the outcome of the Ontario NDP leadership convention reported the kidnapping of James Cross. In the ensuing days, Canadians watched in dismay as events they had associated with remote Latin American dictatorships took place in their own country. Political terrorism, blackmail, a revolting murder, mass arrests, troops with steel helmets and machine guns, the startling activation of the half-forgotten War Measures Act: here, with a vengeance, was that "smack of firm government" Trudeau had represented for Canadian voters in 1968.

In retrospect, it became easy to say that the government had raised an enormous hammer against a handful of unbalanced fanatics, acting out the revolutionary fantasies of the nationalist elite. The extraordinary proposal for a special government to take over Quebec, associated with Claude Ryan, was nothing more than another manifestation of the self-importance of that same Montreal elite. As for the evident psychological collapse of the Bourassa government or the need to shock would-be revolutionaries from dreams back into reality, these were reasons for the War Measures Act which the Trudeau government could hardly be expected to articulate in public. In the absence of such an explanation (or perhaps even if it had been offered), sixteen members of the New Democratic Party caucus rose alone in the midst of the clamor to oppose the federal government's action.

At a time when a tired prime minister spoke of "bleeding hearts," when Robert Stanfield, whatever his private reservations, stood with the majority, when Réal Caouette demanded that the revolutionaries be shot by firing squad, it was an act of collective courage. Coast to coast, most powerfully in Quebec itself, Canadians backed the government and vilified the NDP as an alliance of cowards, traitors and secret separatists. To an impressive degree, the party membership stood firm. It understood the position of those who had sided with the government; it admired the sixteen who had not. Some were reminded that, in 1942, the CCF had also been vilified for its protests when Japanese Canadians had been subjected to mass deportation under the same War Measures Act. It was one of the stands that had added distinction to the CCF's record. By November, when the party accepted the principle of the Public Order (Temporary Measures) Act as the price imposed by the government for withdrawing the War Measures Act, the civil libertarians had been aroused and even turned on the NDP for its apparent surrender. The public mood changed more slowly. A December Gallup poll showed the Liberals at an almost unprecedented fifty-nine per cent and the NDP slumped from twenty to twelve per cent. By the spring, though, the party had recovered and, in a by-election in the Ontario constituency of Brant on May 31st, 1971, captured a traditionally strong Liberal seat. There is nothing so mutable in politics as the public's memory.

Paradoxically, the party's position in the October crisis damaged it nowhere so much as in Quebec. Since 1968, the NDP's affairs in the province had deteriorated sadly. Ill and exhausted, Robert Cliche could no longer afford to carry on as leader. His successor, Roland Morin, an interpreter and former union official, persuaded a reluctant party to contest the 1970 provincial election. The result was a humiliating disaster. Between them, the party's thirteen candidates collected a derisory 4,130 votes − 0.15 per cent of the total. The strong separatist showing in the 1970 election and the ensuing October crisis ended a bitter dilemma for many of the faithful CCF and NDP supporters. Despite NDP efforts to appeal to French Canadians, it had remained dependent on English-speaking Montrealers for most of its money, members and energy. The rise of the Parti Québécois meant, for many of them, that the NDP was a luxury they could no longer afford. The party's pathetic showing in the April election indicated the disaffection. The October crisis confirmed it: even the veteran CCFer, Frank Scott, reluctantly agreed with the Trudeau government's response. So, too, did Michael Oliver, the NDP's first president.

When the remnants of the NDP gathered in a church basement in Montreal on February 19th-21st, 1971, it had become a very different organization. Most of the leading figures of the previous eight years were gone. Robert Cliche appeared, almost out of loyalty, to lend a symbolic presence but a new leader and a changed mood were symptoms of change. Raymond Laliberté, the latest Quebec president, had impressive credentials as the former head of Quebec's militant teacher's union, the C.E.Q. A thin, intense intellectual with a wispy beard and a grating voice, he was a self-persuaded socialist, immune from most of the pragmatic gradualism of those who had grown with the faith. His chief lieutenant, Emile Boudreau, a Steelworkers official in Montreal, held an executive position in the Parti Québécois. In an attempt to appeal to those who might be attracted to the NDP by its stand in October,

convention organizers had proclaimed an "open" meeting:
anyone who came could vote. The resulting influx facili-
tated the transformation; it probably did not change it. It
was an invitation to those who had felt themselves
"radicalized" by the October events, to those who had
hitherto felt themselves too radical for the NDP and to
those who now felt that the NDP might be able to carry
the twenty-three per cent separatist vote in federal
elections.

Less than two hundred delegates and hangers-on went to
the week-end meeting but they transformed the NDP in
Quebec. When they emerged, a coalition of quasi-
separatists had taken over the party, forged an alliance
with the Waffle group and presented, virtually as an
ultimatum, what should be the NDP's next policy on
federalism. The "Canadian party," as the federal NDP
was now called, must recognize the unfettered right of
Quebec to self-determination. The phrase was not new. It
was hallowed in innumerable United Nations resolutions,
approved by Claude Ryan and *Le Devoir* and endorsed,
long since, by the Waffle. Its meaning, robbed of the
exquisite rhetoric which soon embellished it, was that
Quebec would have the unilateral right to decide whatever
she liked inside or outside Confederation. To illustrate the
theory by practice, the Quebec party proclaimed that it
was entitled to its own constitution, that it would offer its
own programme and that the "Canadian party" could
conform or not as it pleased.

The church basement convention got national publicity.
Waffle spokesmen proclaimed a major triumph and the
news media echoed the claim. Inevitably, the reports and
the claim ignored some of the complicated details. The
NDP had not, for example, actually been captured by the
Parti Québécois itself. Laliberté was not precisely a
separatist; he was prepared to accept a loose, almost

diaphanous, federalism. His chief feeling was that the entire national issue had to be cleared from the agenda of Quebec politics before socialism could be seriously considered. Others, even Boudreau, had become somewhat disillusioned by the P.Q. – not for its nationalism, of course, but because it was insufficiently radical. For the NDP across Canada, as for the press and the public, these were nuances which hardly made much difference. The notion that "self-determination," once obtained, might never be exercised, was urged by Waffle leaders and by Laliberté himself. All that meant, surely, was that Quebec would have a weapon to obtain the best of both federalism and independence. Across Canada, the party would be condemned for making a treasonable deal with Quebec separatists in the hope of a handful of extra seats in parliament.

In retrospect, the NDP might simply have disavowed its troublesome Quebec section. A year later, it would do precisely that with its vestigial New Brunswick section when it briefly fell into the hands of a coterie of Fredericton revolutionaries. What was the Quebec NDP, after all, but a few hundred paid-up members and an annual subsidy of $15,000? In the winter of 1971, such forcefulness was inconceivable. On the eve of a possible federal election, it would expose the party's claim to a Quebec wing as the Potemkin village it really was. It would have endangered the chances of running a few score of token candidates in French Canada on which the NDP's claim to national party status depended. It would have provoked an open battle with the Waffle for which neither the party nor its leaders were prepared. Above all, it would have demanded tough, concerted leadership at a time when it was not available. Allan Blakeney, the party president, was immersed in preparations for his forthcoming Saskatchewan election, while T. C. Douglas had seen his role, quite properly, as virtually a caretaker leader since his return to Parliament in 1969; if his successor chose to deal with the Waffle or Quebec, he would at least find them in the party. Ever since Douglas had announced in October, 1969, that he was definitely stepping down, the federal party secretary, Clifford Scotton, had been fully engaged in preparing for the Ottawa leadership convention. It was an undertaking comparable in scope and complexity to the original New Party Founding Convention.

By the winter of 1971, the NDP's leadership race had acquired all five of its contestants. To ensure fairness, the party drew up elaborate rules and illustrated its own principles of campaign finance by allowing each candidate a thousand dollar grant and limiting him to a maximum expenditure of $10,500. To help further, the five were shepherded through a schedule of all-candidate meetings across the country. Ed Broadbent had been the first to declare, basing his claims on his credentials as an academic radical, his success in getting elected and his links with a number of trade unionists. John Harney, the bilingual former Ontario secretary, had worked publicly at Winnipeg and quietly thereafter to extend his support, particularly among consituency moderates who saw Lewis as too old, Broadbent as too woolly and Laxer, the Waffle candidate, as political suicide. James Laxer had been fielded only after much Waffle strategical pondering: cool, articulate and disarming, he was undoubtedly their most attractive personality. Frank Howard, a veteran loner in the caucus since his election in 1957, was the only candidate who did not come from Ontario. All four were overshadowed by David Lewis, the Polish immigrant boy who had risen from Montreal's Jewish ghetto through a Rhodes Scholarship and his own brilliance and toughness to become the undoubted guiding force of the CCF and the NDP since the 1940s. No one could doubt his qualifications or his claims to the party leadership; some could wonder about his age, his flexibility and his strength. Far more serious as an obstacle were the bitter, remorseless enemies he had acquired in thirty-five years of fighting to impose his own concept of social democracy on the party. Lewis might be the ablest, the most clear-minded, the most forceful leader the CCF or the NDP had produced; he was not the best-loved.

Lewis's chief antagonist at the 1971 convention would be the Waffle group. Encouraged by success in polarizing debate within the party and by the realization that the party leadership was on the defensive, the group organized vigorously. Its prime target was the weaker constituencies and those where, perhaps, barely a tenth of the member-ship appeared for a general meeting. Concentrating its strength, caucusing in advance, it was not difficult to dominate the delegate elections or to win approval for Waffle resolutions. If regular members were not prepared to sit through interminable debates, procedural wrangling and florid rhetoric, that was their problem. It rapidly became the concern of a group of moderates, based on the party's federal council, who decided that in the Ottawa convention the Waffle would not win by default. An array of draft resolutions, matching the Waffle formulations, was presented through sympathetic constituencies and affili-ated organizations, plans were laid to provide speakers before and at the convention and limited efforts were made to ensure that sympathetic delegates were elected, all independent of the leadership campaigns. To show its flag, the group presented its philosophy in a booklet entitled *NDP NOW*. Launched only a few months before the convention, the NDP Now group, like the Waffle in 1969, was no more than a cadre of like-minded people in search of wider support.

It found it, initially, in a sharp, pre-convention battle

for control of the resolutions committee, the funnel through which material was transmitted to delegates for their decisions. When the smoke cleared, the Waffle had won only a quarter of the positions on the committee and convention resolutions were accordingly bereft, as a Montreal reporter commented, of "the rhetorical symbols — words like imperialism, exploitation or even socialism — which turn on the Wafflers and, probably, turn off the voters." Control of the drafting of resolutions by moderates meant that the Waffle was compelled to rally support to "refer back" statements for the incorporation of its own ideas and verbal symbols. That gave Waffle spokesmen the advantage of the offensive but it provided the NDP Now organizers with a simple signal system — all references back were to be defeated. Apart from some symbolic victories — banning candidates' signs and placards from the convention floor, changing the timetable for a demonstration — the Waffle, for the first time, encountered an impermeable wall of opposition to its policies.

The Quebec resolution could not be disposed of so simply. For the first time, delegates were not prepared to give a blank cheque to upholders of the latest nationalist slogan. Experience with "special status" in 1968 had not been forgotten. The open alliance with the Waffle cost Laliberté and his group the previous automatic sympathy of party leaders. Still, the urge to find a compromise remained almost desperate. A major leadership convention, with extensive national coverage, was hardly the moment to unveil the disintegration of NDP support in French Canada. After anguished sessions, the resolutions committee grudgingly accepted a laborious statement which acknowledged that if "one of our provinces were to choose to separate freely and democratically, it would be madness to attempt to restrain it by force." With Waffle encouragement, the new Quebec leadership rejected the compromise out of hand. Briefly, the majority view hardened and a fresh version of the statement appeared, implicitly rejecting the earlier formulas of "two nations" and "special status" and asserting: "There is no question of the right of Canadians to question Confederation. Nor is there any doubt that the existence of our country depends on the free consent of all our people. The unity of our country cannot be based on force. However, the business of the NDP is to work for a united Canada, on a basis which will do full justice to all our people." After checking to see that Mr. Trudeau had made an identical observation, the drafters further conceded that Canada could not be held together by force.

Compromise resumed as more moderate leadership candidates were consulted and tacit approval was obtained from those Quebec members who might be needed to put together a new party if the Laliberté group bolted. That meant a further, lengthy statement promising that the federal and Quebec parties would continue, after the convention, to try to resolve their differences. The final version was taken before the full convention, exposed to the kind of full-dress, televised debate which the Waffle and "United Canada" resolutions had received at Winnipeg, and adopted 853 to 423. Having won its policy victories, the NDP Now group publicly announced its dissolution.

In contrast to Liberal and Conservative conventions, the leadership race was virtually sandwiched between policy sessions. Nomination speeches, a final debate and occasional interventions in policy debates had helped Laxer and Harney and probably Howard, confirmed Lewis in his traditional role as a convention "heavy" and fatally damaged Broadbent's chances. When balloting began on the afternoon of April 24th, the ranking was predictable; the relative strengths were not. At 661 votes, Lewis's support showed the absence of a hundred or more trade union delegates whose promised presence might have given him a badly-needed first ballot victory. Laxer, with 378, was second; Harney had 299, Broadbent 236 and Howard had 124, more than predicted but too few to stay in the contest. Surprise came with the second ballot. Instead of a rush to Lewis to end the race, the four remaining candidates kept their places, with Harney gaining proportionately and Broadbent falling: the results were Lewis, 715; Laxer, 407; Harney, 347 and Broadbent 223. On the third ballot, a natural switch between middle-of-the road candidates could have put Harney in second place and perhaps won him the contest. Instead, a hundred Broadbent people went to Laxer, driven by a surprising bitterness between the two closest camps. The results were Lewis, 742; Laxer, 508; Harney, 431. A fourth ballot ended it as two generations of Lewis enemies moved out to grab yellow Laxer badges, the leading Harney supporters headed for Lewis and their candidate sat grimly alone with his shattered ambition. The final count was 1046 for Lewis, 612 for Laxer, a shabby triumph for a veteran who deserved better from his party. As Laxer supporters pounded their feet and shouted "Power to the People" in the approved American style, their candidate headed for the podium to make the graceful gesture of declaring the vote unanimous.

When the convention dissolved, two critical pieces of unfinished business remained: the Waffle and Quebec. Neither problem had been much improved by the unexpectedly prolonged leadership contest.

On the Quebec NDP, Lewis faced the choices the party had avoided in February: he could ignore the Laliberté group and try to patch together the earlier Quebec NDP or he could seek to negotiate. He chose the latter course, armed with the implied blank cheque in the second half of the convention resolution. He found Laliberté and Boudreau in a more accommodating frame of mind. The former had decided that a promise not to support civil war was not so far from self-determination after all and, in any case, his group's claim to policy autonomy had not yet been challenged. Boudreau, for his part, had tried the political water in a by-election in Chambly on May 31st and discovered that the riding's separatists would not, after all, support the NDP. After six laborious meetings, much drafting, and toing and froing between Montreal and Ottawa, a brand new policy and the latest slogan, *"une constituante,"* had emerged. To resolve the problems of Canada, the NDP would call a grand constitutional conference at which all Canadians would be represented — governments, oppositions, provinces, cities, even the native people "in a manner determined by themselves." Like many political compromises, the new formula was absurd and naive. It ignored the problems which a large and disparate assembly would face in arriving at agreement in a public forum. It ignored the problems of ratification. It ignored the problems of content. Instead, it patched over a problem, restored the illusion that the party was a factor in French Canada and preserved what a Quebec NDP spokesman, sociologist Gabriel Gagnon, admitted to be a pre-election truce.

The Waffle problem could not be resolved by words. Two years of conciliation, accommodation and hope had broken down on the eve of the 1971 convention. For the Waffle, four days of non-stop policy setbacks were forgotten after Laxer's unexpectedly powerful showing. News coverage of the convention emphasized the polarization of the party and suggested that Lewis would have to conciliate his left wing to bring the NDP back together. Promptly, he made it clear that he would do no such thing. Convention delegates elected only a single Waffler to the party's new executive. With the former Ontario leader, Donald MacDonald, as the NDP's new president, Lewis could count on firm executive support.

For two years, party battles would be essentially provincial. Before the 1971 Saskatchewan election, Waffle leader Don Mitchell announced that the party would get no help from the group unless it pronounced its more radical policies with the requisite firmness. Blakeney ignored the ultimatum. In Ontario, Stephen Lewis was not so nonchalant. On Feburary 21st, 1971, he launched his first public attack on the group and its public utterances. A month later, the Waffle's Ontario chairman, Stephen Penner, riposted with a well-publicised attack on the party's official programme, terming it dishonest and complaining that the word "socialist" appeared only once in its seventy-three pages. As the provincial elections approached, some Wafflers went after key nominations. Penner captured the candidacy in the downtown Toronto riding of Dovercourt; Bruce Kidd, a well-known athlete and Waffler, defeated the party's research director, Marion Bryden, in a contest for the party-held seat of Beaches. In the autumn election, Wafflers fought almost autonomous campaigns, collecting sympathisers from other constituencies to work in favoured areas at the expense of other candidates and to the particular benefit of Penner. Other Wafflers made sure that Stephen Lewis, at public meetings, was regularly questioned about more controversial features of the NDP program such as nationalization of resource industries and abortion on demand.

In the dreary aftermath of the Ontario campaign, Stephen Lewis had plenty of opportunity to recall the Waffle contribution — and the embarrassing fact that Penner had only been narrowly defeated in Dovercourt. Waffle activities were no longer limited to conferences, meetings and internal party agitation. Increasingly, the group marched into labour battles under its own flag, grabbing headlines and attempting to impose its own strategies. There was a growing affinity between Waffle leaders and J. Kent Rowley, an inveterate left-wing foe of the mainstream Canadian labour movement who had suddenly become a darling of the nationalists through his raids on international unions. After the 1971 election, the Waffle voice in the Ontario NDP grew stronger. Election-oriented members and supporters resumed their normal lives, leaving the usual small band of militants and faithful to carry on the chores of a political party between campaigns. Waffle activity, for both newcomers and jaded veterans, was an appealing alternative to collecting memberships, selling dance tickets, organizing raffles and the other indispensable drudgery of a self-financed political organization.

Lewis's own work of rebuilding and maintaining the party ran into road-blocks. At a party meeting in St. Catherines, Wafflers jeered and heckled him, virtually driving him from the platform. A Waffle conference in Windsor in January, 1972, designed to extend the group's trade union following, provided a platform for labour malcontents of every political persuasion. Press reports revelled in denunciations of international unions and their leaders. For the party's key labour supporters, the Windsor meeting was a catalyst for growing misgivings about Waffle activity. Indoctrinated in the political stereotypes of the American union scene, few political commentators seemed aware that most Ontario labour leaders had even deeper roots in socialism than in unionism. Men and women like David Archer, president of the Ontario Federation of Labour, Iona Samis, secretary of the Canadian Food and Allied Workers or Lynn Williams, the cool, articulate former graduate student who was soon to take over District 6 of the Steelworkers, had spent their youth in the CCF or its radical youth movement. Almost consciously, they had turned to the labour movement rather than to politics in the late Forties and Fifties because they saw it as the only framework for the mass base on which democratic socialism could be built. Others, with roots in the British Labour Party, shared their goals. Increasingly, they perceived the Waffle as a threat to their strategy. After two years of reluctance to get involved, the party's trade union leaders saw the January meeting in Windsor as a challenge. If Lewis was prepared to fight, they would see the battle through to a finish.

A constituency resolution addressed to the Ontario NDP council meeting in Oshawa on March 18th, 1972, condemning the Waffle, provided the opportunity. With both sides warned, attendance was heavy at the drab union hall but few were braced for Stephen Lewis's forceful and uncompromising attack. The Waffle, he proclaimed, had poisoned the atmosphere of debate within the party, had maintained the separate structure of a party within a party and had displayed a "sneering, contemptuous attitude towards official trade unionism and the labour leadership." Much of his ammunition was drawn from reports of a secret Waffle meeting in Hamilton only a few weeks before. A long and bitter debate ended only when the party secretary, Gordon Brigden, moved that the problem be referred to the Ontario NDP executive for a report. A vote of 157 to 62 suggested the relative strength of the forces.

For the next three months, the Ontario party was in turmoil. A three member committee, headed by the provincial president, Gordon Vichert, and including the party treasurer, John Brewin and the former Waffler, Gerald Caplan, toured the province to hear opinions. The Waffle, by no means meekly submissive, crowded the committee meetings, shouted down opposing voices and flatly rejected Lewis's criticisms. The group's 8,000 word brief uncompromisingly asserted the Waffle's right to exist, denounced the party leadership and implied that the real villain was, of course, the trade union leadership. If polarization had been intended by both Lewis and the Waffle, it happened. A neutral, even mildly sympathetic committee returned traumatised by the vitriolic mood it had encountered. Instead of the expected compromise, the ensuing report announced that the issue was no longer about democratic debate or whether the party should be radicalized; it had become a question of whether the majority in the NDP could tolerate a ceaseless assault on its principles, policies, structures and leadership. "Our party exists to fulfil certain purposes which have been decided upon by a majority of its members. In our judgement, the fulfilment of those purposes takes precedence over any absolute rights of unfettered freedom, and when the assertion of such rights threatens to undermine the Party's overriding function, the party is entitled, even obligated, to assert its rights." The committee proposed a membership-controlled study of party operations, communications, even the trade union relationship, but it concluded, unequivocally, that the NDP could no longer afford organized, structured opposition groups. The Waffle would have to dissolve.

The report, issued on May 6th, only added to the clamor of the struggle. Urged on, perhaps a little hypocritically, by the newspapers, individuals and groups thrust themselves forward in the role of peacemaker. Two former federal leadership aspirants renewed their rivalry as spokesmen for different plans. John Harney proposed that the Waffle become an affiliated organization, forcing it to reveal its strength but liberating it for its own activities. It was an ingenious scheme which, however, found favour with neither side. More common were proposals for codes of conduct to help guide groups and individuals within the party. It was Ed Broadbent who helped to steer through the so-called Riverdale motion which formed the basis for the eventual party decision. Its principle was simple: the rights of groups to caucus and organize to change party policies and leader had to be recognized. In the angry mood of the party, that would only be possible if the name Waffle disappeared. For the Wafflers, compromise had not seemed necessary or appropriate. Insistent claims that they were being "purged" encouraged press and party members alike to cast them in the congenial role of martyr. Only in the final weeks, at last realizing that they had painted themselves into a corner, did Waffle leaders even consider concessions. Party leaders and the executive moved first, persuaded that the Riverdale motion reflected a basic uneasiness in the riding associations. The Waffle, which by now faced only a reprimand and loss of its name, refused. Instead, it came to Orillia on June 23rd more intransigent than ever.

The meeting next day in the sleepy little Ontario city climaxed three of the most searing months in the Ontario party's history. For five hours, the compromise resolution was denounced as "the War Measures Act" of the NDP and defended as the minimum condition for restoring civilized relations within the party. "I, too, am a socialist who wished to fight for a free Canada," Stephen Lewis hurled at his critics, "but I want to fight without the Waffle forever an encumbrance around my neck." By a vote of 217 to 88, he had his wish.

For almost two months, the Waffle kept the Ontario party waiting for its reaction to the demand for dissolution. Two Toronto riding associations announced that they were on strike, refusing to pay their debts to the provincial organization. The Quebec NDP, momentarily forgetting its insistence on provincial autonomy, condemned the Ontario section and, in Saskatchewan, the Waffle announced that it would do nothing until the Ontario NDP rescinded its decision. Four constituencies which had nominated prominent Wafflers for the forthcoming federal election waited with rising impatience until mid-July when all four announced that they would not run. A month later, on August 19th-20th, the group held its last meeting as part of the NDP. By then, it had already split. With an election approaching, many of its fringe supporters had glumly accepted the Orillia decision. Others, led by Stephen Penner, announced that they would cling to the party to disrupt it in every way possible. A few of them were arbitrarily excluded when the meeting opened in a hall in Delaware, a small town outside London. A majority of those who attended agreed to follow Laxer and Watkins out of the party and into a "Movement for an Independent Socialist Canada." The initials of the new organization, MISC, did little to encourage even sympathisers to take it very seriously.

Like most great political dramas, the Waffle affair ended in anti-climax. It was a misfortune for both the NDP and the leading Wafflers but it was probably inevitable. If the group had dissolved in 1969, as the NDP Now group did at the end of the 1971 convention, both its influence and its potential would have remained. By persisting, its leaders, despite their media reputation as political tacticians, were to qualify as losers. After three years, according to their own insistent judgement, they left the NDP even more "reactionary" than they had found it. The leading Wafflers had begun with positions of prestige and influence in the party; systematically, they had lost them. The transformation of a powerful pressure group, mobilizing a third of the voting strength of a national political party, into a sectarian study club, meeting in closed session to avoid capture by Trotskyites, must count among the more dramatic reversals of fortune in recent Canadian political

Backed by the righteous dogmatism of student radicalism in the late 1960s, James Laxer led an effective challenge to the NDP's cautious social democracy. While Laxer and the Waffle were defeated, many of the ideas and some of the militants remained.

history. The NDP, too, had suffered. It could not afford a hemorrhage of young and vigorous supporters, or the bitterness of many veteran members who could not easily understand why decisive action had been necessary. Despite the obvious decision by the Waffle supporters to remove themselves from the party, it was easier to believe the claims of Wafflers and news media alike that the party establishment had purged its liveliest critics.

The problem for the NDP was due to its own ambivalence. It was and behaved like a mass party of the democratic Left; it also presented itself as a socialist movement. Those who abandoned traditional allegiances, plucked up their skirts and crossed the Rubicon to true socialism would inevitably find the Waffle more attractive than the messy, compromising New Democratic Party, with its pedestrian concern for fund-raising, canvassing and picking up members. Politics could become a religion, in which even the solemn incantation of the word "socialism" would become mystically satisfying. To the majority in the party, routinely loyal to what was natural, logical and sensible, such a millenarian enthusiasm might seem marvellous and enviable but also a little foreign and suspect. In its lengthy brief to the Ontario party, the Waffle had suggested that solid commitment (among trade union affiliates, for example) was more important than mere endorsement. It was a persuasive argument if the NDP had been basically a dedicated but doctrinaire socialist movement. Eleven years of history and a Canadian political culture had already made it something else: it was, structurally, and ideologically, if not yet numerically, a mass party.

For David Lewis, the Ontario preoccupation with the Waffle had been infuriating. An election was certain in 1972; if it had come in the spring, it would have found almost a third of his party deep in fratricidal struggle. In

February, the country had smiled when the New Brunswick NDP had been captured by a tiny clique which travelled even to the left of the Waffle. An embarrassing month ensued before control was recaptured by more responsible leaders. Throughout the Ontario battle, the elder Lewis, refuting his stereotype, urged moderate compromise. And only three days after the Orillia meeting, there was a fresh explosion, this time in Montreal.

For a lump of cosmetic designed to portray the NDP as a truly national party, the Quebec section seemed to have truly carcinogenic properties. Delighted at securing the earlier agreement from the Laliberté group, party leaders overlooked the fact that the Quebec party now felt entitled, as a sympathetic commentator observed, "to preach doctrines about the future of Canada, to say nothing about economic and social policies, which may raise goose flesh in the rest of Canada." And that was precisely what the Quebec party proceeded to do. While the main party produced its own "mini-programme" or platform, Laliberté and Boudreau drafted theirs. Entitled *Il faut prendre le pouvoir partout* it flaunted the phrase "self-determination" at the head of every section. One especially troublesome passage assured readers that when Quebec decided on independence, NDPers in Ottawa would be their most valuable spokesmen. An appalled David Lewis needed no reminder of the significance of that sentiment to his opponents in every part of Canada. On June 26th, the NDP federal officers pleaded in vain for a delay in publication. Three days later, when the booklet was presented to the press, Lewis announced his formal repudiation. For a month, there was a stand-off but both sides had bargaining counters. Without Laliberté's help, there would be no more than a handful of NDP candidates for the seventy-five Quebec seats: without Lewis's formal approval, not a single candidate could place the NDP label on the ballot. While party officials put aside a host of more urgent preoccupations, negotiations resumed. Finally, a patchwork compromise was accepted. Then there were further delays but, in mid-September, a poorly-attended special convention of the Quebec NDP accepted the amendments with an ill grace.

It was a bleak beginning to an election campaign for which the NDP had had more than four years to prepare. A year before, the party had even sneaked ahead of the Conservatives in the Gallup ratings — though only at twenty-four per cent to an abysmal Tory standing of twenty-three per cent. On the eve of the 1972 election, in August, the polls indicated only fifteen per cent support for the NDP. Editors had enjoyed themselves through the summer excoriating the heartless treatment of the Waffle and revelling in the party's plight in Quebec. A party survey, piggybacked on a Gallup poll, indicated in February that support was down in British Columbia and, when Premier Bennett called a surprise summer election, it seemed that the party would find little comfort in the outcome. There was only modest reassurance in a Vancouver *Province* survey suggesting that the NDP stood at a high of thirty-four per cent support among provincial voters. Abandoning a license surely forgiveable in opposition leaders, Dave Barrett forbade party supporters to announce him as the next premier of British Columbia. Why defy credulity?

In fact, though few knew it, Barrett was busy making himself the next premier of British Columbia and beating the unbeatable W. A. C. Bennett into the bargain. Berger, with moderation, patience and systematic organization, had failed. Barrett, with a scratch organization, more limited funds and a bravura personality, succeeded. Berger had tried to ignore Bennett's charges of revolutionary socialism; Barrett laughed them out of the hall. "If he calls me a Waffle," he joked, "I'll call him a pancake. If he calls me a double Waffle, I'll call him a stack of pancakes. And if he keeps calling me a Waffler, knowing his attitude to Quebec, I'll call him a crêpe suzette." When the premier warned that the socialist hordes were at the gates, bumper stickers appeared, boasting of the fact. The tactics worked, partly because Dave Barrett was in the flamboyant tradition British Columbians have always admired in politicians since Richard McBride, Duff Pattullo and Bennett himself; partly because the province was eager for a change. The gas in the durable Social Credit balloon had been prosperity, full employment and ample public works. Now, unemployment was rising, the province's resource industries seemed to be in the doldrums and Bennett, to aggravate matters, had antagonised most of the pressure groups in the province, from organized labour to the school teachers. Even business was disenchanted and, in the young Conservative leader, Derril Warren, it thought it had an alternative.

On the night of August 30th, the longest provincial struggle for democratic socialism in Canada entered a new phase. A shocked, slightly exhilarated province discovered that it had given the ebullient Barrett thirty-eight seats and almost forty per cent of the popular vote. Only ten seats were left for Social Credit, five for the Liberals and a meagre two for the Conservatives.

Within a few weeks, the 41-year old social worker had formed his government, spreading portfolios across the factions of the party, summoned the new legislature and demonstrated that a new era had come to British Columbia. A tenants' bill of rights, plans for urban rapid transit, a ward system for Vancouver and a guaranteed $200 income for old age pensioners were all hurried into law. The province's wealthy mining and forest industries learned that the era of sweetheart royalty deals was over and the insurance industry discovered that Barrett had plans to go even farther into public insurance than Saskatchewan and Manitoba.

The British Columbia victory, on the eve of the twenty-ninth federal election, could not have come at a better moment for a divided and depressed party. It was not the only fillip for the party faithful. In a month-long pre-election tour, David Lewis had developed the issue which suddenly shot him and his party into the running.

Preparations for the 1972 campaign had so far been distinctly lacklustre. The February survey indicated little perceptible improvement in the party's prospects over the 1968 result, no widespread enthusiasm for the NDP's new leader and even greater public disapproval of trade unions than of the Waffle, an organization of which surprisingly few had heard. The party's advertising agency, approached for fresh ideas, could offer only a variant of the 1968 slogan: this time, the party would proclaim "Canada needs More New Democrats." After the Waffle imbroglio and the Quebec conflict, Canadians might reasonably wonder why.

All at once, David Lewis gave them a reason. The previous spring, in an overdue attempt to restore the prosperity Canadians had traditionally associated with Liberal governments, the federal finance minister, John Turner, had announced surprisingly generous tax concessions to corporations. With the promised largesse, free enterprise would presumably create jobs and reduce an embarrassing seven per cent unemployment rate to a more acceptable level. The government's benevolence evoked NDP criticism at the time but it also sent the party's federal research director, Boris Celovsky, digging into other examples of Liberal benevolence to private companies. The result, backed with names, figures and a brilliant slogan, gave Lewis his issue. Launched at a crowded rally in New Glasgow, Nova Scotia, the image of

"Corporate Welfare Bums" penetrated the headlines, sent journalists scurrying along the NDP's pre-campaign trail and delighted party supporters. Whatever its effect in converting masses of voters — it was minimal — the corporate tax rip-off was the kind of issue which only a party like the NDP could raise. Thousands of party members who had forgotten why they belonged suddenly remembered. Editors and journalists, delighted to find snap and crackle in the early stages of a dull campaign, gave the NDP unprecedented publicity. Party researchers, in turn, became so entranced with the so-called corporate rip-off that they stopped in mid-campaign to put together a book on the issue.

By then, the issue had begun to pall. Robert Stanfield and his local campaigners shortened the slogan and used it as a sadly effective weapon against the poor and the jobless, insisting that they lived on government largesse. Lewis and his entourage turned slowly back to other, more familiar NDP issues and slogans. Loaded aboard an aged Handley-Page Herald for the last few weeks, the leader's tour at last could claim its own aircraft and an esprit de corps which compensated for an absence of fresh ideas but some of the momentum obviously went out of the campaign.

Perhaps it hardly mattered. As in previous federal contests, the essential NDP campaigns were local constituency battles in which the morale and organization of the party's volunteers could alone help to determine the outcome. For that, the combination of Lewis's fiery attacks on favourite NDP enemies and the thrill of the British Columbia victory were sufficient. In the 1972 election, the party campaigned, almost for the first time, without illusions. Ritual visits to Quebec were brief, sadly disorganized and soon forgotten. Lewis went where the party had votes and the potential for more — to the West, to northern Ontario and the industrialized south, and, fleetingly, to the Atlantic provinces. The NDP campaigned, as it always had, for its only realistic federal goal — an effective balance of power in Parliament. Regularly, as in earlier elections, pre-election punditry predicted that outcome. On October 31st, the experts seemed to be flabbergasted that that was precisely what happened.

In Ottawa, where Mr. Trudeau waited complacently for his majority, there was dismay. In Halifax, where the returns had begun to promise Mr. Stanfield the majority he had privately barely expected, there was a rough, angry disappointment as the prize was pulled away. In Toronto, in the shabby ballroom where defeated NDP candidates and their workers had come to share the smell of victory with the lucky few, there was a mixture of exultation and realism. 1,7000,000 Canadians, 18.1 per cent of the voters, had given Parliament more New Democrats — thirty-one of them, even one from the huge, empty North-West Territories. It was the beginning of a new challenge.

Dave Barrett. A shocked, slightly exhilarated province discovered that the longest provincial struggle for democratic socialism was over. The flamboyant tradition of Richard McBride and Duff Pattullo had found a new standard-bearer.

VIII. Performance

The architects of the New Democratic Party had had a plan to turn their dream of power into reality. Canadian history had taught that federal power was built province by province and the NDP accepted the lesson. Meanwhile, the NDP contingent in Ottawa would show Canada where their party stood on national issues and, when the opportunity came, it would seek the balance of power in order to extort what policies it could

In the aftermath of the 1972 election, the strategy seemed to be working. There were already NDP governments in three western provinces, and now the strongest caucus in the House of Commons that the CCF or NDP had ever sent to Ottawa could choose between the Liberals and the Conservatives. But the power base was fragile. In two of its three provinces, the NDP was in power only because the anti-socialist forces had split. Federally, the party remained just below its familiar plateau of eighteen per cent of the popular vote. The Left had gained its critical influence only because so many Canadian voters had moved away from the Liberals to give the Progressive Conservatives an extra thirty-five seats.

David Lewis and his colleagues had a well-known model for how they should behave in such circumstances. There

was no more precious document in the NDP's archives than
the 1926 letter from W.L. Mackenzie King formally com-
miting his minority Liberal government to introduce old
age pensions in return for support from J.S. Woodsworth.
This classic of righteous *realpolitik* had become a major
myth in the CCF-NDP tradition, cleansed of the troublesome details that the pensions were meagre, means-tested
and rejected by the Senate. Moreover, they had not even
been established until after King got his majority in the
1926 election. These details might have made the NDP
more modest in its expectations but it was the myth of
Woodsworth's achievement which mattered. Nearing the
end of his political career, David Lewis was entitled to a
comparable legislative landmark as a testament of his service to ordinary Canadians.

Bargaining requires a choice of customers. Confident
that victory was within their grasp the Conservatives determined in advance that they would make no concessions to
the despised socialists. An early election, they believed,
would destroy the Trudeau government and annihilate the
NDP in repetition of the Diefenbaker landslide of 1958.
Surveying the scene, particularly in western Canada where
Conservative strength was rising fast, Lewis and his colleagues came to the same conclusion. Clinging to office and
playing for time, the Liberals soon realized that they could
count on NDP support. Because the Tories refused to bid
for NDP support, the Liberals were spared the humiliation
of either private negotiations or open concessions. They
could afford to give less to the NDP. If David Lewis waited
for a private call from Sussex Drive, it never came. Instead,
he had to depend on the media, with all their capacity for
distortion and mischief, to carry his messages to the Prime
Minister.

When Parliament met in January, 1973, the NDP influence was soon apparent. Family allowances were tripled,

and there was no more talk of an earlier plan for a complicated and discriminatory system of means tests. Instead, the benefits would simply be taxable. If old age pensioners were guaranteed $100 a month, it was half what the NDP had sought but, as the *Globe and Mail*'s Geoffrey Stevens noted, it was a lot more than they would have received from a majority government. A government bill designed by critics of unemployment insurance was quietly dropped when the NDP indicated its hostility. As supermarket prices soared in a new burst of inflation, NDP influence shaped a special House of Commons committee. In turn, a Food Prices Review Board was launched in late April, empowered to prove the familiar NDP thesis that inflation was fuelled by corporate profiteering.

The Review Board also illustrated the frustrations of the NDP role. Having helped to launch the Board, NDP members squirmed when its government-appointed chairman, Beryl Plumptre, directed most of her fire at farmers and their new marketing boards rather than at the supermarkets. Having neatly separated his corporate welfare measures from his budget, the Finance Minister, John Turner, manoeuvred them through Parliament with help from grumbling Tories. As the session wore on, Lewis and his colleagues began to realize that their balancing role imposed great responsibilities with very little power.

It was in the provinces that the New Democratic Party possessed both. Across western Canada, three governments could give a better idea of what the NDP was about than the mountain of speeches, resolutions and news releases accumulated since 1961. Schreyer, Blakeney and Barrett were as diverse in background, style and outlook as their respective provinces. What they shared was a common indifference to ideology, a model in the successful Douglas government of Saskatchewan and a commitment to specific, practical programmes, each designed to stand on its own merit.

If Schreyer and Blakeney bore at least an external resemblance to the youthful, carefully dressed executives who ran Canada's provinces in the Seventies, Dave Barrett was the exception. Brash, self-confident and outspoken, he made it clear that he would not tiptoe to re-election. In 1972, the first flood of measures — the Mincome programme for the elderly, Canada's highest minimum wage for the working poor — had been of immediate benefit to NDP federal candidates. The surge of activity continued and a Vancouver newspaper noted that the new government had committed itself to forty-two policies in its first fifty-five days in office. As in the other provinces, there was no significant turnover of civil servants; as in the Saskatchewan model, NDP influence was exercised through appointments to ministerial staff, a number of outside advisors and the creation of new departments for housing and consumer affairs.

While there were significant differences in the priorities and pace of change in the three NDP provinces, common to all were policies of cautious income redistribution, improved public service and a pay-as-you-go fiscal orthodoxy. The next stages in achieving comprehensive medical care were Pharmacare — free prescription drugs for the elderly — and free dental care for children. Those who demanded immediate and comprehensive drug and dental plans for the whole population were firmly reminded that the cost would be unsupportable and qualified professionals were not yet available.

A standard feature of democratic socialism is support for public ownership. In Canada, it is an idea shared by the record of other parties. Conservatives can take credit for Ontario Hydro and the CNR; Liberals created Air Canada and most other federal crown corporations; even Social Credit in British Columbia had nationalized the ferries and B.C. Hydro without batting an eye. More common in

Canada has been the arrangement Ed Schreyer described as "mongrel enterprise," with taxpayers providing most of the capital and shareholders getting all the profit. The principle built the CPR in the 1880's, maintained Denison Mines in the 1960's and kept much of Canadian business happy in the intervening years.

While the "mongrel" principle satisfied a widespread belief that no government can or should make a profit, it meant little to NDP politicians. Schreyer's most disastrous inheritance from the Roblin era, Churchill Forest Industries, was a model mongrel enterprise, with Manitobans providing millions of dollars to a shadowy consortium with a numbered Swiss bank account. In Saskatchewan, the Blakeney government took power in time to stop what might have been a similar adventure. All three NDP governments saw nothing wrong in investing public money in useful private undertakings. The difference was that they insisted on the same equity and voice in management that any prudent investor would demand. One painful political consequence was that voters could learn what they had won or lost by their investments. In all three provinces, the cost of propping up ailing industries to save jobs or to preserve a community's economic base has sometimes been high. In other provinces, the voters' ignorance of the fate of grants and "forgiveable loans" has been a politician's bliss.

In all three NDP provinces, public ownership was more often a policy tool than an ideological imperative. Government car insurance was a partial exception. A brilliant success in Saskatchewan, it was now almost an obligatory feature of any NDP government. Even when it promised to move beyond automobiles to other forms of insurance, the Insurance Corporation of British Columbia encountered less political resistance than its Manitoba equivalent. Instead, the province's thirty-seven insurance companies fought it through the courts. More often, nationalization was a response to an emergency or an economic threat. The Blakeney government invested heavily in a Regina steel plant and a Saskatoon meatpacking operation to forestall alleged takeover bids from eastern Canada. When Crown Zellerbach condemned the pulp and paper town of Ocean Falls to sudden death, the Barrett government paid out a million dollars for the aging complex – just as pulp and paper prices began to soar. A month later, the government announced acquisition of seventy-nine per cent of Columbia Cellulose, a major processer of the province's forest resources. As Canadian Cellulose, the operations of the new company extended as far as a mill in Belgium. Like other NDP governments, the Barrett regime established its own Development Corporation, designed to help small- and medium-sized businesses with everything from loans to managerial expertise. Instead of nationalizing British Columbia's privately-owned telephone company as he had promised, Barrett watched while share prices plummeted. As they hit bottom, he moved in to buy up as much as the province could afford. Party purists were shocked at a socialist premier playing the stock market.

While most of the policies of the three NDP governments of the 1970's bore a close family resemblance to those of the CCF in Saskatchewan, there were some differences. The CCF's streak of conservationism had become a broad band of concern for the environment. Federal and provincial New Democrats had denounced the Columbia River treaty with its permanent sacrifice of Canadian water and hydro potential. The party's energy critics had warned against long-term contracts to sell oil and natural gas to the United States, questioning company claims that we had more than adequate reserves. In varying degrees, all three NDP governments owed their election to growing public concern about disposal of resources at fire-sale prices and about the environmental consequences.

With their lobbies in Ottawa and Washington, their multinational connection and their hammerlock on thousands of jobs and the prosperity of hundreds of communities, the resource industries represented the most powerful challenge to the NDP governments. Almost as important as their substantive power was the accompanying faith that resources existed only to be torn from the ground and hurried into use and that in Canada's limitless domain, there was always more. It was a challenge the NDP governments faced with varying degrees of caution. After exacting higher royalties and setting up Mineral Resources Ltd. to lead Manitoba's hunt for new ore bodies, Ed Schreyer contented himself with appointing the former federal Liberal cabinet minister and increasingly radical economist, Eric Kierans, to analyze the province's future. In Saskatchewan, Allan Blakeney moved in his first session to reclaim ninety per cent of the province's oil reserves and set up the Saskatchewan Oil and Gas Corporation to provide an alternative if higher royalty payments persuaded the private oil companies to walk out.

The toughest fight was in British Columbia, a province largely built on primary resource extraction, with an economy and a political system shaped by the demands of the big companies. While the forest industry and the mining companies braced for battle and a New York financial magazine, Barron's, described Dave Barrett as an Allende of the North, the issue in 1973 was energy. When demand from the United States threatened to leave British Columbia consumers short, Barrett promptly bought into Westcoast Transmission, the pipeline company that carried gas and oil through the province from Alberta. By the year-end, he had created British Columbia's own petroleum corporation with power to buy, sell and deal in natural gas and oil.

Closely related to the resources battle was a struggle to save agriculture. In Manitoba and Saskatchewan, Liberal and

Tory politicians had moaned publicly that they could not interfere with the market forces that doomed the family farm. Privately, they condemned the small farm unit as an economic anachronism. In British Columbia, Vancouver's surburban sprawl regularly gobbled acres of rich Fraser Valley land to the dismay of environmentalists and farm organizations and to the private pleasure of willing buyers and eager sellers.

By December, 1972, Barrett had frozen conversion of agricultural land. Within months, a five-member Land Commission assumed control of land-use in the entire province, with power to overturn municipal by-laws. The former premier, W.A.C. Bennett, raged at "confiscation without compensation" and farmers and their developer allies demonstrated at the legislature. Procedures were softened but the principle survived. To control the disastrous income fluctuations which drove even the best farmers from the land, Agriculture Minister Dave Stupich pioneered a unique farm income stabilization plan. Based on the costs of efficient producers, the farmer-controlled scheme used insurance principles to guarantee a basic income.

In Manitoba and Saskatchewan, where farms were closing down at a rate of a thousand a year, the key problem was to keep people on the land and to make it possible to take over a farm without acquiring a crushing load of debt. Manitoba's "Stay" option used public funds to buy up farms, retire their aged owners and transfer the land to younger farmers eager to get started or to expand their operation. Producer-controlled marketing boards, cheaper crop insurance and a Farm Machinery Act, compelling implement dealers to stock spare parts, tackled problems of the farm economy. Funds to revive struggling prairie towns, special training for small town school teachers, even subsidies to television repairmen servicing rural areas, were part of an imaginative programme to improve the amenities of rural life. In neighbouring Saskatchewan, the Farmstart programme and a controversial land banking scheme over-rode bitter Liberal objections. So did legislation to keep out American-based farming corporations and absentee landlords by restricting the sale of agricultural land to non-residents. Without romanticising rural life or ignoring the prairie desire for industrialization, both the Blakeney and Schreyer governments had tried to reverse a trend and to do whatever a government could to support the small town and the family farm.

As it happened, 1973 was an ideal year for governments determined to save agriculture, regain control over natural resources or perhaps even to get re-elected. Across Canada, inflation suddenly replaced unemployment and recession as the economic obsession. In the United States, long-predicted shortages of oil and gas suddenly came true but in Canada it was food which led the consumer price index with a seventeen per cent increase over the year. Wheat prices, already at a postwar high of $2.15 a bushel, pushed to $4.92 in a year of generally high yields. Across Canada, unemployment fell – fastest of all in British Columbia. Saskatchewan's potash industry, struggling for years at half its potential production, lumbered into a higher gear as farmers looked for more fertilizer. For every province of western Canada, 1973 was a boom year. The worldwide energy and resources' shortage gave them a status and a bargaining power they had rarely possessed in Confederation.

While Dave Barrett had refused to play beyond a single term of social and economic changes, Ed Schreyer had determined from the beginning that he would try to make his party the accepted government of Manitoba. Given the chance, he had assured voters in 1969, he would complete the normal four years before calling an election. He kept his word. After fulfilling his election promises, Schreyer allowed a couple of quiet sessions of the Legislature while voters forgot the earlier turmoil and opposition politicians complained that the NDP had run out of ideas. The 1973 session saw a conventional pre-election budget with medicare premiums abolished, pensions increased and taxes cut. When the election was called for June 28th, Manitobans could weigh the merits of a government which could reasonably claim that it had kept its promises, presided over unprecedented prosperity *and* left taxes for anyone earning less than $20,000 lower than they had been in 1969.

In the circumstances, some NDP organizers and a good many journalists promised a Schreyer landslide. Instead, the party faced a tough fight. Would-be saviours of free enterprise had wheeled and wheedled from the sidelines to persuade Liberal and Conservative voters to gang up on the NDP. In Winnipeg, a business-backed coalition had effectively shut out NDP candidates from municipal influence and a Group for Good Government tried to transfer the technique to provincial politics, fingering the Liberal or Tory candidate most likely to beat the New Democrat. Winnipeg newspapers amplified the chorus against the NDP and the message was taken up, in an odd counterpoint, by Joe Borowski, running as a law and order independent, and by Cy Gonick, editor of *Canadian Dimension,* who had flounced out of politics altogether.

On election day, 78 per cent of the electorate (compared to 64 per cent in 1969) turned out to give the NDP an added four per cent in popular vote, increased Conservative strength by a point and left the Liberals with barely 19 per cent. The New Democrats held 31 seats, their opponents 26, although several contests were close enough to be settled in the courts. If Schreyer had proved that an NDP government was no longer an aberration in Manitoba, he had also discovered that even his cool, social democratic approach had left a majority of Manitobans unconverted.

Victory in Manitoba at least guaranteed that delegates to the NDP's seventh federal convention at Vancouver would see a full contingent of three provincial premiers. They would not see much of the Waffle Group. In Ontario, leaders of the Movement for an Independent Socialist Canada (MISC) grew tired of their near-eclipse from the news media and promised to enter electoral politics. So did their cousins in Saskatchewan, John Richards, a university lecturer and sole Waffle sympathiser in the Saskatchewan legislature, abandoned the NDP caucus to sit as an independent. In both provinces, reactions from former Waffle sympathisers were generally frosty. As for the "crazies," as Mel Watkins had termed the dissenters from his own leadership, they had returned briefly to throw the Ontario NDP's 1972 convention into chaos and disappeared again into the "Revolutionary Marxist Group." What the Waffle left behind in the NDP was a serious generation gap in the party's intellectual wing and a nervous awareness of the dangers of policy discussion. In exchange, the Vancouver convention suggested a party at peace with itself. Although a small, predictable minority denounced Lewis for collaborating with the Liberals, an overwhelming majority endorsed his parliamentary strategy, beat back a hard-line demand for total nationalization of Canada's energy industry and backed an official proposal that mixed regulation with public ownership, Douglas Campbell, a Mississauga taxi driver, poet and inveterate leadership challenger, could muster only 79 votes to Lewis's 719. Even dissolution of the party's youth section, ostensibly on the grounds that the eighteen-year-old voting age made it redundant, failed to produce conflict. Journalists, who had headed west for the usual fun, almost wondered how to justify their expenses. None of them noted the real story of the convention.

Remembering the bitter polarization of the previous convention, David Lewis came to Vancouver armed and ready not only to defend his support of the Trudeau government but also to announce that it was virtually at an end. Alone or with his few trusted confidants, he had concluded that there was no more to be expected from the minority Liberal regime. Further support of Trudeau would contaminate the NDP with his unpopularity, particularly in western Canada. Rising food prices might please Manitoba farmers but they were the leading edge of an inflation which was beginning to disturb Canadians. It was an issue for which the NDP had few popular answers and it would be wiser to force an election in the summer or fall of 1973 before the problem got much worse. In a characteristically blunt and belligerent speech to the convention, Lewis gave public notice that the NDP would not tolerate a Trudeau government much longer and that further concessions, if they came, must meet the NDP's condemnation of corporate welfare. Constituencies must prepare themselves. The contest would come soon.

Lewis had spoken clearly. His problem was that few delegates took him seriously. As they rose dutifully to the customary standing ovation, his words joined the windy rhetoric of threats, boasts and denunciations which fill all political conventions, to be forgotten under the trees and sunshine of the University of British Columbia campus. If Lewis had given up on the minority government, most delegates had not. Nor had most Canadians. In the summer of 1973, the New Democratic Party appeared to command an influence in Parliament and a prestige across Canada which it had never possessed before. These were not assets to be cheerfully put at risk.

In August, Lewis summoned his caucus to an emergency meeting. Soaring food prices would be a legitimate reason for bringing down the government. The caucus disagreed.

Few had been consulted about their leader's newly militant strategy and they could not see the point. Some were annoyed at their leader's attempts to pick a fight with the Liberals. Instead, fresh demands were presented to the Liberal government and, to Lewis's disappointment, largely accepted. The Food Prices Review Board secured greater resources for research. Government subsidies held down the price of bread while cost of living adjustments helped the poor and the elderly. Meanwhile, the party had a graphic lesson in the political dangers of continued inflation. When a series of rotating strikes developed into a national rail strike, Parliament was summoned. While Lewis addressed a demonstration, promising the NDP's support for the best possible settlement, angry strikers broke away to invade the Parliament Buildings themselves. A predictable wave of public indignation only foreshadowed the hostility organized labour might attract as it sought inflation-proof wage settlements. It was an antagonism that would easily be redirected against labour's political arm.

There was one issue which could have forced an election in 1973. For years, T.C. Douglas and other NDP spokesmen had condemned the subjection of Canadian energy policy to the advice and consent of the huge multi-national oil companies. It was the oil companies which dictated that eastern Canada would be dependent on oil imports while Alberta wells were drained to supply the United States market. No one cared about NDP warnings when the companies boasted that Canada had limitless reserves of oil and natural gas.

In a few months of 1973, the props of that national energy policy collapsed. In January, Alberta crude sold at $3.00 a barrel; Iranian oil stood at $2.50. By summer, as Canadians discovered the Organization of Petroleum Exporting Countries, world prices had risen fifty per cent and Alberta oil sold for $4.00 a barrel. The Arab boycott after the Yom Kippur war of October, 1973 sent the world price to $7.50. As for the Canadian reserves, they turned out to be barely enough to carry the country through the 1980's. With the cheapest, most accessible gas and oil draining away as exports, the oil companies now insisted on massive price increases to finance frontier oil exploration and to justify exploitation of the Athabaska tar sands.

Even from a minority Liberal government there were no apologies. In September, it hurriedly authorized completion of a pipeline from Sarnia to Montreal, imposed a tax on exports of oil and imposed a temporary price freeze. After the Arab oil boycott, the export tax increased, the price freeze in eastern Canada ended and a government advertising campaign told Canadians how to save energy. Canadian oil and gas prices might not quite reach world levels, the Prime Minister told Canadians on November 22nd, but they were going up: "the days of cheap and abundant energy are over."

Like other Canadians, New Democrats might accept the inevitable; they could not ignore where the blame for Canada's plight lay. With the government's life depending on a vote of confidence on December 10th, the NDP caucus drafted a series of proposals which would either give Canada a national energy policy or a winter election. There was no case, the NDP insisted, for imposing the world price on domestic oil and gas supplies extracted at half that cost. There must be no end to the domestic price freeze and there must be a national petroleum corporation which, for the first time, would give the government accurate information about the oil industry and some leverage to affect its practices. Caucus members left Ottawa for a week-end of speeches and politicking: some of them were convinced that it might be their last free week-end before an election campaign. They returned to discover that the Liberals had accepted virtually every line of their ultimatum. Henceforth, the Prime Minister promised, Canada would have a single national energy policy. It would have a national petroleum corporation and the oil price freeze would extend throughout the heating season. For good measure, although not on the NDP list, there would be money for oil sands development and there would be approval of a Mackenzie Valley natural gas pipeline. For David Lewis, waiting at Fort McMurray in the heart of the Alberta tar sands, the government statement was "a victory beyond my expectations." More privately, the NDP leader suspected that he had been robbed of a campaign-worthy issue.

Whether or not the NDP would have benefited from a winter election, it might have been spared some of the strains of the ensuing six months. It would also have missed the maturing experience of a national party confronting its own regional differences. A federal party whose repertoire of federal-provincial issues had been limited to the grievances of Quebec had to learn for itself some of the strains in Confederation.

No provincial section had been a more loyal and consistent backer of the national party than Saskatchewan. The politics of oil now found the Blakeney government in an uneasy alliance with the Conservatives of Alberta. While Premier Lougheed was more eager to protect the oil companies, both were determined to appropriate the windfall oil profits for their own people. For Blakeney, whose province's oil was almost entirely refined by a special process in the United States, the export tax was federal discrimination while the price freeze was an attempt to force the West to subsidise the industrial East. Both policies had been argued forcefully by David Lewis and the federal NDP. When Blakeney came east early in 1974 to present the West's case, one stop was an NDP federal council meeting in Toronto. The outcome was a bitter, emotional debate between the Saskatchewan premier and David Lewis.

It was not the only case of federal-provincial friction. Long before the Conservatives had discovered wage and price controls in the winter of 1973, Ed Schreyer had been an open advocate. The notion of public influence on income and price determination had struck him as an appropriately socialist policy. To restrict only prices, as current NDP policy suggested, struck him as unbalanced and unfair. As the inflation threat grew, other NDP premiers offered a muted support for Schreyer's view. At Vancouver in 1975, in a debate led by Terry Grier, now a Toronto area M.P., the New Democrat convention furiously denounced any control programme. Controls had failed in Britain and the United States, Grier insisted, and they would freeze existing inequities in Canada. While the federal NDP position echoed the views of most academic economists, it also proved indistinguishable at a distance from the policy of the federal Liberal party. Since the views of Schreyer and his fellow premiers were no secret to the press, the New Democrats were in danger of being openly divided on what had become, by 1974, one of the few salient political issues in the country.

With a tiny staff, a number of touchy individualists in his caucus and all the incessant preoccupations of party management, it was understandable that Lewis made few efforts to consult with the NDP premiers or even with some parliamentary colleagues. It would also have been foreign to his style. As CCF national secretary, he had despatched his unsought advice to a CCF premier of Saskatchewan; as NDP federal leader, Lewis expected the premiers to conform to the party's federal policies or, at the least, to conceal their differences. When Dave Barrett had flown to Montreal in November of 1973, to persuade René Levesque of the Parti Québécois that he was all but a New Democrat, Lewis had raged privately at the indiscretion. Publicly, he disclaimed its significance.

Barrett, who never forgot that one of the Lewis clan had backed his rival, Tom Berger, was unlikely ever to become a confidante of his federal leader. That was unfortunate because far more serious for the NDP than differences with Blakeney or Schreyer was the state of the party on the west coast. By 1974, British Columbia's honeymoon with the Barrett government was over. So was the resources boom. As the economies of most western countries sagged into recession, markets for lumber, paper and most minerals dried up. Layoffs were blamed on the socialists at Victoria, not on corporate miscalculations or world conditions. Increased mining royalties sent only a few hundred protesting miners to the Legislature but others stayed behind to meditate on company handouts. Organized labour was angry too, at a new labour relations act which made it easier to organize and harder to stop a strike but which also made it easier to raid and which left some restrictions on picketing. Barrett, who had bypassed labour leaders in winning power, paid little heed to their protests. Instead, they joined the cacophony of a province in which everyone suddenly seemed to have a grievance against the government. Under a new leader with a familiar name, W.A.C. Bennett's son, Bill, Social Credit was fighting back. So were Liberals, Conservatives, newspaper editors and an earnest lobby of disgruntled businessmen called the Majority Movement for Freedom and Private Enterprise.

In the midst of this sea of troubles, David Lewis could have been forgiven for assuming that the time to force an election had passed. Despite his fears, there was no evidence of plummeting public support for his party. Polls from 1972 to the spring of 1974 fluctuated from a low of sixteen per cent (after the NDP had opposed capital punishment) to a high of twenty-one per cent. This was political capital which, a shrinking group of "doves" in the NDP caucus

insisted, could be used to press still further policy concessions from the Liberals. That, after all, was the role New
Democrats had promised the 1972 electorate that they
would perform. The signs were clear that most Canadians
understood and appreciated the NDP's federal role. At the
end of 1973, a survey indicated that two-thirds of the
people believed that Parliament should carry on – with
intended NDP supporters almost as strongly in favour as
were Liberals. In another poll, more than two-thirds of
the respondents felt that the NDP would continue to support the government. They were wrong.

Lewis had not changed his mind. By March, most caucus
members had been persuaded that an election was inevitable and even morally necessary. From Manitoba and
Saskatchewan came suggestions that if the NDP would not
fight the Liberals, support could slip permanently away to
the Conservatives, who were increasingly seen as regional
guardians against the Quebec-backed Liberals. With a
political skill refined over almost forty years, Lewis had
gathered his majority, isolated a minority of barely three
or four caucus "doves" and won his point. By the end of
March, when Liberals and Conservatives united to prevent
review of a 1973 package of tax concessions to corporations, only a pretext for defeating the government remained
to be found.

Among the Liberals, NDP intentions were no secret. Unlike Mackenzie King, who had liked Coldwell and welcomed
the CCF threat as a weapon against his own party's reactionary wing, there had been respect but no affection for
Lewis from Trudeau and his front bench. Among Liberal
backbenchers there was growing exasperation at their
occasional humiliations. As the Liberal strategists had
hoped, time had paid off. Public and private surveys indicated growing support. They also suggested that the Tory
proposal for wage and price controls could be turned into

a major liability for Stanfield. If the NDP wanted to defeat the government, that was fine with the Liberals. All that mattered was to ensure that David Lewis got the blame for killing the Twenty-Ninth Parliament.

April was a month for manoeuvring. Before a CTV audience, Lewis reeled off the demands the NDP would make in return for continued support: an end to land speculation, an excess profits tax, aid to small business, lower NHA mortgage rates, a prices review board with powers to roll back price increases. In Mississauga on April 19th he already blamed the Liberals for forcing an election: "They are unable to make the necessary and fundamental changes required if we are to deal effectively with pressing issues like the rising cost of living." The Liberals fought back. In Winnipeg, John Turner compared Lewis's attack on the corporations to "half-witted Ned Ludd." In Hamilton, Trudeau claimed that Lewis was threatening to break up Parliament "because that is the only way he can get headlines and be in the limelight."

April was also a month for provincial elections in Nova Scotia and Prince Edward Island. Both were clear Liberal victories but there was encouragement for the NDP as well. On April 2nd, Nova Scotia voters doubled their support for the NDP from 6.6 per cent in 1970 to 13.7 per cent and Cape Breton sent another member to join Jeremy Akerman's tiny caucus. In Prince Edward Island, the party presented its first provincial candidates and collected six per cent of the vote, mostly at the expense of the Liberals. There was nothing in either result to deter Liberals or New Democrats from a federal contest.

The government would fall on its budget, due on May 6th. By late April, that fate was virtually foreordained. For the New Democrats, it was a chance to present three conditions which the budget would have to include and which Turner was virtually certain to reject: a two-price system

for Canadian commodities like oil, gas and lumber, a substantial increase in corporation taxes and a government-
subsidized six per cent mortgage rate. For the Liberals, it
was a chance to muster some of their most attractive draft
legislation and march it into Parliament. If Parliament
died, the NDP would be guilty of killing an excess profits
bill, a small business loans act, a fisheries improvements
loans act, a farm improvements loans act and aid to Air
Canada and the Canadian National Railways. There was
even a hastily conceived bill to protect Canadian football
from the threatened depredations of a World Football
League.

To most Canadians, removed from the drama and postur-
ing of Parliament, the Turner budget was welcome news.
It claimed that Canada had emerged from a frightening
winter with its prospects buoyant and its inflation under
control. It gave modest but specific blessings: 300,000
Canadians would no longer pay income tax and everyone
was spared sales tax on clothing and shoes; would-be home-
buyers could tuck away a tax-free thousand dollars every
year and there was higher interest on their savings bonds.
If anyone really shared the NDP's concern about hitting
corporations, Turner could claim that they would have to
cough up an extra $800 million a year, largely through a
tax on the royalties that oil companies paid to the
provinces.

To Lewis and his colleagues, it all seemed trivial and
specious. In a private preview of the budget, the NDP
leader discovered not only that Turner had ignored his
demands but that the Finance Minister had done his best to
make the budget unacceptable to the New Democrats.
Whatever the country might think, Lewis finally had his
pretext. Next day, backed by a united NDP caucus, he
raked the budget with scorn and demolished it with anger.
When inflation robbed the average family of a thousand

dollars a year, what relief was there in handing back a dollar a week? Most of the tax concessions were the work of a wrong-way Robin Hood, taking from the poor and giving to the rich. As for taxing royalties, that would take $400 million from Alberta and Saskatchewan, not from the oil companies. "There are some people in this country who suggest that the time has come for a Tory government," Lewis declared. As the Conservatives erupted with desk-thumping, he turned to them. "I want to say to the members of this Parliament and to the people of Canada that a Tory government has already arrived."

It was almost over. It remained for the Prime Minister to answer outrage with ridicule of "David, the daisy, picking his petals one by one: will we have an election; will we not have an election." At last, there was Real Caouette, the aging, ailing Creditiste leader, rising to warn that the NDP was heading to its own destruction: "Mr. Speaker, I met with some York South constituents, workers who are members of the NDP and have never been Social Crediters in their life. They told me that they would vote against the leader of the NDP ... who would not return here after the election."

In early May, that seemed highly improbable. While Lewis expected that the NDP would lose some seats, particularly in British Columbia, the polls showed public support at the familiar level of eighteen per cent. Election planning was complete. While publicity and organization had been more decentralized than usual in response to provincial insistence, advertising, printing and a new party logo were ready. Even in Quebec, where a bare shadow of an organization survived under the leadership of a young mathematics professor, Henri-François Gautrin, nominations had proceeded well. In Cape Breton, in the wake of its recent provincial gains, the party persuaded Father Andy Hogan, an outspoken, popular community leader, to help win back its Atlantic foothold.

Yet, from the outset, something was wrong. Perhaps it was symbolized by the party's election slogan, "People Matter More." It was not so much limp as meaningless. Was it possible that the NDP had forced an election only to find that it had nothing new to say?

Exhausted from the 1972 campaign and eighteen months of non-stop parliamentary manoeuvring, an aging Lewis gathered his advisors and emerged with a theme: who controls Canada? Designed to hammer the Galbraithian theme that corporate power was the major cause of inflation, it was the core question for a series of attacks on development companies, industry conglomerates and multinational resource empires. Tested in a series of speeches in southern Ontario and particularly at the campaign kick-off in Toronto, it flopped. To the media, it sounded like a tired revival of the corporate welfare bums. The alternative, tried out with union audiences and unveiled at the Canadian Labour Congress convention in Vancouver, was an assault on the Conservative plans for wage and price controls. The speech got an unexpectedly cool audience to its feet to cheer. With much of his itinerary in areas of western Canada where New Democrats were busy battling the Tories, Lewis had plenty of chance to repeat his denunciation of the Stanfield proposals. Only by mid-campaign, when he paused to assess his progress, did Lewis realize that he was doing the Prime Minister's work for him.

By then, it was probably too late. Having defeated the government on the Turner budget, NDP spokesmen promptly forgot it. It was left to the Liberals to claim that Lewis had left $800 million in the coffers of the corporations or that three hundred thousand Canadians were still forced to pay taxes. Convinced for six months of the need to defeat the government, Lewis and his advisors forgot that few Canadians had followed the parliamentary game and that dissolution had not seemed to them inevitable or proper. There might be good reasons for the party's strategy but NDP candidates could rarely provide them. Instead, they wrestled with statistics about company profits and tried to argue that six per cent mortgages were realistic when even savings accounts earned a higher interest. The party had seized on Trudeau's sneer at "David, the Daisy," adopting the flower as a campaign emblem, christening the leaders aged chartered aircraft "Daisy Air." It was no answer to the only question that voters really wanted to put to the party and its leader. It hardly mattered whether Lewis attacked corporations or controls. Having failed to persuade most Canadians that he had been right to force an election, both he and his party became sadly irrelevant to the contest. Journalists might have asked the questions and even provided the answers but that was hardly their responsibility. They preferred to record the Prime Minister's promises and to admire the campaigining skills of his young wife.

Left to themselves, NDP candidates struggled with the usual regional and local issues. In British Columbia, there was public dismay at the Barrett government's reported hundred million dollar over-run in welfare spending. In Saskatchewan, the NDP suffered when companies halted oil exploration and when bad weather promised the poorest wheat yield in years. In Quebec, where Lewis pleaded with Parti Québécois supporters to consider the social and economic programme of his party, the Quebec Federation of Labour only hesitantly echoed the appeal. Its president, Louis Laberge, pointedly commented that NDP lack of understanding of Quebec's "national question" was "just as reprehensible as that shown by the other federal parties." The endorsement made little difference in Quebec and did no good elsewhere.

On July 8th, the dull, depressing battle was over. By

election eve, the opinion polls had promised a Liberal victory and it came. For the NDP, there was an early triumph when Andy Hogan captured his Cape Breton seat. Then came the grim news. In Toronto, the NDP lost three seats and barely clung to two more. Caouette had been right. In York South, the NDP vote fell a stunning thirteen percentage points to cost David Lewis his place in Parliament. In the West, the news was worse: one loss in Manitoba, three in Saskatchewan. Finally came British Columbia where only two of the party's eleven seats remained. Ridings which had withstood the Diefenbaker landslide of 1958 tumbled to unknown Liberals. As the bleak reality settled on waiting New Democrats, there was one modest comfort: in the huge North West Territories, Wally Firth had kept his seat and raised his majority.

It was a bitter night for Robert Stanfield. It was the Liberals, not the Conservatives, who had trampled the NDP in western Canada and, in Ontario, they had demolished the Conservatives as well. Once again, Pierre-Elliott Trudeau could govern with a majority – 141 Liberals against 95 Conservatives, 11 Creditistes and only 16 New Democrats. Across Canada, the NDP had attracted only 1,476,350 votes, 15.1 per cent of the total, its lowest share since 1963.

Later, David Lewis would explain his belief that "it was our duty to think of the long term position of the NDP and that that required an assertion of principle and courage rather than the traditional preoccupation with electoral calculations." Now he had led his party back into the wilderness and he had been chief among those who had suffered its humiliation. Even opponents would pause to regret that so brave a fighter had gone down.

IX. Frustrations

"Recrimination is the least fruitful product of election analysis" warned the NDP's official post-mortem on the 1974 debacle. In fact, bad feeling was easily absorbed by the swift and dignified departure of David Lewis. At 65, with a record of six defeats in ten attempts, he had fought enough elections. He retired to Ottawa's Carleton University, to his memoirs, and to the failing health that troubled his final years.

For its third leader, the NDP would have to choose someone who had not been trained and nurtured in the ranks of the CCF. Tommy Douglas, approached to act as interim leader, insisted that the caucus look to its younger blood. Among only sixteen MPs, the choice fell on Ed Broadbent, one of the few New Democrats to improve his vote in 1974. In his rumpled, friendly way, Broadbent had proved to be an ideal candidate for his mixed middle-class and autoworker constituency of Oshawa-Whitby. A worker's son who had escaped the assembly line to become an academic political philosopher, Broadbent had an independent mind, faith in himself, and astonishing rapport with all sorts and conditions of humanity. He lacked the rhetorical skills that Robert Michels had once defined as essential in a socialist leader; he had little patience or skill in the weary negotiations imposed by the NDP's intricate structure, and he had to shake memories of his dismal performance at the 1971 leadership convention. A pedantic speech and some naive horse-trading had dropped him to fourth place and almost cost him his federal seat.

As House leader, Broadbent faced trial by ordeal if he wanted to inherit Lewis's mantle. Characteristically, he was not prepared to be a caretaker. To Broadbent, the central problem of the NDP was its provincial orientation. Between federal elections, a national organization barely existed. The federal headquarters depended on contributions, often far in arrears, from provincial sections. Even victory in the three western provinces proved troublesome to the national party, absorbing funds and talented candidates and strengthening rival power bases in the organization. Broadbent set out to buck the trend. His lever was the new election expenses act that NDP pressure had helped push through the previous minority parliament. Since contributors to national parties could now deduct much of their gift from their federal income tax, Broadbent proposed that the NDP would henceforth have a central treasury and an easy way to fill it. At a federal council meeting in Halifax in October, 1974, provincial representatives, with their own plans for spending the federal windfall, gave Broadbent an embarrassing rebuff.

It was a bad beginning for an interim leader, made worse when details of the dispute spilled into the press. It was also a reminder that New Democrats were still looking for a sufficiently eminent successor for David Lewis. For most members and certainly for the NDP's leaders, Saskatchewan's Allan Blakeney would have been ideal. He had made Medicare work and he had emerged as a tough but responsible bargainer for control of his province's resources. He was also alone among the three NDP premiers in sparing much attention for his party's federal wing. However, with a provincial election due, Saskatchewan had no intention of allowing another popular premier to be shanghaied to Ottawa. Manitoba's Ed Schreyer, with his broad appeal to moderates was an obvious alternative, but he would not budge. The search went on. Professor Charles Taylor was the preferred candidate for those who demanded a bilingual leader. Even Eric Kierans, the former Liberal cabinet minister and stock exchange president, who had impressed some western NDPers, was considered.

Amidst growing amusement among media watchers, the futile hunt persisted until January 17th, 1975. In a brief announcement, Ed Broadbent declared that he would not seek the leadership. A contented family life and a newly-adopted daughter were attractive enough alternatives to the quarrels, aggravations, and lost weekends of leading a party that preferred other choices. A shocked federal council considered deferring the contest to 1977 when a provincial premier or some other star might be available. The possibility was rejected. Already one candidate was mustering support — Rosemary Brown, a member of the British Columbia legislature. To delay a choice when the only available contestant was a black woman would guarantee charges of sexism and racial prejudice.

Brown was attractive, eloquent, and instantly appealing to the righteousness and romanticism of middle-class New Democrats. She would also be a quixotic choice for a party with troubles enough. In an impressive if belated display of solidarity, Lewis, Douglas, all three NDP premiers, and most of the other influential figures in the party joined in persuading Broadbent to reconsider. On March 26th, he announced that he was back in the race. In most other parties, such solid establishment backing would have guaranteed victory; in the NDP, it could also be a liability. When the two front runners, joined by Saskatchewan's Lorne Nystrom, John Harney, and two fringe candidates, set off on a planned itinerary of debates, there was little response. Tiny gatherings — 200 in Toronto, 165 in Winnipeg — robbed the party of internal excitement and media coverage. After so many defeats and disappointments, it was by no means clear that the NDP's establishment could deliver victory to a candidate who plainly did not hunger for it.

As usual, when delegates crowded into Winnipeg's new convention centre on July 4th, organizers insisted that leadership was a subsidiary to the main role of an NDP gathering: debating policy. Bearpit sessions and nomination speeches were sandwiched between debates on multinational corporations and a proposal to nationalize the CPR. Perhaps the only surprise of a convention held in International Women's Year was a determined and successful attempt by some women delegates to modify the NDP's pro-choice stance on abortion. Yet it was the leadership contest that drew 1661 delegates to Winnipeg, almost as many as had filled Ottawa's Civic Centre in 1971. By now, there were only five candidates, with Broadbent playing the front-runner's role, well aware that the rhetoric that provoked NDP cheers might cost the party wider support. Rosemary Brown was a second Jim Laxer, with more fire, fewer facts, and a dependence on trite platitudes that troubled even some of her own followers. Nystrom, in 1968 the youngest MP in history, was earnest and well organized, straining to catch Brown supporters if, as he hoped, she fell behind. Harney's wit and bilingualism could not overcome his 1974 rejection by voters in Scarborough West.

As in 1971, the contest went the full distance. Douglas Campbell, a Mississauga taxi-driver, tested even NDP tolerance for eccentricity, but he served his purpose by showing the field: Brown was second, safely ahead of Nystrom, close enough to Broadbent to dream of victory. Harney's followers split evenly among the three survivors; Nystrom's backers went mainly to Broadbent. It was no easy acclamation.

Leadership ballots at the 1975 convention

	I	II	III	IV
Broadbent	536	586	694	948
Brown	413	397	494	648
Nystrom	345	342	413	
Harney	313	299		
Campbell	11			
	1618	1624	1601	1606

Whatever the process of victory, Broadbent had inherited the mantle of Woodsworth, Coldwell, Douglas, and Lewis. He had argued consistently and without compromise for a more powerful federal presence for the party, for concentration on the fifty or sixty seats the NDP could hope to win in a 1978 election, and for a national economic strategy that might give coherence to the NDP's enormous accumulation of programmes and policies. By 1976 he had established an Election Planning Committee headed by Terry Grier, the former federal secretary and now a rising academic administrator at Toronto's Ryerson Polytechnical Institute. Just as important was a Policy Review Committee, headed by Steven Langdon, a Carleton University professor with a special expertise in Third World development. Langdon's committee began fashioning the documentation for an industrial strategy that would form the keynote of Broadbent's speeches from 1977 on.

As usual, the NDP's provincial preoccupations superseded federal priorities. For most of Canada west of the Ottawa River, 1975 was an election year. In an encouraging prelude, a Yukon NDP organization, born at a tiny convention in

June, 1973, contested three seats on November 18th, 1974 and won two of them. In the neighbouring Northwest Territories, NDP and NDP-backed candidates won five of fifteen seats on March 10th, 1975. In southern Canada, 1975 proved a hard year for incumbent governments. The euphoria of the Trudeau victory had passed quickly. Canadians once again wrestled with double-digit inflation, unemployment, and growing pockets of economic stagnation. A majority government felt no special need to respond.

Organized workers, struggling to keep pace with inflation, sacrificed 9.2 million days in strikes in 1974 — a near-record — and lost 10 million days in 1975. As major employers, NDP governments found themselves caught between striking workers and voters demanding fast, hard-line settlements. The provincially-owned British Columbia Railway was paralyzed by rotating strikes through much of the summer of 1974. Having rescued Flyer Coach from bankruptcy, the Manitoba government faced an interminable strike by its workers. Saskatchewan Power Commission workers chose sub-zero weather in January, 1975, to withdraw their services. The Blakeney government summoned the legislature and ordered the electricity workers back to their jobs. "There is a point in any type of human activity at which the public interest becomes paramount," insisted Roy Romanow, the Saskatchewan attorney general, "The government thinks this is such a point."

In the West, labour disputes mattered less than resource policies. In his post-election budget, John Turner revived the Liberals' tax on oil royalties. Promptly half the wells in Saskatchewan shut down and the oil industry took its grievance to Regina. Next door, in Alberta, Premier Peter Lougheed propped up the huge Syncrude project, proclaimed himself the saviour of the province's energy industry and, on March 26th, 1975, won a landslide. The NDP, which had run five more candidates than Social Credit and

Ed Broadbent defeated British Columbia MLA Rosemary Brown to become the NDP's third federal leader. Broadbent combined philosophical sophistication with strong union backing.

billed itself as "The Only Real Opposition," was lucky to save its leader, Grant Notley, by a margin of 99 votes.

For Blakeney, faithful to the CCF-NDP tradition of a June election every four years, prospects looked grim. The 1974 wheat harvest had been bad, back-to-work legislation had angered labour, and Saskatchewan had neither Alberta's one-party tradition nor its deferential media. The fact remained that Saskatchewan was an oasis of low unemployment, a budget surplus, and the fastest growing public revenue in Canada. A suggestion by Otto Lang, Saskatchewan's voice in the Trudeau cabinet, that the cherished Crowsnest Pass freight rate deal should be scrapped gave Blakeney an issue. The campaign surprise came from the Conservatives. Led by Richard Collver, an evangelist of right-wing nostrums, and backed by a concerted effort from the province's Tory MPs, they produced a full slate of candidates. The results, on June 11th, 1975, demonstrated that there was more than one way to show anger at Ottawa. NDP support slumped from 55 per cent to its former base of 40 per cent but the party held 39 of the 61 seats. The Liberals, with 15 seats, fell to 32 per cent while Collver's campaign won an unexpected seven seats and 28 per cent of the vote. While Blakeney could boast of "an unequivocal victory," the NDP had lost heavily in the southern and western regions where oil development had come to a halt. With the Tories, a new force had entered the provincial scene.

A three-party arrangement might not be fatal; it had been the secret of Ontario Tory longevity since 1943. Yet, in the mid-1970s, polls were showing Ontario's Liberals in the lead. Ontario's accustomed prosperity had been shaken by the energy crisis. Inflation generated crippling strikes, soaring rents, and tripled house prices. The Liberals were willing beneficiaries of electoral grumbles about taxes and education spending. In 1973-74, they had captured three safe Tory seats in by-elections. The NDPers' prospects were bleak. For months during 1973, Stephen Lewis, the provincial leader, had questioned whether he could lead an Ontario party to victory. When he returned from his self-imposed retreat, he had given Ontario voters a chance to forget the strident, aggressive politician of 1971. He set off to get to know the small towns of the province, doing little talking and much listening to groups of parents, farmers, business people, and editors. In October, 1974, the NDP took Stormont in a by-election and came close in Carleton East, ridings where the party had barely made a showing before. Party strategists were grateful for signs that something was working. It was not much.

By mid-August, 1975, when Premier William Davis finally called the Ontario election, the Liberal-Tory struggle had turned into a noisy, scandal-waving affray. Tory polls showed the government still trailing the Liberals while the NDP had slipped far behind. NDP statisticians were worried too. They had counted on the Tory machine to demolish the Liberals, as it had done before, leaving dissatisfied voters to turn to the NDP as a responsible, constructive opposition. Every feature of the campaign, from Lewis's issues of conserving farmland and improving industrial safety to the election colours — a warm shade of brown —had been chosen for their reassuring qualities. Despite secret pleas from the Tories to attack the Liberals, Lewis and his advisors stuck by their strategy. In the end, with no one else willing to demolish the Liberals, Premier Davis did it himself, in a brutal television debate that damaged both traditional parties in the regions where the broadcast was seen. On September 13th, the Conservatives had their poorest showing since 1943, only 51 members, 35.9 per cent of the votes. For once luck and electoral geography favoured New Democrats. With 28.8 per cent, they won 38 seats, mostly in major industrial cities and suburbs and in the North. The Liberals had 34.2 per cent of the votes but only 36 seats. By a squeaky margin of a couple of seats and a few hundred well-placed votes, the NDP was back where the CCF had been twice before, as official opposition in Ontario.

Throughout the Ontario campaign, NDP candidates had waited nervously to be deluged with damning facts and figures from British Columbia. Perhaps because Tories were preoccupied by Liberals, the barrage never came. The threat was real. If 1974 had been bad in British Columbia, 1975 was worse. Disastrous prices in the mining and lumber industries pushed unemployment above the national average. Dave Barrett's government raided its reserves to produce a $3.2 billion budget, with $70 million for job creation, but the liberalized legislative procedures allowed the Social Credit opposition to stall NDP programmes. Strikes closed super-markets, breweries, sugar refineries, schools, and the new Insurance Corporation of B.C. Most serious was a struggle between the newly nationalistic pulp and paper unions and their employers. Environmental groups denounced the NDP for planning a provincially-owned oil refinery. Landlords blamed Vancouver's housing shortage on NDP rent controls. Native groups switched their angry demands for a land settlement from Ottawa to Victoria.

Most democratic governments survive troughs in popularity and some even plan for them, counting on voters to have short memories. With a divided opposition, Barrett would still have a fighting chance. Liberal and Tory leaders each insisted on playing St. George to the socialist dragon. Not until 1975 had the business community concluded that Social Credit, led by the colourless but stubborn Bill Bennett, was still the only opposition. By May, the Conservatives had disintegrated; in September, 1975, the Liberals followed. Three MLAs, including a former Trudeau cabinet minister, Jack Davis, proclaimed their faith in the mysteries of Social Credit.

With his enemies closing in, Dave Barrett decided to fight. He set off for the interior, seizing time on open-line shows and drawing crowds that were larger than anyone would have imagined. He boasted of his achievements, denounced right-wing wreckers and, in early October, conducted a long overdue cabinet shuffle. On October 7th, he summoned an astonished legislature to end strikes in the forest industry, the supermarkets, and the B.C. Railway. When he returned from a federal-provincial finance ministers' conference on October 25th, Barrett had fresh announcements: a freeze on the price of food, energy, prescription drugs, and other essentials until January 1st, increases in Mincome and the minimum wage, and lower rent-control ceilings.

There could only be one more announcement: that British Columbians would vote on December 11th. The issue, claimed Barrett, would be the inequities of federal wage and price controls. Of course, that was not the real issue, nor was socialism versus free enterprise, as newspaper editorials insisted. At stake was the premier — "Little Fat Dave" as he called himself — and his record. The NDP insisted that it was a fight of "the people against the big vested interests." Legislation to curb campaign spending was a casualty of the sudden dissolution of the legislature, and the Social Credit war chest spread its wealth to candidates and to an array of anti-socialist allies ranging from the "Concerned Citizens and Foresters" to the "Women's Mining Association." By common consent, Barrett won the campaign but Bill Bennett, wisely avoiding public debate or intra-party squabbles, won the election. With just under half the votes, Social Credit won 35 of the 55 seats; only 18 New Democrats survived the debacle though the NDP's vote was virtually unaltered from 1972 at 39.4 per cent.

Defeat in British Columbia, however predictable once polarization had set in, was a deep humiliation for a party accustomed by long years of power in Saskatchewan, and even by the narrow 1973 re-election in Manitoba, to assume that voters would be grateful. It was meagre comfort to watch B.C.'s vulnerable economy wallow into even deeper trouble under Bennett's new government. In an effort to prove the disastrous state of the NDP-created Insurance Corporation, the new regime noisily transferred $181 million to its account, only to borrow back the money since it was not needed. Eccentric government book-keeping was an old British Columbia tradition but the experience of 1972 to 1975 entrenched another tradition even more deeply. Inept, absurd, or corrupt the Social Credit regime might be, but it was not the NDP. For enough British Columbians, that was all that mattered.

For most Canadians during the 1970s, other provincial elections were overshadowed by contests in Quebec. In 1970 and in 1973 Robert Bourassa's Liberals had held the separatist Parti Québécois at bay but huge legislative majorities concealed the steady growth in PQ popular support. By 1976, the PQ's combination of nationalism and reform had swept up most of Quebec's French-speaking intellectuals, labour leaders, and students, as well as a healthy share of workers and the middle class. It did not seem enough for victory, even with the new pledge that any decision on independence would be made by a referendum. Bourassa and his government, pilloried and besieged by strikers and media critics, might still survive. Even the Olympic games, a debt-ridden flop, could be blamed on Montreal's Mayor Jean Drapeau.

Then came the affair of *les Gens de l'air*. The issue seemed trivial: should air traffic control in the skies over Quebec be conducted in French as well as in English? *Les Gens de l'air*, a union of French-speaking aviation workers thought so; so did Jean Marchand, Trudeau's transport minister. The proposal provoked a chorus of protest from English-speaking pilots and air traffic controllers: any concession to bilingualism in the air would imperil safety. When protesters chose to strike, the NDP endorsed their concern. So did Tories and many Liberals. The government retreated to the refuge of an official inquiry and English Canada promptly forgot the issue. Quebec did not. The Bourassa government had squandered support by timidity, mismanagement, and a bungled language law; the issue of language in the air was a final blow. On November 15th, 1976, Quebec gave the PQ 71 seats and the Liberals a meagre 26.

Almost everywhere, Canadians were traumatized. National disintegration seemed imminent. Pierre Trudeau may have contributed to the crisis, but suddenly Canadians turned to him as a saviour. As in most Quebec-Canada crises, the NDP seemed impotent, irrelevant, and slightly foolish. A few prominent party members applauded the PQ victory. Dave Barrett rushed to Montreal to remind the Parti Québécois that another Canadian party shared its social-democratic ideals. These were not messages most NDP supporters wanted to send. They ignored the fact that national independence, not social reform, was the PQ's prime concern. Ed Broadbent had a point when he blamed the Lévesque victory on an inflexible federal government and a mismanaged economy, but it was both vulgar Marxism and ill-informed to insist that unemployment was the root cause of separatism. Lacking credible leadership in French Canada, the NDP still relied on editorials in *Le Devoir* and a kind of left-wing "bonne ententism."

The NDP found itself hardly better equipped for political argument when Ontario's William Davis received polls claiming that his Tories could win an easy majority and promptly called an election for June 9th, 1977. Tough times and jitters created by the Lévesque victory helped the Davis government to concentrate its fire on Stephen Lewis and the New Democrats. This time British Columbia was an issue in the Tory ads that blasted the NDP, but New Democrats

Stephen Lewis's oratorical brilliance both charmed and frightened Ontario
voters in the 1970s. In the end, their fears and his own discouragement helped
stall NDP advances.

contributed to their own problems. As leader, Lewis demoralized militants by disavowing the NDP's explicit promise to nationalize Ontario's resource industries. Next, he gave a feeble defence of the party's commitment to a $4 minimum wage. In the North, a defence of native rights and denunciation of environment damage cost votes. It was the Liberals, with an inexperienced leader and seemingly no chances, who collected support while the Tories, as lack-lustre as the NDP, saw their winning margin evaporate. Instead of an easy victory, Bill Davis emerged on June 9th with only 58 seats, ahead of the Liberals' 34 and the NDP's 33. For the NDP, the loss of five seats and second place was cause for frustration. Lewis promptly quit as party leader, leaving his party more or less where he had found it in 1970 but much deeper in debt. His successor, Mike Cassidy, a former journalist, was a decent, utterly uncharismatic figure, quite unable to rally the party's dispirited membership.

The NDP's disappointments were not yet complete. In Manitoba, Ed Schreyer's cautious, consensual regime seemed as secure as any government in Canada. Tories, unable to attack premium-free medicare, no-fault government auto insurance, the "stay" option for farmers, could complain only of high taxes and "bloated bureaucracies." In Sterling Lyon, the Tories had found a leader who boasted of his right-wing views. He seemed a hopeless adversary for a government that almost religiously shunned the reforming spirit of its youth. Yet Schreyer knew he was in trouble. Polls suggested a Tory sweep. Conservative meetings were packed. The Liberals had ceased to exist. Labour backers smarted at memories of the Griffin Steel strike, an ultimate union defeat in which the government had refused to intervene. Schreyer and his ministers were testy under criticism. "You've got the best labour laws in the country," Schreyer told one union meeting. "What more do you want from us, for Christ's sake?" The answer came in the form of catcalls.

Schreyer postponed the election from June to October 11th, and government advertising boasted that the NDP had "turned Manitoba into a Business Success." Autopac, the government insurance scheme, boasted that it spent half as much as private insurers, 17 cents per premium dollar, on administration. The Tories displayed a benevolent Sterling Lyon speaking to children and pledged an income tax cut, a reduction of the civil service, and an inquiry into the government's major corporations. The outcome was a clear Tory victory: 49 per cent of the votes, 33 seats to the NDP's shrunken total of 23 (a single Liberal remained in the legislature). A suddenly unbenign Sterling Lyon fired officials, froze spending, and suspended the family law reforms that had been almost the only substantive pre-election achievement of the NDP. Personal and corporate taxes were cut by 2 per cent and overtime pay was cut to time-and-a-half. Right-wing ideology triumphed with a vengeance. New Year's celebrations at the posh Manitoba Club, noted a commentator, were "unusually cheerful."

New Democrats had no such comfort. For a time in the early 1970s, it had seemed that the NDP had been on the march, collecting the provincial victories that party strategists considered the necessary prelude to federal success. Now the movement was in retreat. Even worse than the setbacks themselves, for a party that prided itself on coherent policies, was the sense that New Democrats had no persuasive or unifying solution to the combination of stagnation and inflation that troubled Canada. If their opponents were no better equipped with ideas, blaming unions and "big government" for economic problems won echoing applause from the troubled heirs of a fading prosperity.

X. Reappraisal

In his 1965 study of the origins of the New Democratic Party, Gad Horowitz had warned that Canadian labour had a success psychology. If the experiment in creating a political party had achieved success within fifteen years, labour might well look for another political vehicle. Horowitz's notional deadline would come in 1976.

No aspect of the NDP's 1974 debacle troubled party leaders more than the drop in union support to a mere 22 per cent. Some observers claimed to have noticed the symptoms when a few delegates to the 1974 CLC convention sat out the ritual standing ovation to David Lewis. Officially, CLC leaders were as staunch as ever: two-thirds of the $300,000 spent for the NDP's central campaign in 1972 and in 1974 came from union treasuries. The break came lower down the hierarchy. In most unions, political action had been a marginal activity, limited to a handful of stalwarts. A change of leadership could bring a dramatic change in attitude. Under Fred Dowling, the United Packinghouse Workers had been a major pillar of the CCF; his successors, now part of the Amalgamated Meatcutters, showed no such enthusiasm.

Although representatives of the twelve major union affiliates sat on the NDP's federal council, formal links with the Canadian Labour Congress were frail. Regarding itself as midwife rather than mother to the new party, the Congress avoided formal liaison with the NDP. Lewis recalled a single meeting with CLC executive officers during his term as leader. In provinces with NDP governments, relations ranged from the close contact between Schreyer and Len Stevens, president of the Manitoba Federation of Labour, to the ill-concealed hostility of the B.C. Federation of Labour towards Barrett and his labour minister, Bill King. Each NDP government had reformed labour relations law, improved job security and safety legislation, and raised the minimum wage, but none had given unions all they demanded.

Rebuilding grassroots labour support became an NDP priority after the 1974 election. The job was given to Michael Lewis, David's second son and an able organizer in his own right. Summer schools and weekend seminars targeted a rising generation of local union leaders, few of whom knew anything about the NDP. Federal Liberals had a more discreet strategy. Having held the allegiance of far more union members and their families than the NDP, the governing party now aimed at separating the union leadership from the NDP. Trudeau's minister of labour, John Munro, was a veteran Hamilton politician, vulnerable to NDP strength yet well aware of some of the frustrations union leaders felt about their socialist link. A new Canada Labour Relations Council, with government, business, and union representatives, allowed labour leaders to rub shoulders with Ottawa power brokers. A few veteran unionists were invited to consider Senate seats.

Munro's courtship of labour was complicated by his colleague, John Turner. As inflation soared, the Liberal diagnosis changed. Business might blame the problem on slack government purse strings, but official economists defined the villain as "cost-push" — specifically excessive price increases and wage demands. Turner's answer was voluntary restraint: if Munro's union leaders wanted to share in the power structure, let them qualify by persuading rank-and-file unionists to tighten their belts. This was easier said than done. The CLC might be the political voice of labour, but its power over its affiliates was negligible. Given the extremely decentralized pattern of collective bargaining in Canada — itself the product of deliberate government policy — even national and international union leaders had trouble influencing their locals. Joe Morris, the CLC president, shrewdly avoided responsibility by offering Turner a nine-point counter-proposal, ranging from rent controls to lower unemployment rates, as the price of CLC support. By September, when Turner quit the government, he had nothing to show for his time in the finance department save the genesis of an ultimately enormous federal deficit.

In 1974, post-election wisdom decreed that Canadian workers had heeded NDP attacks on the Tory wage and price freeze policy, but that they had switched to the Liberals to save themselves. Though very few voters could ever be found to have followed this ingenious strategy, the myth became all the more convenient when the Trudeau government itself decided to steal the Stanfield policy. The workers' opposition to controls was easy to understand though few took the trouble. Locked into two- or three-year contracts while prices and taxes soared, union members had to wait to recover their losses until their contracts expired. By then, inflation had become a crisis and early winners had pocketed their gains. The spot-light of criticism had time to focus on workers demanding thirty to forty per cent settlements as their way of building real wage increases on top of catch-up. On October 13th, 1975, at the end of the Thanksgiving weekend, the prime minister used national radio and television to announce the most pervasive controls on prices and incomes peacetime Canada had ever known.

For Ed Broadbent, the issue and the opportunity were

clear. For sixteen months, the NDP federal caucus had languished in obscurity, wondering if the country knew it was there — or even cared. Now New Democrats could stand alone against the prime minister's latest switch in policy. They could use arguments Trudeau himself had used against controls, some of them printed in the issue of *Maclean's* on sale as the new programme was unveiled. Controls, Trudeau had warned, would affect wages more than prices. They would generate a tangle of regulations and a river of injustices. They would end in either a desperate struggle to catch-up or a catastrophic recession. If Trudeau had foresaken his arguments, Broadbent would use them and, in the process, rebuild the NDP's flagging union support.

The dangers were less immediately obvious. In fact, a good many ordinary Canadians, including many union members, rejoiced that Ottawa appeared to have done something decisive about inflation. Some New Democrats — by no means doctrinaire — wondered whether labour's devotion to free collective bargaining was more righteous than business's faith in a free and unfettered market. Both forms of freedom ran counter to a socialist faith in planning, rationality, and fairness. Even worse for the party, the issue produced an open federal-provincial split. The Manitoba and Saskatchewan governments announced that they would be full, if reluctant, partners in the Trudeau scheme. Even after its defeat, the British Columbia NDP approved a modified system of wage and price controls.

For union leaders, there were no shades of grey in Trudeau's Anti-Inflation Board. Collective bargaining is the key union function in Canada; suddenly it had been seized, frozen, and handed over to the unpredictable decisions of a jerry-built bureaucracy. As financiers and manufacturers heaped their praises on the Trudeau programme, unionists needed no reminder that wages, not prices, would be the real target of restraint. What was even more humiliating, Trudeau had obviously weighed the predictable labour hostility to his programme in the balance and had ignored it. What more needed to be said about labour's political strategy since 1961? Perhaps, as Horowitz had predicted, unions needed a new vehicle.

It was not easily found. After an angry meeting with the prime minister on October 31st, CLC officers emerged to announce their campaign: a $500,000 war chest, an advertising blitz, a constitutional challenge and, when labour leaders visited Parliament Hill in March, 1976, a mass demonstration would accompany them. By then Joe Morris, the gravel-voiced ex-logger who presided over the CLC, and Shirley Carr, the former Niagara Falls office worker who was the CLC's first woman vice-president, would be national figures.

Amidst the anger, haste, and improvisation, a longer-range union strategy emerged. It was encouraged by Trudeau's year-end musing on the possibilities of a "syndicalist or corporate state." Labour, business, and especially the government would join in controlling the economy. The immediate response of Morris and other union leaders was as apoplectic as those of bankers and business magnates but Ron Lang, the CLC's new legislative director, saw in Trudeau's remarks a springboard for a new political strategy for Canadian labour. Lang's predecessor, Andy Andras, had been a major influence on CCF-NDP thinking, but Lang had reservations about party affiliation. If the Trudeau government was bent on centralizing key aspects of collective bargaining, organized labour would have to follow suit. Instead of being a biennial talk-shop, the Canadian Labour Congress could become the effective bargaining agency for all workers, on the model of the Swedish labour federation, the

LO. By accepting the prime minister's image of a corporate state, Congress officers might gain enormous power over the once-haughty national and international affiliates. Instead of waiting forever for the NDP to form a government and then getting half a loaf, Lang's echo of Trudeau's social corporatism offered the CLC an early and effective voice in shaping social and economic policy.

As the winter of 1976 turned to spring, it was apparent that the Congress campaign against controls was going badly. The advertising campaign was prepared, tested, and dropped as ineffective. CLC lawyers collected briefs from 38 reputable (and largely right-wing) economists, only to find that the Supreme Court of Canada was not impressed by the arguments. Neither was the government, despite the presence of twenty thousand union members to Parliament Hill. By the time CLC delegates met in Quebec on May 17th for their biennial convention, their leaders were angry, frustrated, and empty-handed. It was the opportunity Lang needed. His ideas, embodied as "Labour's Manifesto for Canada," hurried through preliminary committees into the convention. Delegates had no time to reflect on arguments for a "tripartite" approach to planning a post-controls Canada nor even a commitment to a "national wages policy." With a small amendment to remove the words "social corporatism," the Manifesto became CLC policy. So did a proposal for a nationwide general strike on the anniversary of the prime minister's announcement. Such proposals were a predictable ritual at CLC conventions but this time the CLC's Executive Council gave its backing and delegates shouted their approval. Was this a "new vehicle," the old syndicalism, or merely stage management?

Re-christened a "Day of Protest" the strike was all three. It was also evident that convention militants did not speak for the rank and file. The embarrassing truth was that Trudeau's anti-inflation programme was more popular with workers than their leaders. As the day approached, CLC leaders turned desperately to the industrial unions to deliver the million strikers necessary for media recognition. Public sector unions, militant at the convention, proved mouse-like when the testing time approached. On October 14th, 1976, unions came close to delivering the essential million protesters but the penalties exacted in most provinces for staging an illegal strike discouraged any repetition. Fervid pledges of escalation were forgotten. The controls programme remained until mid-1978 when the prime minister returned from the Bonn summit with a brand-new inflation-fighting strategy: monetarism, high interest rates, and a sharp increase in unemployment. Those who had predicted that controls would end in recession would be proved right.

For its part, the NDP was sidelined by the struggle. New Democrats grumbled at a CLC campaign that seemed almost designed to alienate sympathy. Even a fraction of the pay forfeited on the Day of Protest would have given the NDP a fund to match the finances of both traditional parties — and most of the contribution would have been tax-deductible. It was no use: extra-parliamentary activity was something the party's labour allies had to get out of their system. By 1978, the issue seemed to be settled. Lang's Manifesto had swirled away to the oblivion reserved for convention rhetoric. Ed Schreyer's defeat and his subsequent appointment as Governor-General removed the NDP's most conspicuous believer in wage and price controls. Joe Morris, equivocal at best about the CLC-NDP alliance, was replaced in 1978 by the Canadian director of the United Autoworkers. Dennis McDermott had been outspoken about pro-controls heresies in the NDP and he wanted the party purged of "armchair academics and pseudo-intellectuals," but he was also uncompromising about labour's responsibility for helping labour's party.

While labour made its weary political detour from 1975 to

1978, its partner had not been idle. True to his original purpose, Broadbent had set out to endow the NDP with a sophisticated and contemporary economic analysis. Using arguments that such theorists as Robert Reich and Lester Thurow had applied to the United States, a policy review committee headed by Steven Langdon insisted that rising unemployment was caused by deliberate deindustrialization. The short-sighted "paper entrepreneurialism" of huge corporations allowed capital to be wasted in mergers and tax dodges while productive jobs and new technologies moved offshore. Broadbent and Langdon added a Canadian and social-democratic solution to the analysis: an economy "restructured so that Canadian needs will be met from production based on domestic resources." A three-stage programme began with enhancement of three key sectors, housing, transportation, and food, moved on to the industries supplying these basic needs, and finally added selected industries with investment potential. A Canadian Investment Fund, based on a Swedish example, would be built from forced corporate savings in boom times that would be tax exempt if invested according to government guidelines. If multinational firms objected to such a government intrusion in their affairs, the strategy envisaged limited foreign exchange controls on their Canadian earnings.

Even in the NDP, Broadbent's industrial strategy drew mixed reviews. Pleasure at a coherent new economic alternative encountered regional suspicions that Ontario would, as usual, be the beneficiary. Media observers offered limp praise for a party leader capable of articulating fresh ideas but concluded that an increasingly conservative electorate would not be in a buying mood. "Talk of a social democracy and a planned economy turns the public off," declared the *Globe and Mail's* Geoffrey Stevens. "The people want less government, not more. . . ."

Defeat in British Columbia and Manitoba had been warning enough of electoral conservatism. The new Tory leader, Joe Clark, had enjoyed a honeymoon in the polls in 1976. Then, the PQ victory in November had sent support surging back to the Liberals: if Trudeau had called a snap election in 1977 he might have won a sweep. Instead, the prime minister ignored his advisers. National alarm and even interest soon faded from the Quebec situation. The right-wing mood that would elect Margaret Thatcher in Britain in 1979 and would sweep Ronald Reagan into the White House in 1980 became more easily visible in Canada. Among government initiatives, only lotteries — the "voluntary taxes" Jean Drapeau had inaugurated to finance his Montreal Olympics — seemed popular. Opinion polls showed renewed hostility to unions, support for capital punishment, and deep divisions about access to abortion. The post office, plagued by internal conflict and a bungled attempt at automation, became a national symbol of anger at public institutions. Government itself, not merely mistaken policies, had become a villain pursued by editors, business leaders, and a growing share of the electorate. Conservatives obviously benefited from the chase; equally obviously, New Democrats did not.

By the autumn of 1978, Trudeau had lost his opportunity for an easy victory. Instead of a general election, he announced by-elections for fifteen long-standing vacancies, most of them Liberal. The results, scattered across seven provinces, would be a foretaste of the election to come. On October 16th, Conservatives swept ten of the seats, Liberals and New Democrats held two, and Social Credit retained a lone seat. The Tories were ecstatic; New Democrats were not. In Toronto-Broadview, a youthful Bob Rae had narrowly held a traditional NDP seat. Elsewhere in Ontario, Conservatives had easily beaten strong NDP challenges. The other victory was utterly unexpected: Alphonsus Faour, a young Corner Brook lawyer, had given the NDP its first Newfoundland victory. The success owed less to industrial strategies than to old-fashioned organizing by local unions of fishermen and paperworkers and the candidate's opposition to abortion in a largely Catholic community.

Faour's victory suggested that labour support could make a difference. Early in March, 1979, the CLC's Dennis McDermott summoned a hundred union leaders to Toronto to make sure that no one would ignore labour's political intentions. Instead of its usual discreet role in staffing committee rooms and contributing to local candidates, unions would mobilize a "parallel campaign" to the NDP door-knocking; each union member and family would be canvassed. In larger communities, volunteers would use phone banks to contact every last possible supporter.

When it came to the CLC's strategy, the NDP was a beggar, not a chooser. Misgivings about the state of labour's neglected political organization and the wisdom of claiming a high profile before ensuring the means to deliver were politely squelched. Constituency organizations had to scramble to replace the veteran union activists needed for the parallel campaign. Residual Canadian hostility to unions was all the more easily deflected to the NDP. Perhaps the benefits would be worth it.

Terry Grier's election planning committee had other concerns. Chief among them was the need to establish that the NDP, despite the dismal 1974 showing, was still fully the equal of its two rivals. For the first time, thanks to election finance legislation, the party could mount a serious advertising campaign. Instead of fighting airline schedules and the propeller-driven frustrations of "Daisy-Air," Broadbent's tour would race to rallies and photo-opportunities by chartered jet. Whatever traditionalists might claim about the importance of policy or grassroots organization, the leader was once again the vehicle for NDP electoral hopes. Ed Broadbent fitted the bill. Once orthodontic surgery had closed a gap in his front teeth, the NDP leader was ruggedly telegenic. Campaign ads, prepared by Lawrence Wolf's Toronto ad agency, focussed on an earnest, friendly Broadbent, promoting chunks of his industrial strategy, from mining machinery to a merchant navy, according to the appropriate backdrop.

Moreover, within the modest limits the NDP planners set for themselves, the campaign worked. Policy issues for all parties faded into a battle of personalities. Conservatives, convinced that victory depended on keeping a fumbling leader out of trouble, only managed to reinforce doubts about Joe Clark's competence. Trudeau, alone and defiant before a giant Canadian flag, could restore only the once-faithful. Broadbent emerged from relative obscurity to reassure voters dismayed by their choice of leaders. Granted equal status in the first leaders' debate since 1968, he easily established the NDP's credentials and ensured systematic coverage by the most influential political medium, network television news. By late May, euphoric New Democrats could almost believe that their final television advertisement might work:

A lot of Liberals and Conservatives believe that Ed Broadbent would make the best Prime Minister. They say if Ed Broadbent were the leader of their party, he'd win the biggest landslide in Canadian history. People don't have the same nagging kind of doubts about Ed Broadbent they have about Trudeau or Clark. Maybe it's time to put aside the old Liberal and Conservative myths and simply vote for the best man. If enough people did that, Ed Broadbent would be the next Prime Minister of Canada.

Television, a shrewdly-devised campaign and his own personality had made Broadbent a powerful political asset for his party but not even personality politics could make the NDP acceptable to most voters. On May 22nd, 1979, a full slate of NDP candidates harvested 18 per cent of the ballots, the party's pre-1974 plateau. Trudeau's unpopularity outside Quebec ensured a Liberal defeat; Joe Clark's stilted performance prevented a Tory landslide. In a parliament of 136 Conservatives, 114 Liberals, 26 New Democrats, and a Social Credit rump of 6 seats, Clark could only form a minority government.

The new prime minister believed that he could repeat Diefenbaker's two-step march to a majority but he lacked his predecessor's political flair. As Canadians anxiously watched the effects of a second oil price shock inspired by an Iranian revolution, Clark's government spent a leisurely summer feeling for the levers of power. Interest rates began to soar. Financiers belatedly condemned the more profligate of Clark's election promises. Alberta's Peter Lougheed proved as intransigent on oil revenues to a fellow Tory as he had been to the Liberals. When Clark made concessions to Alberta, he outraged an equally Tory government in Ontario. Within weeks, the new government's honeymoon was over; by September polls showed Clark lagging far behind the Liberals. That had not been Diefenbaker's experience in 1957.

For New Democrats, the post-election mood was almost as quiescent as among the Tories. Relief at reversing the 1974 decline was mingled with frustration that apparent momentum had delivered so little. A surge of support in Nova Scotia and New Brunswick had not added to Andy Hogan's single Cape Breton seat. In Newfoundland, NDP support tripled to 30 per cent but only Faour had repeated his by-election success. It was the West that gave the party its gains, particularly in Manitoba and British Columbia, where the seven seats of 1974 grew to eighteen. In Ontario, where campaign resources had been concentrated, a mere two per cent increase was offset by a comparable loss in Quebec. Without the veteran Andrew Brewin and Max Saltsman to hold them, two of the eight Ontario seats had been lost. A weary party waited for Parliament to resume, wondered what it could do next time and set about paying its debts.

When Parliament finally met in November, Clark's boast that he would govern as though he had a majority had begun to look like nervous bluster. After months of waiting, he had no deal with Alberta, no shake-up of a Liberal-dominated bureaucracy, and very little of his promised legislation. Then, on November 21st, 1979, Pierre Elliott Trudeau announced his retirement from politics. Amid the eulogies, politicians of all parties relaxed. John Crosbie, the Tory finance minister, added flourishes of austerity to his budget, including an eighteen cent-a-gallon excise tax on gasoline. As a means of financing subsidies to eastern Canadian consumers of imported oil, this was more welcome to the oil industry than fresh taxes on their lucrative U.S. exports, but consumers were not pleased. Ontario's Premier Davis, with his own minority position to improve, made his angry disapproval audible.

Clark was not unduly perturbed. Bob Rae, as an impressive newcomer, would move the NDP's ritual vote of non-confidence in the budget but the leaderless Liberals would hardly want to precipitate an election. In any case, Clark would surely get the votes he needed from the *Créditistes*. The scenario was logical; it was not historical. Allan MacEachen, the wily Liberal House leader, suddenly sensed a winning issue. Liberal M.P.s absorbed liquid courage at a pre-Christmas caucus party. Clark, barely aware of his danger, stubbornly refused to curry favour with *Créditistes* or even to summon a handful of absent Tories. Rae's motion gained unexpected momentum. By December 14th, the NDP could take the credit or the blame for defeating a Tory government.

Clark seems to have been content. It would, he insisted, be 1958 again, or better since his main opponent was gone and the Liberals would be wracked by the rivalry of John Turner and Donald MacDonald, Trudeau's would-be successors. Clark failed to note two more important differences: he was not John Diefenbaker and his party now lagged twenty percentage points behind the Liberals. Moreover, within a few days, Canadians had the leader Clark had never been. After proving to Liberals that they had no alternative, Trudeau had modestly resumed his post. In a television age, mid-winter campaigning was no longer the appalling ordeal of John A. Macdonald's age. Trudeau's handlers kept him from crowds or controversy. Why imperil the Liberal lead? Editorials might denounce a useless election; on the whole only Tories — and weary election workers — generally agreed.

For the NDP, as for its rivals, campaigning had to be a matter of recycling the speeches, candidates, and strategies of the 1979 campaign. Terry Grier summoned an election planning committee that had not met since the early summer, took what comfort he could from polls that showed the NDP at 23 per cent, and chartered Broadbent another jet. The beauty of federal election expenses legislation was that winnable ridings with sensible campaigns were almost wholly in the black by December and well able to establish a new line of credit at a bank or credit union. Postponing serious campaigning to the new year cut the costs of the leader's tour and left just enough time to prepare materials normally completed well in advance of a routine campaign.

In some respects, the 1980 campaign was different. The CLC's highly-touted "Parallel Campaign" in 1979 had drawn plenty of anti-union criticism and only some localized surges of support. This time, it was more muted, though hardly more effective. Locals used their customary freedom to ignore Congress dictates. In 1979, Broadbent had avoided defence and foreign policy, areas that normally won the NDP few friends and many enemies. The Soviet invasion of

Afghanistan forced a response. Broadbent's prompt denunciation of Moscow's imperialism inspired an equally prompt disavowal from NDP doves, led by Pauline Jewett, running in New Westminister. Fortunately attention soon shifted. Robin Sears, the NDP national secretary, patched up a private truce on Cold War issues. Publicly, he impressed media commentators with the professionalism and relative affluence of the NDP campaign. Having spent $1.2 million on media in 1979 (to the Tories $2.47 million) the NDP actually raised its total in 1980 to $1.4 million. Certainly television was more vital in a winter campaign; more important, no one could claim that the NDP lacked the lungs for the second race.

The toughest campaign problem was an old one: which party was the NDP fighting? By January it was evident that Trudeau and the Liberals were winning but most NDP incumbents were in the West, fighting Tories. The strategy — a renewed array of Broadbent ads selling NDP policies, notably on energy issues — avoided the problem without solving it. By February, NDPers felt vulnerable, particularly in Ontario, when Trudeau blandly co-opted large chunks of their party's policies on labour, energy, and tax reform. Having besieged every possible Tory seat, the Liberals had turned their sights on the NDP.

On election day, February 18th, 1980, Broadbent and New Democrats had reason for modest rejoicing: twenty per cent of the vote and 32 seats across Canada was the best showing for the NDP or the CCF in any Canadian general election. British Columbia, Saskatchewan, and Manitoba had given half their seats to the NDP. Yet the Liberal strategy paid dividends. In Ontario, NDP strength had dropped by another seat and the hopeful 1979 bridgehead in Atlantic Canada had utterly disappeared. Faoure and Hogan both lost; if NDP support still nudged upward in New Brunswick and Nova Scotia, Newfoundland's thirty per cent in 1979 dwindled to only seventeen in 1980. In Ottawa, the NDP had once again become a regional party, with an Ontario leader and a young, impatient western caucus.

New Democrats were not alone in their plight. Trudeau's 147 seats gave him an easy majority without a single seat west of Winnipeg. Joe Clark's 103 members included a single lonely Quebecker. The *Créditistes,* deprived by death of their creator, Réal Caouette, had ceased to exist. The new Parliament faced some of the most historic and turbulent years in modern Canadian history. Its weaknesses, frustrations, and enormous potential were fully mirrored in Ed Broadbent's parliamentary following.

XI. Regionalism

In his final prime ministerial metamorphosis, Pierre Elliott Trudeau could do as he pleased. His majority gave him power and he would not face Canadian voters again. Marc Lalonde, Jim Coutts and Tom Axworthy could implement what they had borrowed in mid-campaign from the NDP; their leader would mastermind the defeat of René Lévesque's referendum, end the nation's fifty-year constitutional imbroglio and give Canadians the charter of rights that would secure Trudeau his historical niche. Then he could depart, leaving politicians of all parties to scramble for his inheritance.

For New Democrats, the Liberal majority and their own revived strength seemed a new opportunity to grow. There was sneaking embarrassment that so much had depended in 1979 and 1980 on Broadbent's image. Trudeau's agenda was not so much wrong as irrelevant to a country whose economic vulnerability owed as much to multinationals as the Parti Québécois. In Quebec, the tiny NDP remnant had somehow doubled the popular vote from five to ten per cent between 1979 and 1980 but it was hard to see why. A unilingual Broadbent could urge Quebeckers to stay with Confederation but local supporters were more likely to be separatists.

The NDP's highest hopes in the 1979-80 elections had risen in Atlantic Canada. Could federal votes be translated into provincial seats? A 1980 Newfoundland election proved a crushing disappointment. Even with Fonse Faour as leader, a cheerfully ramshackle campaign harvested a mere four per cent of the vote. New Brunswick was slightly more hopeful. In 1978, against Richard Hatfield, NDPers had collected six per cent of the votes; four years later, in 1982, the share was a modest ten per cent, but Robert Hall, a high school teacher, won Tantramar, the first New Brunswick seat in the party's history. Two years later, the Labrador riding of Menihek gave a narrow margin to Peter Fenwick, the NDP's latest Newfoundland leader.

In contrast, the Nova Scotia NDP fell victim to the regional jealousies and economic frustrations of Cape Breton and the mainland. By 1978, Jeremy Akerman's long struggle had won the NDP four Cape Breton seats in the Assembly. By 1980, he had had enough. John Buchanan's Tory government made room for Akerman in its bureaucracy. Free from Akerman's restraint, his abrasive lieutenant, Paul MacEwan, noisily blamed Halifax NDPers for his friend's frustrations and alleged that Trotskyites had infiltrated the party executive. Within a week, MacEwan was suspended. A stormy provincial council meeting in July 1980, with David Lewis presiding, turned suspension into absolute expulsion. In November, Nova Scotia NDPers met to choose Alexa McDonough as their new leader.

The first woman to head an NDP provincial section, McDonough faced a brutal apprenticeship. Articulate, likeable, and tough, she had already won a national profile as a two-time NDP candidate in Halifax. She inherited half the caucus. MacEwan, whom Buchanan moved to a prominent place at the Speaker's left, focussed his remarkable talent for vitriol and invective on McDonough and her father, a leading Nova Scotia socialist and industrialist, Lloyd Shaw. A

As leader of the Nova Scotia NDP, Alexa McDonough survived a bitter, intensely personal campaign to destroy her. Her reward was growing strength on the province's mainland and a national reputation as a strong, principled political leader.

1981 election allowed McDonough to win Halifax-Chebucto, but the NDP's delight at its first-ever mainland victory was offset by loss of both the remaining Cape Breton seats and by MacEwan's re-election. Without help or even party status in the legislature, the NDP leader faced three lonely years of MacEwan's vicious assaults. The Assembly enjoyed the fun.

New Democrats could do little about Nova Scotia and federally they soon had other preoccupations. Among the promises that pursued Quebeckers in the referendum on May 20th, 1980 was a pledge of prompt constitutional reform, endorsed by virtually every national and provincial leader save René Lévesque. After a convincing "Non" victory, work began. All summer, a team of Jean Chrétien, federal justice minister, and Roy Romanow, Saskatchewan's NDP attorney-general, toured Canada trying to shape a proposal. As the referendum crisis faded, so did unanimity. A televised constitutional conference in September showed everyone that the premiers had abandoned none of their old demands, from Brian Peckford's claim to the continental shelf to Bill Bennett's insistence on senate reform. Since any premier could apparently stop progress with a veto, the impasse was as complete as ever.

There it might have remained. Canada's constitutional arrangements might be untidy, but they had worked. That was no longer tolerable to Trudeau. He had predicted a stalemate and, on October 2nd, he broke it. The new Parliament would proceed unilaterally to impose an amending formula and a Charter of Rights and Freedoms. With a Liberal majority in both Houses, it would pass. Already Trudeau had the backing of Ontario's Bill Davis and New Brunswick's Richard Hatfield. He also had the NDP's Ed Broadbent.

The NDP decision had seemed easy. Summer caucus sessions had explored innumerable scenarios and given Broadbent a mandate to support Trudeau if he acted. After all, the prime minister would be doing no less than the Regina Manifesto in 1933, or the NDP itself, in 1961, had demanded. The NDP's priority was to get on with real economic problems. In an hour-long session on October 1st, Trudeau won Broadbent's backing in return for a promise — historic in its significance — to entrench full provincial control of natural resources and to toughen the Charter's provisions.

Across Canada, most NDP and labour leaders approved. Protests from the Quebec NDP could be ignored. What was alarming was the outrage of Allan Blakeney, echoed by Alberta's Grant Notley. Their opposition was due to more than prairie Trudeauphobia. Control of natural resources bit deep in Saskatchewan. In the 1970s, Ottawa Liberals and federal courts had done their best to sabotage Blakeney's attempts to collect oil royalties and to control oil and potash marketing for the benefit of Saskatchewan's people. Court defeats cost the province hundreds of millions. In 1978, Blakeney had won the biggest election sweep in CCF-NDP history on the resource issue. The province's historic Liberal party had virtually ceased to exist as survivors defected to the Tories. Saskatchewan's NDP now had hot competitors in the old game of wrestling with Ottawa. To Blakeney, Broadbent's achievement in getting a resource clause in the new constitution was half-baked meddling. Publicly, the Saskatchewan premier was cautious; privately he seethed. Romanow was despatched to Ottawa to negotiate, partly with Trudeau, partly with his own party.

From the moment Parliament (and his own caucus) returned to Ottawa, Broadbent was in trouble. Faced with reality, not theory, western MPs forgot the scenarios they had accepted in the summer. Lorne Nystrom, mindful of his leadership ambitions and his regional identity, helped muster dissidents. Other NDP members now saw Trudeau's Charter as an exciting opportunity to legislate a better future for women, native groups, and minorities. Most of Broadbent's caucus was new to Parliament and scornful of its compromises. Some, such as Burnaby's Svend Robinson, had served their apprenticeship in the New Left tradition of putting non-negotiable demands. While the federal NDP caucus wrangled, Blakeney weighed in with Trudeau to negotiate his own version of a resources guarantee. For his part, Jean Chrétien did his best to worsen the rift between the Saskatchewan premier and Broadbent. By the end of January, 1981, when Trudeau had failed to get Saskatchewan support, Nystrom and three of the prairie MPs were in ill-concealed opposition to their federal leader. Despite Romanow's assurances to Broadbent, Blakeney ultimately lined up with Lévesque, Bill Bennett, and the other hostile premiers.

Within the NDP, Broadbent had powerful support. Bob Rae, the future Ontario leader, British Columbia's Dave Barrett, and the party veterans Tommy Douglas, Stanley Knowles, and a dying David Lewis backed him. In the end, so did most of the federal caucus. Les Benjamin, the veteran Regina MP and former provincial secretary, paid a price in personal abuse for his support, but he was staunch. So were Dennis McDermott and other CLC leaders. Like the rest of organized labour and, probably, most Canadians, they felt that a deepening economic crisis should have been Parliament's first concern, not a wrangle over a legalistic document few understood. While Joe Clark's Tories dragged parliamentary business to a standstill over the Constitution, Canada staggered into the worst recession since the 1930s.

The NDP's internal divisions were soon public knowledge. At the party's 1981 convention at the University of British Columbia in Vancouver, a full-dress debate on July 4th pitted Broadbent against Blakeney. As the NDP's two most powerful leaders squared off, the prominent names in Canadian socialism lined up on either side. By common account, the dramatic moment of the debate came when a gaunt, sober-suited Stanley Knowles followed Nystrom to the podium. Half a century of oratory had taught Knowles how to seize and hold an NDP audience. Discreetly choosing the detested premier of his own province, he cried, "Sterling Lyon doesn't speak for all the people of Manitoba." The chairman, Robin Sears, called time; Knowles ignored him, thundering his commitment to a charter "that advances the things that we stand for." John Rodriguez, an Ontario ex-MP, followed by attacking Knowles. Delegates booed him. The tide turned. The vote, when it came, upheld Broadbent by almost two to one.

That summer, the Supreme Court wrestled with the constitutionality of Trudeau's procedure. The majority verdict, with the eminent Chief Justice Bora Laskin dissenting, was that Trudeau was defying a convention, if not the law, by his unilateral action. Privately, Broadbent was furious. It was "a stupid goddamned decision" (essentially Laskin's view). Publicly, the NDP leader urged Trudeau to make a last bid for agreement. In November, the premiers once again trooped to Ottawa. Before dawn on November 5th, Chrétien, Romanow, and Ontario's Roy McMurtry had cobbled together a deal: Trudeau's Charter, the premiers' new veto-less amending formula, and a clutch of smaller sections on natural resources, cost-shared programmes, and opting-out. The agreement, concluded without Lévesque who was left sound asleep in his Hull hotel room, became the basis of a constitution. It also became the target of frenzied lobbying by women, native groups, and others whose concerns had been abandoned in the rush. Blakeney, somehow seen as a special defender of their interests, became the special butt of their fury. By April 17th, 1982, the cold, rainy day when the Queen signed Canada's new Constitution Act, most of the pressure groups had been accommodated. Only Quebec, for which the whole process had been initiated, was still excluded.

Superficially, the NDP's bitter split over Trudeau's uni-lateral initiative seemed to do little electoral harm. The Constitution certainly had nothing to do with the outcome of Ontario's March 19th election. When Bill Davis chose February, 1981, to announce his second bid for a majority, most experts predicted disaster for the Liberals. Instead, with a spirited campaign and Trudeau's continued popular-ity, Ontario Liberals held their own. It was the NDP under Michael Cassidy, oddly ineffective and demoralized even before the campaign, who suffered the brutal setback. While Davis and his party won an easy victory, the NDP lost three seats to Liberals and nine to Tories. The popular vote, 21 per cent, was the lowest since 1963. A frustrated Cassidy resigned. His successor, after a campaign marked by little of the hard feelings of earlier contests, was Bob Rae, a young labour lawyer and a diplomat's son, who had dominated media coverage of the NDP in Ottawa.

Nationally, NDP support slumped a little in 1981 but party morale soared in August when Dan Heap derailed Jim Coutts, Trudeau's powerful aide, in what had been the safest Liberal seat in Ontario, Spadina. A far bigger victory, on November 17th, 1981, saw the NDP topple Sterling Lyon's Manitoba Tories. The NDP had had no easy time. In 1980 Sid Green and two other ex-cabinet ministers defected to form their own "Progressive Party." Green, acerbic and egocen-tric, blamed unions for twice frustrating his leadership ambi-tions and opened the NDP to a flank attack on its trade union ties. Journalists dismissed Green's successful rival, Howard Pawley, as "a touch uninspiring." Maybe that was an asset for voters fed up with Lyon's bluster and Tory austerity. The NDP's bid to restore hope and pride to a province plagued by an exodus of the young helped win 47 per cent of the vote and 31 seats while Lyon was left with only 23 seats. Green and his followers were wiped out. So were the Liberals. Pawley formed a strong government, with Roland Penner, scion of a North Winnipeg radical family, as attorney-general, and an impressive contingent of women ministers.

Manitoba had been regained, Ontario would surely recover, and Blakeney would surely be safe in Saskatchewan. The constitutional debate had given him and Romanow national stature. Certainly there was discontent in Saskatchewan — environmentalists deplored the government's pro-nuclear policy; militant unionists demanded higher pay — but surely such people would not abandon the NDP for the Conservatives. The new Tory leader, Grant Devine, with his genial admission of being "a farm boy who just happened to get a Ph.D." appeared unimpressive. With the province prosperous amidst a recession-wracked Canada, and Ottawa threatening the sacred "Crow's Nest Rate," it seemed a good time for Blakeney to call an election. Striking hospital workers were brusquely ordered back to their jobs and a vote was called for April 26th, 1982.

Not even NDP veterans foresaw their problems. CUPE pickets dogged Blakeney. Provincial employees echoed CUPE's anger. Saskatchewan's prosperity seemed to justify their demands. It also allowed Devine to promise sweeping tax cuts, rate freezes, and generous new spending programmes. As for the "Crow rate" it was no issue. "Sell Blakeney, not the Crow," shouted opposition politicians, mimicking the 1980 NDP slogan that had urged voters to sell Joe Clark, not Petro-Canada. On election day, Grant Devine drew the biggest margin in Saskatchewan history, 55 per cent of the votes to the NDP's 38 per cent; 55 seats to a meagre 9 for Blakeney. In Saskatoon, a token Tory candidate beat Roy Romanow.

Disaster in Saskatchewan rocked the NDP everywhere. When neighbouring Alberta voted on November 2nd, voters gave Peter Lougheed his largest (and last) majority. There was a small comfort that the final disintegration of Social Credit and a second NDP seat, won by Ray Martin in

Edmonton, made Grant Notley leader of the opposition. With 18 per cent of the vote, and 20 of 79 seats in which NDP candidates had saved their deposit, the party had a shaky claim to second spot.

The NDP's last hope of early gains was British Columbia. By 1983, those hopes were bright. Recession and Bill Bennett's management had reduced the province to an economic wreck that no one could blame on socialism. Lavish junkets by Socred ministers fed voter wrath. The NDP had a strong caucus and a leader who had humbly repented past errors. A nervous Bennett, advised by borrowed Tory experts, delayed the election past B.C.'s normal three-year term. When the campaign finally began in April, 1983, the province had not seen a budget in eighteen months. It was a classic recipe for defeat — but not in British Columbia. In the shortest campaign in memory, Social Credit unleashed an old-fashioned socialist-bashing blitz. Bennett bluntly denied NDP warnings of impending user fees and hospital charges. Trapped into condemning wage restraint for public employees, Dave Barrett found himself on the unpopular side of public opinion. He and New Democrats flailed wildly in self-defence. Voter confidence dissolved as NDP candidates contradicted each other. On May 5th, 1983, voters handed four NDP seats back to Social Credit. Bennett collected half the votes in the province. A weary, disillusioned Barrett quit as leader and MLA to become an open-line talk show host. Perhaps, in B.C.'s political circus, that was where power lay.

In seven years, Bennett had done little to dismantle the reforms of the brief NDP era. That quickly changed. On July 7th, British Columbia finally got its overdue budget. It was an agenda for a right-wing revolution. B.C.'s rentalsman, human rights commission, and other agencies were wiped out. Public employees, from professors to ferry workers, could be dismissed regardless of cause. Municipalities and school boards lost their fiscal autonomy. Protesters thronged to mass rallies. Art Kube, the new head of the B.C. Federation of Labour, took a lead in forming Solidarity, a coalition of aggrieved groups. As the rest of Canada reacted in shock to Bill Bennett's radical agenda, federal Tories tried to distance themselves from the political fallout.

The B.C. premier was utterly unrepentant. Political polarization guaranteed his continued power. Workers in B.C.'s troubled resource industries, with their own jobs lost or in jeopardy, had little sympathy for relatively affluent teachers or civil servants. While the NDP opposition futilely filibustered at Victoria, by-election voters in the lower mainland stripped the federal NDP of its seat in Mission-Port Moody. Solidarity held to its course, pledging mass strikes at the end of October. When the time came, most government employees walked out. A week later, B.C. teachers defied the law and followed suit. On November 13th, as a third phase was about to begin, Jack Munro of the Woodworkers union was summoned to Bennett's home town of Kelowna. He returned with a deal: seniority would be respected in the government layoffs; there would be money to save teachers' jobs; there would be compromises on human rights and landlord-tenant legislation.

Munro's deal ended the strikes, dissolved Solidarity into furiously resentful fragments, and cracked even labour's unity. Kube, who had been too sick to go to Kelowna, protested that he would never have signed such a deal. The next Federation of Labour convention saw Munro and his powerful union decamp in a dudgeon. A delighted Bennett pressed on, opening B.C.'s Expo '86 site to non-union contractors, crushing protests, and humbling a once-proud labour movement. Canadians who wanted evidence of the sudden rightward plunge of political attitudes needed only to look to the west. In 1983, the right-wing reached a new apogee of power and self-confidence.

Union members protest federally-imposed wage controls in 1976. Frustrated by electoral failure, Canadian labour soon found even greater frustration in the old weapons of strike and demonstration.

Ironically, the NDP had planned its 1983 convention as a celebration of socialist progress in the fifty years since the Regina Manifesto. The 1400 delegates crowding into Regina could instead mourn Blakeney's and Barrett's defeat. Pre-convention opinion polls showed the national NDP at a meagre 15 per cent. True to form, the party's left-wing offered nationalization of all five major chartered banks as a solution. A majority of delegates settled for one of them. Majorities, in a militant mood, condemned Manitoba's NDP government for upholding Canada's abortion law, demanded a Palestinian state, and reiterated the old NDP policy of getting out of NATO.

A major task at Regina, accepted two years earlier, was the adoption of an up-to-date Manifesto. Ontario's Socialist Caucus had matched the official version with its own, more radical document but the real alternative, concocted by Blakeney and Grant Notley, arrived long after the official resolutions deadline. By dint of publicity and their own prestige, the two western leaders forced consideration of the document. Broadbent and union leaders were doubly angered: not only had the westerners forced a bending of the rules, but their insistence on a "social contract" and incomes policy would certainly be interpreted as NDP endorsement of Liberal and Tory wage controls. While the convention delegates listened to the well-worn arguments of left and right, the real convention fight raged in nearby hotel rooms where Broadbent, Blakeney, and their respective emissaries wrestled for a compromise.

In the end, it was found: a form of words that recognized regional and provincial rights, dropped the "social contract," and was promptly forgotten. After Doug Anguish, a maverick Saskatchewan M.P., dropped his challenge, Broadbent won an uncontested fifth term. Delegates desperately wanted reconciliation. On July 2nd, an evening in honour of Tommy Douglas allowed the old veteran to issue a passionate valedictory to his party. Desperate to believe again in themselves and their cause, two thousand New Democrats cheered, wept, and applauded during fifteen emotional minutes. Finally, Douglas forced them to stop. The morning after, both the nostalgia and the bitterness remained.

In 1980, prospects for the NDP had looked bright. Thereafter, as one commentator noted, the party had gone through hell. By 1983, even Manitoba looked hopeless for the NDP as the Pawley government awkwardly struggled, amidst mounting public hostility, to do justice to the province's French-speaking minority. Despite the alternative, the useless but court-imposed translation of ninety years of provincial laws, Tories, a few dissident NDPers, and most of the audible voices in Manitoba forced the government to back down. Polite support for Pawley from federal Liberals and from the new Tory leader, Brian Mulroney, was not much help.

Outside Manitoba, whatever modest attention Canadians gave to politics had been focussed since 1982 on the self-immolation of Joe Clark, the Tory leader, and the rise of his crafty successor. Virtually unknown until 1974 outside Conservative backrooms and the Montreal legal fraternity, Brian Mulroney owed his prominence to junior membership in a provincial royal commission into labour violence headed by Robert Cliche, the former Quebec NDP leader. That had been enough to make him a contender against Clark in 1976. Handsome, smooth-voiced, colloquially bilingual thanks to a Baie Comeau boyhood, Mulroney captivated Canadians in 1983 as Trudeau had fifteen years before. The extra four years of Liberalism, marred by flawed policies and arrogant displays of power, would have been too much for Canadians even without a harsh recession. Media attention and Mulroney sent Tory fortunes soaring as high as 60 per cent; they ended the year at 53 per cent.

Yet there were lingering doubts about Mulroney's experience, his links with the Tory right wing, even his integrity, whenever the choirboy exterior slipped to reveal the political operator underneath. The Liberals, too, could change leaders. After a well-publicized world tour for peace somewhat improved his ratings, Trudeau chose a February 29th snowstorm to decide on retirement. The Liberals were finally free to recall their leader-in-waiting since 1975, John Napier Turner. The years away among bankers and brokers, his discreet barbs at Trudeau's staff, and the eclipse of a populist Jean Chrétien would position a Turner-led party where a more conservative electorate could support it. Liberals, after all, were the natural majority party and big business's natural ally. So it looked, in early 1984, as Liberal fortunes turned and climbed. In April, the Liberals passed the Tories in the polls. By the June convention, when Turner triumphed over his populist rival, Chrétien, his party boasted an eleven-point edge over the Conservatives.

Meanwhile, if anyone noticed, hell for the NDP had turned even hotter. After 23 per cent support in August, 1982, the polls began to turn steadily down. For Broadbent, the decline was a challenge to rebuild the party organization and to refurbish NDP policy for greater strength and relevance. Against advice, he appointed Jim Laxer, the ex-Waffle leader and a university professor, as caucus research director, the key official in NDP policy creation. When Robin Sears left to work for the Socialist International, western members of the NDP federal council urged that Cliff Scotton, a former federal secretary, CLC official, and displaced Saskatchewan civil servant, take over as the party's top official. Broadbent insisted on his own nominee, Gerry Caplan, the ingenious but abrasive architect of Stephen Lewis's political career. By a margin of one, Caplan got the job, and the West got another grievance.

Laxer was no longer a radical. His ideas, reflecting the

imprint of American neo-liberalism gave a renewed vigour to Broadbent's speeches on industrial strategy, but Laxer got little welcome from other caucus members, preoccupied as they were with western concerns and their own shrinking prospects for re-election. A Broadbent speech in October, 1982, admitting that Canada's soaring deficit imposed policy problems, produced furious protests from union researchers as well as from party militants. Praise from such media commentators as Richard Gwyn that Broadbent had finally dragged his party into the centre of the economic debate was offset by harsh warnings that the NDP had also forfeited its distinctiveness. In January 1984, Jim Laxer complicated matters by issuing a massive report, denouncing NDP policy as short-sighted, old-fashioned, and contradictory. A copy was delivered to the Toronto *Globe and Mail*. Laxer also resigned to give his critique maximum publicity. When the NDP tumbled a further couple of points, to 13 per cent in February 1984, angry New Democrats knew whom to blame. After party officials foolishly tried to suppress Laxer's report, he published it anyway. As with most such books, it gained brief notoriety and then vanished rapidly into limbo.

Across Canada, and perhaps especially in Ottawa, the Laxer episode fed a sense of panic. Nystrom and other Broadbent critics openly endorsed the critique. As the inevitable election approached, the polls showed NDP support plummeting to a mere ten or eleven per cent, worse than anything since the NDP began. The few media commentators who even noticed the NDP predicted that it was now likely to lose the minimum twelve MPs needed for party status. For his part, Caplan proclaimed that the NDP was losing its soul. Broadbent, in turn, began to question his own advocacy of Caplan's political genius.

It was Terry Grier, experienced and perhaps a little cynical, who grasped the problem: media preoccupation with Mulroney and Turner. The NDP had simply vanished from television. Policy-making, even the Laxer furore, made no difference: there were no pictures. In 1983, Grier recalled, in the wake of the NDP's convention and Douglas's emotional farewell, party standing had bounced briefly to 20 per cent. When the elections came, Grier insisted, the NDP would bounce again — if it kept its nerve.

How to do that emerged almost by accident. Far from floundering, Grier's election planning committee committed half a million dollars for a pre-election media campaign in four key provinces and fifty priority ridings. To get opinion soundings, the committee had hired a Regina pollster, Larry Ellis. In October 1983, after many problems, Ellis reported that voters had no faith in the NDP as an economic manager but they did trust the party to stand up for the little guy. The NDP, Ellis insisted, should try to repair its weakness by stressing its economic ideas. It was tempting advice for a party that took policy seriously and for a leader who had spent almost eight years propounding an industrial strategy. In the circumstances, Grier and Caplan agreed, it was also stupid advice.

NDP election planners used Ellis's findings, not his wisdom. The "little guy" evolved into a slogan of "Standing Up for Ordinary Canadians." George Nakitsas, the bright, practical union researcher hired to replace Laxer, began churning out the ideas and facts to back up a campaign based on tax reform, jobs, small business, and the needs of women in the labour force. The NDP quietly crossed the border to recruit Vic Fingerhut as a pollster, a Washington-based expert who had done brilliant work for the Democrats in battling right-wing referenda in California. Fingerhut's specialty was "turning people around": he was just what the NDP needed.

It also needed luck. In June, it got some. Once exposed to public scrutiny, it was evident that nine years in corporate boardrooms had cost John Turner his political timing. The

Through the 1980s, Ed Broadbent's pugnacious intelligence remained one of the NDP's major assets. In an age of doubts about political leadership, he ran well ahead of his party. He also tried to endow the NDP with fresh, relevant ideas.

embarrassed Liberal establishment delivered him the leadership on June 16th, but the loser, Jean Chrétien, had the party's populist soul and, as time would tell, most of its Quebec support. Instead of waiting to demonstrate his new governing style, Turner interpreted the fat Liberal lead in the polls as an argument for a quick election. Only then did he find that Trudeau had left him no plans, little organization, and an ugly plethora of patronage appointments. While Turner was mired in difficulties, Mulroney merely smeared himself, unwarily confessing his delight at political patronage and then, unctuously, apologizing when the media pack turned righteous.

Within days of the campaign outset, Broadbent had emerged as more honest, appealing, and attractive than his two rivals. The NDP chose Bay Street, the heart of Toronto's financial district, to launch its campaign theme. Crowds cheered and laughed as Broadbent, amid the office towers, invited Turner and Mulroney, the "Corporate Clones", or "Bobbsey Twins of Bay Street," to come down from the 45th floor to see the problems of ordinary Canadians. It was a theme with variations that the NDP leader carried across Canada, helped by Nakitsas and his principal secretary, Bill Knight.

Television, still willing to treat the NDP as almost equal, allowed Broadbent fair coverage and a full share in the campaign's three national debates. In French, Broadbent was painful, but at least Quebeckers could understand him. With women's issues an NDP focus, he had no trouble winning the largely feminist audience for the final debate. By August, the NDP was back at 17 per cent. Local candidates and campaigns, glimpsing victory instead of costly humiliation, began to come to life. As a theme, "ordinary Canadians", as Grier ruefully admitted, might be a lot more populist than socialist, but it plucked a deep chord in the party and among those who had never supported the NDP.

The next problem, as ever in NDP campaigns, was how to build a second charge of energy as election day, September 4th, approached.

Indeed, as the party took heart, a new panic seized some at the centre. The NDP revival coincided with a dramatic Tory surge. At 50 per cent by August, a Conservative landslide of Diefenbaker proportions might annihilate the NDP, whatever its share of the vote. In a campaign memo, inevitably leaked to the press, Gerry Caplan ordered an all-out attack on the Tories as the only means of self-preservation. For Broadbent, notified too late to intervene, it was a gross error. To the very end, both the "Bobbsey Twins of Bay Street" remained in his sights.

As it all turned out, Mulroney's victory was of a 1958 magnitude, but it was the Liberals who came close to annihilation, with a mere 40 seats to the Tories' 211. With 30 seats and 19 per cent of the vote, the NDP ended its four years of misery more or less where it had started. In the West, the Tory tide had snatched away six seats; in Ontario, the Liberal debacle had added four. "Pleasure," wrote Grier, "is often the absence of pain; success might well be said to be the absence of failure." New Democrats had earned another tomorrow; it was more than some of them had expected.

XII. Prospects

For seventeen years, Canadians had responded to the whims and fancies of Pierre Trudeau, a political master. Despite his lopsided majority, Brian Mulroney could not help being a lesser figure. Associates knew him as "Bones," remembered him as a convivial plotter in Tory back rooms, and wondered whether he had ever had an idea of his own. To win the leadership of his party and of Canada, Mulroney had scattered scores of pledges, many of them contradictory. It was the Tory right wing that gave him victory at the 1983 convention but Mulroney insisted that universal social programmes were "a sacred trust", that world peace was his highest priority, that wealthy tax-avoiders would be made to pay their fair share.

New Democrats had painted Turner and Mulroney as twins but they saw the Tory leader as the special friend and servant of American corporations. Among Mulroney's childhood recollections was singing for Colonel McCormick, the right-wing Chicago newspaper magnate who owned Baie Comeau's only industry. In 1976, Mulroney had taken over the Iron Ore Company of Canada, a subsidiary of the Hanna family of Cleveland. At their orders, he had shut down Schefferville, a company town much like Baie Comeau, though he managed the deed with such smoothness that even displaced workers bore him no grudge. Mulroney himself boasted of his friendship with Ronald Reagan, cancelled all that he could of the economic nationalism of the previous government, and launched his young government on a bid for continent-wide free trade. With their own economy recovering, Canadians began to have second thoughts about their new government and its ingratiating but shallow new leader.

If Mulroney made a single substantive promise in the 1984 campaign, it was to reunite a divided country and to make the Progressive Conservatives its natural government. It was easier said than done. Where they could, provincial Tories hastened to profit from the Mulroney honeymoon, aware that it could not last. In Nova Scotia, John Buchanan hurried into a November election and emerged with a landslide of 52 seats. Alexa McDonough, with her own version of the "ordinary Canadians" theme, found herself with a caucus of three, and renewed party status in the legislature. It was blessed relief in her struggle with the durable and abusive Paul MacEwan. Next door, New Brunswick might have followed Nova Scotia, but embarrassing revelations of marijuana in his luggage gave Richard Hatfield second thoughts. Resentful voters in a Saint John East by-election picked an astonished NDPer. Within months, he had shifted his allegiance to the Liberals, leaving the New Brunswick legislature with a lone New Democrat.

By 1985, even before his inevitable mid-term slide, Mulroney's coattails had begun to shrink. Granting Newfoundland virtually all it had ever wanted for its offshore resources should have given Brian Peckford a sweeping victory on April 2nd. Instead, voters remembered the dismal Tory economic record and years of broken promises. Peckford won, but Liberal fortunes revived. Peter Fenwick, the NDP's provincial leader, hung on to his Labrador seat and narrowly missed gaining a partner in Grand Falls. The NDP vote revived from 4 to 14 per cent, a frail base, but moving, NDP organizers boasted, "in the right direction." Two weeks later, at the opposite end of the country, the party could even boast a new government. In the Yukon, native people and union members gave the NDP eight out of sixteen seats. It was a narrow triumph — the NDP's 41 per cent of 10,618 voters was smaller than the Tory share — but it was enough to make Tony Pennikett leader of the territorial government. New Democrats could be grateful for small mercies.

Ontario should have been proof against national trends. When Bill Davis quit in October 1984 after thirteen years of power, he left Tories with a plump majority in the polls and every hope of extending their hold on power to a full half-century. In fact, party delegates had chafed under Davis's long middle-of-the-road management and they handed the succession to the most right-wing of the contenders, Frank Miller. Instead of waiting to tone down his image, Miller imitated John Turner by calling a snap election. Confident that the NDP could now win its share of the province's broad centrist consensus, Bob Rae waged a deliberately low-key campaign. Party strategists underestimated the Liberal alternative. With promises deftly snatched from the NDP's collection, David Peterson moved into the middle ground. With no Trudeau government to act as an albatross, with too many voters still nervous about the NDP radicalism, inexperience, and union ties, it was Peterson who made the gains.

The May 2nd Ontario election gave Miller 52 seats but fewer votes than Peterson with 48 seats. The NDP gained only four more seats with a popular vote of 24 per cent. There would be a minority government but the form would be original, imaginative, and controversial. Instead of the shaky, frustrating arrangements of the 1970s and a formal coalition that would chain NDP ministers to the decisions of

Howard Pawley brought the NDP back to power in Manitoba and won re-election in 1986. His unflamboyant earnestness was a style Manitobans generally seemed to welcome in their political leaders, regardless of party.

a Liberal majority, Rae offered each of the larger parties a formal accord based on a specific agenda of reforms. The Tories, unable to grasp that forty-two years of power might be at an end, refused to negotiate; the Liberals seized the chance. On July 1st, David Peterson became Ontario premier in return for an agreement to carry out the promises he had borrowed from the NDP, to wait a minimum of two years before the next election, and to allow legislative defeats without invoking a premature dissolution.

Disillusion with Mulroney's fumbling and amateurish government had played a part in the Ontario outcome; it remained to be seen whether disenchantment would invade the former Tory heartland of western Canada. A Conservative party with a Quebec Irish leader and a massive swathe of seats in central Canada looked more like the former Liberals than the party of John Diefenbaker. Deregulating the West's oil industry from Trudeau's hated National Energy Policy had looked marvellous in 1984 but disastrous a year later as world oil prices tumbled and the great Alberta bonanza dried up. Widespread drought, dust storms, and low world wheat prices were hardly Mulroney's fault, but no one could claim that Tory victory had brought good times.

By 1986, polls indicated that New Democrats could probably take three of the four western provinces. Manitoba's Howard Pawley, apparently doomed only two years earlier in the heat of Manitoba's language dispute, took his chances and went to the polls on March 18th, 1986 with a vigorous programme of reforms and a boldly controversial defence of his province's massive hydro-electric development. The New Democrats held power, though more narrowly than they had expected: 30 seats to 26 for the Tories and a lone Liberal.

Alberta's election on May 8th, 1986 produced a far more astonishing result. Grant Notley, the architect of all that the NDP represented in the province, was tragically killed in an air crash in 1984. His sole colleague in the legislature, Ray Martin, took over the leadership, but the usual experts predicted that the NDP might well be finished. That prospect seemed even more certain when an aging and tired Peter Lougheed gave way to Don Getty in 1985. Yet when the election came on May 8th, exasperated Albertans gave Martin and the New Democrats 16 seats and more than 29 per cent of the votes. It was still a Tory victory, but most of Edmonton and even part of Calgary had voted NDP. It was the kind of breakthrough that had heralded changes of government before in Alberta.

By the summer of 1986, New Democrats elsewhere in the West were still waiting for their chance. Trapped by economic and political troubles, Grant Devine's lopsided majority in Saskatchewan looked vulnerable. A province that had been declared "open for business" looked more like a candidate for a firesale. Allan Blakeney waited for vindication. In British Columbia, the glitzy splendours of Expo '86 could have only one aftermath; the question was whether voters would be appeased by a summer of circuses. Twelve hundred NDP delegates had chosen Bob Skelly as Dave Barrett's successor. Quiet, self-effacing, a deliberate contrast to the ebullient "little fat Dave," Skelly offered patient reassurance as the antidote for a polarized electorate. Reporters claimed that he was dull; perhaps they missed the point.

Across Canada, New Democrats were making gains with the old strategy Tommy Douglas and David Lewis had designed to give the NDP national power. In every province but Quebec and Prince Edward Island, the NDP was a major political factor. It had also established its identity in most of the major cities of Canada where New Democrats served as mayors, councillors, aldermen, and trustees. New Democrats at all levels of government identified with tenants, immigrants, the elderly, and the unemployed as well as with unions, co-operatives, and farm organizations.

For a few captivating moments, the 1984 federal election had offered New Democrats the dream that they might supplant the Liberals as Canada's alternative party. Except in western Canada, that has not happened. It was also evident that New Democrats themselves were not prepared to make the compromises necessary to conciliate a broad middle range of opinion. Almost perversely, delegates at the 1985 convention defied Ed Broadbent and even Pauline Jewett by reiterating their determination to get Canada out of NATO. A more moderate and realistic industrial strategy was sent back to incorporate ritual commitments to public ownership, workers' control, and opportunities for women. Delegates made sure there would be no short-cut to power.

At its quarter-century, the New Democratic Party has not realized its early dreams of power. It has failed to bridge the gulf between progressive forces in French and English Canada. Even the trade union links that made the NDP a labour party are still imperfect and controversial.

Yet, like the CCF before it, the NDP has helped dictate and determine the politics of change in Canada for the past half century. The timidity of the Mulroney government in its first years of power was testimony to the influence of the New Democratic Party and the potential support it could gain from millions of "ordinary Canadians." The national distinctions that most Canadians cherish as they worry about the Americanization of their country were often based on the programmes of the CCF-NDP. Medicare, public broadcasting, unemployment insurance, and access to free collective bargaining are among the institutions in jeopardy if Canada's social-democratic tradition is buried.

In its quarter-century, the New Democratic Party has won no quick or easy victories. New Democrats have learned patience and fortitude. At the same time, few Canadian observers would still consider the NDP a minor party. Those who had drafted its obituaries hide them. No political party can live forever. Any group committed to change and to visions of a better world is fuelled by a dynamism that can easily explode. Yet, over the years, the New Democratic Party has succeeded in changing radical dreams into acceptable reality and it is likely to go on doing so.

Since politics is about leadership as well as policies, it is relevant that the NDP has been able to make a transition from an older generation to a new one. Ed Broadbent proved to be a worthy successor to Lewis, Douglas, Coldwell, and Woodsworth and there will be powerful contenders for his succession. New Democrats can claim some of the most impressive talent on the Canadian political stage, from trade unionists such as Shirley Carr and Bob White to big-city mayors like Vancouver's Mike Harcourt or the ex-mayor of Ottawa and now national party president, Marion Dewar.

A quarter-century has taught Canada's New Democrats the importance of political professionalism. The NDP has been as innovative and aggressive in absorbing modern techniques of communication, fund-raising and opinion analysis as it has in exploring the modern implications of its democratic socialist philosophies. However, techniques and policies alike are the servants of ideals. New Democrats remain united behind the noble vision of making Canada "a society of friends." Through all the distractions of image-making, electioneering, and political controversy, this is the vision that gives a purpose to the politics of change.

Appendix. Structure

The history of the New Democratic Party presumes some slight familiarity with its structures. New Democrats cherish the conviction that their party is somehow different and finer than its rivals. The older parties, they insist, are autocratic organizations in which policy is determined by a leader's whim, memberships are sold in bulk by aspiring candidates, and funds are collected by discreet bagmen. In the NDP, by contrast, policies are adopted by the mass membership, leaders must renew their mandate at regular conventions, and financial support is provided openly by hundreds of thousands of Canadians.

While wishful thinking and over-simplification contribute to the contrast, the NDP *is* different. Certainly democracy in the NDP observes the normal rules of political behaviour. Leaders prefer to have their own way. Majorities shirk the obligation to sit through endless meetings; minorities are prone to claim that their rights have been trampled when they merely did not get their way. Democracy depends on membership participation. Unlike earlier Canadian socialist parties, which forced would-be members to pass an exam, the NDP's criteria are modest: would-be New Democrats must be residents of Canada, over fourteen years of age, and not a "member or supporter of any other political party." Membership dues vary considerably from province to province with federal and provincial tax legislation often offering substantial rebates to encourage contributions. The NDP boasts the most widespread, though by no means the richest, network of contributors among the three major Canadian parties.

As of 1986, the NDP boasts about 120,000 regular members across Canada, most of them in Ontario, Saskatchewan, and British Columbia. A more controversial category is affiliated membership. Theoretically open to any kind of organization, from a credit union to a ratepayers' association, the option has most often been exercised by trade union locals, ranging from a handful of firefighters in Corner Brook, Newfoundland, to huge steelworker locals in Hamilton and Sudbury. NDP rules require affiliation to be approved by a general membership meeting and for opponents to be allowed to opt out. In practice, unions affiliate for less than their full membership, saving dissenters any need to make themselves known. In 1986, the NDP claimed more than a quarter-million affiliated members, a modest share of a labour movement that numbers close to four million men and women.

Throughout its history, the NDP has varied in its enthusiasm for special organizations of women and youth. In the early years, when such groups were established, their ablest leaders soon fled to the mainstream policy-making bodies of the party, leaving separate organizations to wither or to be infiltrated by the NDP's perennial parasites, the Trotskyites. In more recent years, enthusiasm for separate youth and women's caucuses has revived, largely as a means of pressuring councils and conventions in the name of feminist and youth concerns and, on the whole, for the sake of a more forceful socialism.

In structure, unlike the highly-centralized CCF, the New Democratic Party is a federation of quite autonomous provincial parties. As Ed Broadbent complained, provincial parties remain responsible for federal as well as provincial organizing within their boundaries. Federal and provincial election finance legislation in the 1970s enormously complicated an NDP financial structure that purported to integrate federal, provincial, and constituency financing. The major benefits, as befit a federal law, seem to have accrued to the NDP's federal office and staff in Ottawa. On the other hand, hard-pressed provinces owe heavy debts to the party's central treasury.

The governing structure for the federal NDP and for most of its provincial sections is roughly identical. Formally, the supreme body is an annual or (in Ontario and federally) a biennial convention. Representation is based on membership in constituency and affiliated organizations: the federal NDP allows a delegate for each fifty members of a riding association and a delegate for each thousand members of an affiliate. Since conventions are self-financing, attendance tends to be limited by the cost of registration fees and travel expenses. At a typical convention, constituency delegates outnumber union delegates by about two to one, though many riding representatives will, themselves, be unionists in good standing.

As policy-making bodies, NDP conventions have severe limitations. Gatherings may include a thousand or more delegates. Despite winnowing by resolutions committees, scores of complex and controversial matters come before the convention. Delegates must thumb through mountains of printed and photocopied resolutions (in both official languages at federal conventions), lose their places, get distracted, and, often, vote on cue from more experienced neighbours. The mood is almost always purposeful and even a little solemn — NDP conventions limit their jollification and pep rallies to an occasional evening session. While conventions are troubled by procedural exhibitionists and occasional disruptions, they also reach high drama, as in the debate on "self-determination" at Ottawa in 1971 or on the Constitution at Vancouver in 1981.

Like other parties, the NDP uses conventions to choose leaders. While New Democrats often insist that resolutions and other formal policy-making takes precedence, no quantity of resolutions can anticipate all the issues on which leaders must take stands and on which parties will be judged. So far, no incumbent leader has been driven from office by an NDP federal or provincial convention, but the prospect of a divisive and potentially successful challenge has persuaded a number of leaders to retire.

More influential than conventions as a forum for the democratic control of the NDP are federal and provincial councils. The federal council is dominated by provincial representatives while constituency officials dominate provincial councils. In both bodies, affiliated trade unions have a limited representation. Assembling three or four times a year with members well versed in party affairs, councils tend to be more consistent and knowledgeable in debate and more penetrating in calling leaders to account. Though subordinate, in theory, to a convention, NDP councils can do almost anything but choose a new leader. Meetings adopt policy statements, scrutinize budgets and reports, and hear appeals on party discipline. It is the councils that pass at least preliminary judgment on matters of controversy within the NDP.

Federal and provincial executives in the NDP include party officers elected by a convention and members in most cases delegated by the councils. They meet frequently and, with their committees, form a central authority for the federal or provincial NDP. Until recently, New Democrats have resisted specific quotas of men, women, youth, or unionists. Instead, balance was sought through "slates," lists of appropriate executive teams balanced, in a time-honoured Canadian way, by sex, age, region, and affiliation. Groups ranging from the current party leadership to the party's left wing, sponsor rival lists. While most of the members of the "official" slate normally succeed, one or two others usually manage to "break the slate" and become, willy-nilly, part of the party "establishment."

Because of the NDP's structure, most members have their closest identification with their provincial constituency association. *Ad hoc* committees from ridings within a larger federal constituency manage its affairs. Whatever the level, candidates must be chosen only by NDP members living within their electoral boundaries. A thirty-day cut-off for new members discourages the old Canadian custom of packing nomination meetings. Party candidates require formal endorsement by a provincial council. The addition of party names to the ballot in 1974 made approval necessary from the federal leader as well. Formal rejection has been rare, though a few would-be candidates have received quiet warnings that they might not be found suitable.

Like other Canadians, New Democrats seem to feel that candidate selection is a local prerogative. With much diplomacy, party officials may try to "place" an impressive candidate with no home base but such attempts are rare. The party may also compel a constituency association to present a candidate though, again, such coercion has been unusual. Like other parties, the NDP makes a special effort to field qualified women candidates; unlike its rivals, it also seeks out able trade unionists.

Party fundamentalists often complain about the NDP's preoccupation with elections and parliamentary politics. The party is regularly urged to devote more resources to community organizing, peace movements, and tenants' groups. The problem is that elections and legislatures tend to be the NDP's primary concern, devouring all the energy, funds, and talent that the party can muster, particularly in larger cities where municipal contests have become as preoccupying as federal and provincial struggles. Unlike some of its socialist precursors, the NDP does not pretend to provide its members with a comprehensive political life: it can keep them very busy with elections at all levels, meetings, conventions, memberships, and financial drives and regular calls to share in the parades, rallies, dances, garage sales, and other activities of the NDP and its allies.

Critics may suspect that the combination of television and large public subsidies will make a mass-based democratic party obsolete. The contrast between the NDP's socialist economic strategy — reinforced by the radical mood of the party's 1985 convention — and very different perceptions of the party by the electorate risks a split between ideologues and election managers.

The core issue in party democracy is the respective power of the membership and the wider electorate. Out of office, a party may please itself with its policies and pay the price of impotence if it does not please the voters. In office, a government is responsible to at least a plurality of the electorate. Perhaps polarization was inevitable in British Columbia politics, but the Barrett government almost certainly accelerated the process by its political style. In the heyday of the Saskatchewan CCF-NDP, party membership formed such a significant bloc of the population — approximately one voter in ten — that it could fairly claim to represent at least that substantial part of the electorate that accepted the party's agenda. When Manitoba New Democrats complained, as they often did, that the Schreyer government did not measure up to its rigorous standards of socialism, the premier's implied response was that an organization of a couple of thousand militants was less than *vox populi*. When, after strenuous organizing, the Manitoba party grew to a membership of 13,000, conventions seem more often to have approved Schreyer's cautious reforming style.

A quarter-century after its creation, the NDP remains firmly in the social democratic tradition. If party leaders dreamed briefly in the wake of the 1984 election of supplanting the Liberals as a major national party, convention delegates in 1985 firmly rebuffed any watering of the party wine. The rest of North America might, however superficially, be in love with privatization, deregulation, and the "downsizing" of government; NDP delegates remained faithful to public ownership, economic planning, and a concern for justice and equality over the competitive joys of free enterprise and devil-take-the-hindmost.

Ideological purists would find NDP thinking a puzzling mixture of imports and home-brew. Its socialism has less to do with Marx, Engels, and even the British Fabians than with J.S. Woodsworth's notable reminder that the word socialist derives from "the good old Latin word for 'friend'." In a society of friends, peace would be a natural priority. The "needy" would not be segregated and stigmatized by categorical programmes, however benignly conceived. The needs of the poor, in the words of Canadian Catholic bishops, would take priority over the wants of the rich. Among friends, private choices and public dissent are tolerated and respected.

Such a political faith has a soft exterior and a tough core. The values and achievements of the New Democratic Party have become part of the Canadian fabric, helping to define the uniqueness of a separate North American society. Without the NDP, how many of the institutions and values that distinguish Canada from the United States would remain?

Further Reading

Whatever its other deficiencies and deprivations, the Canadian Left cannot complain of scholarly neglect. Its bibliography is long and the cast of participants impressive. They include such ill-matched intellectuals as O.D. Skelton and Stephen Leacock, Liberal and Tory, united only in their determination to battle the spreading heresy of socialism.

Those who want to know more about the roots of the Canadian Left might start with Paul Fox's essay, "Early Socialism in Canada" in J.H. Aitchison's *The Political Process in Canada* (Toronto, 1963). The most thorough account, if bearing the flaws of a pioneering work, is Martin Robin's *Radical Politics and Canadian Labour* (Kingston, 1968). Anyone interested in the mental processes of those early Canadian radicals should look at the new edition of T. Philip Thompson's minor classic, *The Politics of Labour* (Toronto, 1975), originally published in 1887.

An enormous outpouring of Canadian labour history has supplanted the few dreary classics available ten or fifteen years ago. Modesty does not deter me from recommending the further reading sections of my own book, *Working People: An Illustrated History of the Canadian Labour Movement* (Ottawa, rev. ed., 1984). Others may admire Bryan Palmer's *The Working-Class Experience* (Toronto, 1983). Additional contributing streams in Canada's left-wing tradition may be pursued in W.L. Morton's *The Progressive Party of Canada* (Toronto, 1950), W.C. Good's self-portrait, *Farmer Citizen: My Fifty Years in the Canadian Farmers' Movement* (Toronto, 1958), and, for a stream that diverged, see Ivan Avakumovic's *The Communist Party in Canada* (Toronto, 1975). A view that puts Marxism at the core of Canadian socialism is Norman Penner's *The Canadian Left: A Critical Analysis* (Toronto, 1977).

Much has been written about the CCF in all its aspects. Kenneth McNaught provided a full-length biography of J.S. Woodsworth in *A Prophet in Politics* (Toronto, 1959). David Lewis, in some ways Woodsworth's younger foil, lived long enough only to complete the first of two volumes of autobiography. Few books capture an author's character as well as *The Good Fight: Political Memoirs, 1900-1958* (Toronto, 1981). The most important overall book on the CCF was by the late Walter Young, *The National CCF: Anatomy of a Party* (Toronto, 1969). A number of newer themes are pursued in J. William Brennan's *Building the Co-operative Commonwealth: Essays on the Social Democratic Tradition in Canada* (Regina, 1985). Provincial supplements are provided by Gerald L. Caplan's *The Dilemma of Canadian Socialism: The CCF in Ontario, 1932-1945* (Toronto, 1973) and Nelson Wiseman's *Social Democracy in Manitoba: A History of the CCF-NDP* (Winnipeg, 1983).

The tribulations of a CCF leader in Quebec were described by the late Thérèse Casgrain, *A Woman in a Man's World* (Toronto, 1971). Michiel Horn's *The League for Social Reconstruction* (Toronto, 1980) depicts in detail the early intellectual guides of the CCF. Some of the work of its most prolific member may be found in F.H. Underhill's *In Search of Canadian Liberalism* (Toronto, 1960).

The CCF's major achievements were in Saskatchewan. The most thorough study of the prairie phenomenon was

Seymour Martin Lipset's youthful work, *Agrarian Socialism: The Co-operative Commonwealth Federation in Saskatchewan* (Los Angeles, rev. ed. 1967). A more popular account, by Chris Higinbotham, is *Off the Record: The CCF in Saskatchewan* (Toronto, 1968). Higinbotham also conducted the long personal interviews with T.C. Douglas, more recently edited by Lewis H. Thomas as *The Making of a Socialist: The Recollections of T.C. Douglas* (Edmonton, 1982). Some specific aspects of the CCF government as experienced by insiders may be found in Laurier LaPierre et al., eds., *Essays on the Left* (Toronto, 1971). The party's concern for accountability is discussed by Evelyn Eager, "The Paradox of Power in the Saskatchewan CCF, 1944-1961", in J.H. Aitchison, *The Political Process in Canada*. A broad-ranging look at Saskatchewan is available in Eager's *Saskatchewan Government: Politics and Pragmatism* (Saskatoon, 1980). Memories of the Medicare crisis are found in Robin Badgley and Samuel Wolfe, *Doctors' Strike: Medical Care and Conflict in Saskatchewan* (Toronto, 1967). A modern account is in J.L. Granatstein, *Canada, 1957-1967: Years of Uncertainty and Innovation* (Toronto, 1986).

Inevitably, the array of material dwindles as perspective shrinks. Gad Horowitz's *Canadian Labour in Politics* (Toronto, 1968) is a detailed look at the twenty-year process that brought Canadian unions to help create the new party. Horowitz also contributed a provocative explanation of why socialism has survived in Canada while dying in the neighbouring United States. Stanley Knowles, *The New Party* (Toronto, 1961) argued the case for the young party to sceptical Canadians. It is a reminder of old arguments and old hopes. Doris Shackleton's biography, *Tommy Douglas* (Toronto, 1976) is less than the tough-minded biography the NDP leader wanted and deserved. Some of his rhetorical flourish and personal concerns survive in L.D. Lovick's edited collection of speeches, *Till Power is Brought to Pooling: Tommy Douglas Speaks* (Lantzville, B.C., 1979).

The NDP's history after 1961 must, on the whole, be collected from scattered and partial sources, notably from the pages of the *Canadian Annual Review*, fortunately revived in 1960. Wiseman's book on Manitoba's social-democratic history extends to the NDP era while J.T. Morley's *Secular Socialists: The CCF/NDP in Ontario: A Biography* (Montreal, 1984), was written by an involved and partisan participant in his topic. Among scholarly contributions to the topic, see R.U. Miller, "Organized Labour and Politics in Canada" in R.U. Miller and Fraser Isbester, *Canadian Labour in Transition* (Scarborough, 1971). Desmond Morton, "The Effectiveness of Political Campaigning: the NDP in the 1967 Ontario Election," *Journal of Canadian Studies* IV (1969), and John M. Wilson, "The Politics of Social Class in Canada: The Case of Waterloo South," *Canadian Journal of Political Science* I (1968). The Waffle dispute is recalled sympathetically by Robert Hackett "Pie in the Sky: A History of the Ontario Waffle," *Canadian Dimension* XV (October-November 1980), and by John Bullen, "The Ontario Waffle and the Struggle for an Independent Socialist Canada: Conflict Within the NDP," *Canadian Historical Review* LXIV, 2 (June 1983).

The NDP in power may be too recent an experience for objective study, though Barrett's experience in British Columbia was the subject of a major academic study published by Terry Morley, Walter Young, et al., *Reins of Power: Governing British Columbia* (Vancouver, 1983). Less sympathetic but perceptive is Lorne J. Kavic, *The 1200 Days: A Shattered Dream, Dave Barrett and the NDP in BC, 1972-5* (Coquitlam, 1978). A left-wing perspective on subsequent British Columbia affairs was supplied by Stan Persky, *Son of Socred* (Vancouver, 1979) and *Bennett II* (Vancouver, 1983). The Manitoba NDP government's failure to meet a socialist agenda it never embraced annoys James McAllister in *The Government of Edward Schreyer* (Winnipeg, 1984). Russell Doern's *Wednesdays Are Cabinet Days* (Winnipeg, 1982) helps explain why the writer was not invited to join the Pawley government in 1981.

As befits a party preoccupied with ideas, a number of books have claimed to instruct the NDP on its duty. The essays in Michael Oliver's collection, *Social Purpose for Canada* (Toronto, 1961) were contributed by authors ranging from George Grant to Pierre Trudeau. It was followed by a number of books sponsored by the University League for Social Reform, among them Abraham Rotstein, ed., *The Prospect of Change* (Toronto, 1965), T.O. Lloyd and J.T. McLeod, eds., *Agenda 1970: Prospects for a Creative Politics* (Toronto, 1968), and Desmond Morton, *Socialism Canada Seventies* (Toronto, 1969). In the wake of Trudeaumania, Charles Taylor's *The Pattern of Politics* (Toronto, 1970) argued for a more polarized political system. The Waffle's position can be found in Dave Godfrey and Mel Watkins, *From Gordon to Watkins to You* (Toronto, 1970), and in Robert Laxer, ed., *Canada Ltd.* (Toronto, 1973). A different attempt to define the Canadian left was made by John Wilson, "Towards a Society of Friends: Some Reflections on the Meaning of Democratic Socialism," *Canadian Journal of Political Science* III (1970). The aftermath of the NDP-Waffle dispute may have been more tranquil but, in publishing terms, it was also somnolent. However impolitic the circumstances of its publication, Jim Laxer's *Rethinking the Canadian Economy* (Toronto, 1984) represents one of the few book-length intellectual contributions to emerge from the NDP in a decade. A witty, provocative book from a British Columbia perspective is Alex Macdonald, *"My Dear Legs": Letters to a Young Social Democrat* (Vancouver, 1985). A somewhat confusing critique of the NDP by an ex-member and current Tory is Michael Bradley, *Crisis of Clarity: The New Democratic Party and the Quest for the Holy Grail* (Toronto, 1985).

Since these works have been chosen from an already selective list of more than five hundred titles on the history and thought of the Canadian Left, many important books and articles have not been mentioned. Anne Scotton's *Bibliography of All Sources Relating to the Co-operative Commonwealth Federation and the New Democratic Party In Canada* (Ottawa, 1977) is a help though copies are scarce, and the content, inevitably, is dated.

Index

Aberhart, William, 13.
Abortion, 172, 213.
Accord, and NDP, 225;
 and Liberals, 225.
Advertising agencies, 51, 62, 195.
Affiliation, 230, 232.
Afghanistan, 199.
Agriculture, 151-2.
Air Canada, 148, 164.
Aitchison, James, 111.
Akerman, Jeremy, 111, 163, 202.
Alberta, 8, 13, 15, 22, 36, 69, 70,
 75, 111, 117, 151, 157, 159, 165,
 174, 176, 196, 197, 205, 209.
All Canadian Congress of Labour, 13, 17.
Allard, Paul, 83.
Allen Norman, x.
Allende, Salvador, 151.
Amalgamated Meatcutters, 185.
American Federation of Labor, 6.
American influence, 89-90, 96, 227.
American neo-liberalism, 216.
Ames, C.C., ix.
Anderson, Georgie, x.
Andras, Andy, 189.
Anguish, Doug, 213.
Anti-Americanism, 40-2, 76, 91, 93.
Anti-Inflation Board, 188.
Arabs, 157.
Archer, David, 131.
Argue, Hazen, 25, 28, 32, 38, 85, 87.
"Associate status", 57, 60.
Athabaska tar sands, 158.
Atlantic provinces, 17, 120, 142, 199, 202.

Australia, 17.
Auto Insurance, 49, 55, 100, 104-5,
 149, 183.
Automation, 60-61, 193.
Autopac, 184.
Axworth, Tom, 201.

Baie Comeau (Quebec), 214, 221.
Bain, George, 93.
Barrett, Dave, 94, 106-7, 123-41.
 145, 147, 148, 151, 153, 160, 161,
 167, 178, 179, 181, 186, 206, 210,
 213, 226, 234;
 as premier, 148-152.
Barron's Weekly, 151.
Bassett, John, 62.
Beaches (Toronto) by-election (1962), 34.
Beauce, 57, 64, 68.
Beck, J.M., 34.
Belgium, 150.
Benjamin, Les, 206.
Bennett, W.A.C., 29-30, 48, 49, 68-9,
 106, 107, 139-40, 152, 161.
Bennett, William, 161, 178-180, 204,
 206, 210, 211.
Berger, Thomas, 69, 87, 106, 139, 161.
Bilingualism, 45, 100, 101, 180;
 Royal Commission on, 56-7.
Bill 42 (British Columbia), 29, 30, 32.
Blakeney, Allan, 108, 114, 123,
 130, 147-9, 159-61, 170, 174, 176,
 205-7, 209, 213, 226;
 as premier, 149-53.

Bonn summit,   191.
Borden, Sir Robert,   46.
Borowski, Joe,   68, 103, 154.
Boudreau, Emile,   121, 129.
Boulard, Marc,   64.
Bourassa, Robert,   119, 180, 181.
Brant by-election (1971),   120.
Brewin, F. Andrew,   75, 86, 196.
Brewin, John,   75, 132.
Brigden, Gordon,   ix, 132.
British Columbia,   9, 10, 15, 21, 25, 36, 38, 39
    43, 46, 65, 73, 84, 87, 94, 147-8, 149, 151,
    153, 161, 165, 167, 171, 178, 230, 234.
    elections (1963) 47-9, (1966) 68-9, (1969)
    105, 106-9, 114, (1972) 139-42, (1975)
    179-81, 192, 196, (1980) 199, 206, (1983)
    210, 211, (1986) 226.
British Columbia Development Corporation,
    150.
British Columbia Federation of Labour,   186,
    211.
British Columbia Ferries,   148.
British Columbia Hydro,   148.
British Colmbia Legislature,   87, 179.
British Columbia Railways,   174, 179.
British Columbia Telephone Co.,   106,
    150.
Broadbent, Edward,   x, 86, 91, 92, 93,
    124, 127-8, 134, 138, 169, 170, 181,
    187, 188, 192, 194, 195, 198, 199,
    201, 204-7, 213, 216, 219, 220,
    227, 228, 231.
    as leadership candidate,   124, 127-8,
    171-3.
Brocklebank, J.H.   75-6.
Brokenhead riding (Manitoba),   100.
Brown, Rosemary,   171-3.
Bryden, Kenneth,   53.
Bryden, Marion,   x, 89, 130.
Buchanan, John,   202, 222.
Buck, Tim,   30.
Burgess, Tom,   111.
Burnaby (B.C.),   65, 206.
Burnaby-Coquitlam riding,   39, 83.
Burt, George,   30.
Business,   140, 149.
"Business unionism",   30.

CTV network,   62, 163.
Cadbury, George,   89.

Calgary,   11, 12, 13, 69, 226.
California,   217.
Cameron, Colin,   19, 45, 76, 86, 93.
Camp, Dalton,   70, 111.
Campbell, Douglas,   155, 172, 173.
Canada,   4, 8, 10, 176, 180, 193, 196,
    199, 206, 207, 209, 214, 220, 222,
    225-7;
    and English,   180, 181;
    and French,   180, 181, 214, 219, 227.
Canada Labour Relations Council,   186.
Canada Pension Plan,   77, 90.
Canadian Broadcasting Corporation,   24,
    78, 81.
Canadian Cellulose,   150.
Canadian Chambers of Commerce,   27.
Canadian Charter of Rights and
    Freedoms,   201, 204, 205, 207.
Canadian Congress of Labour,   17-18.
"Canadian Development Fund",   24.
Canadian Dimension,   94, 103, 154.
Canadian flag,   195.
Canadian Food and Allied Workers
    (see also United Packinghouse
    Workers),   131.
Canadian football,   164.
Canadian Investment Fund,   192.
Canadian Labour Congress,   18, 20, 25,
    28, 30, 31, 79, 166, 185-7, 189-91,
    194, 198, 206, 215.
Canadian Labour Party,   11.
Canadian National Railways,   148, 164.
Canadian Pacific Railways,   149, 172.
Canadian Union of Postal Employees,   209.
Canvassing,   54-5.
Caouette, Réal,   38, 58, 120, 165, 200.
"Cap-in-hand" sessions,   5.
Cape Breton Island,   4, 17, 37, 43, 111,
    163, 165, 196, 202, 204.
Capital punishment,   161, 193.
Caplan, Gerald,   83, 92, 109, 132, 215-17,
    220.
Carleton East by-election (1974),   177.
Carleton University,   169, 173.
Carr, Shirley,   189, 228.
Carter, Kenneth,   83.
Casgrain, Thérèse,   17.
Cashin, Richard,   111.
Cassidy, Michael,   183, 208.
Catholicism,   6, 52, 194, 235;
    schools,   115.

Celovsky, Boris,   141.
Centennial, Canadian (1967),   72, 79.
Central treasury,   170.
"Centralism",   59-61.
Chambers of Commerce,   45.
Chambly by-election (1971),   129.
Chartrand, Michel,   45.
China,   80, 90;
    immigrants,   9.
Chrétien, Jean,   204, 206, 207, 215, 219.
Churchill Forest Industries,   100, 149.
Cité Libre,   41.
Clark, Joe,   193, 195, 198, 200, 206, 209, 214.
Cleveland,   221.
Cliche, Robert,   57-9, 60, 63, 64,
    76-7, 81, 83-4, 121, 214.
Cold War,   24, 199.
Coldwell, M.J.,   13, 19, 24, 61, 87,
    162, 173, 228.
Collective bargaining,   187, 227.
Collver, Richard,   176.
Columbia River,   150.
Columbia Cellulose — see Canadian
    Cellulose.
Communists,   11, 14, 17, 40, 92;
    and CCF,   17-18;
    and NDP,   30.
Community clinics, campaign for,   67.
Community organizing,   233.
"Concerned Citizens and Foresters",   179.
Confederation of National Trade
    Unions,   30, 41, 64.
Congress of Industrial Organizations, 17.
Conservative Party — see Progressive
    Conservative Party.
"Constituante", une,   129.
Constituency organizations,   194.
Constitution Act (1982),   205-8, 232.
Continentalism,   83, 92.
Controls, wage and price,   160, 166,
    187, 191, 213.
Conventions — see New Democratic Party.
Cook, Ramsay,   76, 83.
Co-operative Commonwealth Federation,
    vii, 5, 9, 13, 14, 20, 22-3,
    24, 27, 28-9, 34, 37, 44, 69, 87,
    96, 110, 124, 131, 145, 146, 150,
    160, 169, 178, 189, 199, 205, 227, 230;
    democracy in,   15, 19;
    history,   12, 18;
    and labour,   17, 18, 19, 21;
    in Saskatchewan,   14-15, 46-7, 51-2,
    69-71, 150, 160, 234.
Co-operative federalism,   56.
Co-operatives,   226.
Corner Brook (Nfld.),   193, 230.

"Corporate Clones",   219.
Corporate tax concessions,   141-2.
Corporation des enseignants du Québec, 121.
"Council of confederation",   43.
Coutts, Jim,   201, 208.
Craft unions,   5.
"Crazies",   155.
Credit unions,   230.
Créditistes,   38, 44, 197, 200.
Creighton, Donald G.,   93.
Crosbie, John,   197.
Cross, James,   119.
Crowe, Harry,   94.
Crown Zellerbach,   150.
Crowsnest Pass rates,   176, 209.
Cuba,   80.

"Daisy Air",   167, 194.
Davey, Keith,   61.
Davis, Jack,   178.
Davis, William G.,   114-16, 177, 181, 183,
    197, 204, 208, 223.
"Day of Protest",   190, 191.
Deficit,   216.
DeGaulle, General Charles,   78.
Deindustrialization,   192.
Delaware,   135.
Democracy,   229.
Democratic Party (United States),   7.
Denison Mines,   149.
Dental care,   148.
Depression,   12, 20.
Deregulation,   235.
Desjardins, Larry,   101, 103-5.
Detroit,   114.
Devillez, Anita,   ix.
Devine, Grant,   209, 226.
Dewar, Marion,   228.
Diefenbaker, John,   18, 21, 27, 34-6,
    39-40, 61, 65, 66, 68, 79, 84,
    86, 87, 146, 196, 198, 220, 225.
Dollard constituency,   81.
Douglas, T.C.,   13, 22, 24, 25, 33, 39,
    44, 50-1, 60, 69, 86-7, 92, 103,
    123, 147, 157, 169, 171, 173, 206,
    213, 214, 226, 227;
    elections,   35-8, 41-2, 61-5, 82-4.
Dovercourt constituency,   130, 131.
Dowling, Fred,   18, 185.
Drapeau, Jean,   180, 193.
Dunsky, Menahem,   62, 72, 82.
Duvernay constituency,   81, 84.

Economic nationalism,   91-4, 116.
Economic planning,   235.

Edmonton, 210, 226.
Election Expenses Act, 170.
Election finances legislation, 198, 231.
Election Planning Committee, 173, 217.
Eliesen, Marc, 91.
Ellis, Larry, 217.
Energy, 153, 157, 158, 199.
"Equal status", 45.
"Establishment", 233.
Ethnic voters, 100.
Exchange for Political Ideas in Canada, 50-1.
Excise tax, 197.
Expo '67, 75, 79.
Expo '86, 211, 226.
Extra-parliamentary activity, 96.

Fabianism, 57, 235.
Family allowances, 146.
Family Farm Protection Act, 114.
Faour, Alphonsus, 193, 194, 196, 199, 202.
Farm Machinery Act, 152.
Farm organizations, 226.
Farmstart, 153.
Federal constituency, 233.
Federalism, 25, 77-9, 159.
Fenwick, Peter, 202, 222.
Finance department, 187, 197.
Financial Times, 77.
Fingerhut, Vic, 217.
First World War, 10.
Fisher, Douglas M., 22, 50, 66, 81, 84, 91, 94.
Fisheries, 111, 164.
Flag debate, 56.
Flyer Coach Co., 174.
Food prices, 153, 156.
Food Prices Review Board, 147, 157.
"For a United and Independent Canada", 94-5, 127.
Foreign Ownership, 24, 61, 76, 83.
Forest Hill (Toronto), 43.
Forgivable loans, 149.
Forsey, Senator E.A., 25, 77.
Fort McMurray, 159.
Fort William, 48.
Founding Convention — see New Democratic Party.
Fox, Paul, x.
Fraser Valley, 152.
Free enterprise, 4, 235.
French-speaking intellectuals, 180.
Frost, Leslie, 29.
Fulton, E. Davie, 48.
Fund-raising, 228.
"Fundamentalists" — see "Left wing".

Gagnon, Gabriel, 129.
Galbraith, J.K., 166.
Gallup poll, 14, 33, 38, 44, 61, 65-6, 79-80, 84, 120, 139, 161-2.
Galt (Ont.), 54.
Gatineau Hills (Quebec), 91.
Gautrin, H.-F., 165.
Gayn, Mark, 50.
General elections, Canada, 16th (1926) 146; 24th (1958) 146; 25th (1962) 34-8; 26th (1963) 39-44; 27th (1965) 61-66; 28th (1968) 80-5; 29th (1972) 139, 141-3, 145, 169, 190; 30th (1974) 164-7; (1980) 199.
Getty, Don, 226.
Gifford, C.G., 64.
Gillis, Don, 31.
Ginger Group, 8, 11.
Globe and Mail (Toronto), 39, 71, 91, 93, 147, 192, 216.
Gompers, Samuel, 6, 18.
Gonick, C. G., 94, 103, 154.
Gordon, Walter, 61.
Grand Falls (Nfld.), 222.
Great Britian, 7, 17, 46, 103, 160, 193.
Green, Sidney, 88, 100, 208.
Grier, T.W., ix, 56, 61, 62, 71, 75, 101, 160, 173, 194, 198, 216, 217, 219, 220.
Griffin Steel strike, 183.
Group for Good Government, 154.
Guaranteed annual income, 126.
Guelph (Ont.), 11.
Gwyn, Richard, 216.

Haggart, Ron, 66.
Halifax, 37, 111, 143, 170, 202, 204.
Hall, Robert, 202.
Hamilton, 14, 31, 43, 54, 117, 163, 186, 230.
Hamilton, Alvin, 40.
Hanley by-election (1964), 54, 55.
Hanna family, 221.
Harcourt, Michael, 228.
Harney, John, 71, 75, 81, 84, 86, 124, 127-8, 133, 171-3.
Hatfield, Richard, 202, 204, 222.
Hawthornthwaite, J.H., 10.
Health insurance, 15, 24, 34, 46-7, 49, 51, 55, 60, 90, 100, 103, 113, 148, 153.
Heap, Dan, 208.
Hees, George, 54.
Herridge, H.W., 19, 32.
Hinman, E.W., 69.
Hilter, Adolf, 14.
Hogan, Andy, 165, 196, 199.

Hooke, A.J., 69.
Horowitz, Gad, 25, 185, 189.
Hospital insurance, 15.
House of Commons, Canada, 11, 32, 85, 145.
Housing, 71.
Howard, Frank, 124, 127-8.
Human rights, 211.
Human Rights Commission, 210.
Hydro-electric development, 225.

"I Believe in Canada", 63.
"Il faut prendre le pouvoir partout", 138.
Immigrants, 226.
Income tax, 170, 184.
Independence, 181.
Individualism, 8.
Industrial strategy, 173, 192, 217, 227.
Industrial Workers of the World, 10.
Inflation, 147, 153, 156, 160, 174,
   176, 186, 187, 191.
Injunctions, 72.
Insurance Corporation of British
   Columbia, 149, 178, 180.
International Nickel Co., 72.
International Union of Mine, Mill &
   Smelter Workers, 31, 37.
International unions, 131.
International Women's Year, 172.
International Woodworkers of America, 211.
Iran, revolution, 196.
Iron Ore Company of Canada, 221.
Irvine, William, 11.

Jaffary, Karl, 96.
Japanese-Canadian deportations, 120.
Jaunszems, Steven, x.
Jewitt, Pauline, 50, 199, 227.
Jodoin, Claude, 28, 31, 80.

Kelowna (B.C.), 211.
Kidd, Bruce, 130.
Kierans, Eric, 83, 151, 171.
King, W.L.M., 9, 12, 14, 146, 162.
King, William, 186.
Kitchener (Ont.), 88, 96.
Kitimat (B.C.), 31.
Knight, Bill, 219.
Knights of Labor, 5.
Knowles, Stanley, 18, 19, 28, 86, 206, 207.
Kube, Art, 211.

Laberge, Louis, 167.
Labour laws, 183.
Labour leaders, 186, 189, 191.
Labour Party (British), 10, 17, 28, 90, 132.
Labour radicals, 6, 7, 9.
"Labour's Manifesto for Canada", 190,
   191.
Labrador, 202, 222.
Lachine constituency, 81.
Laliberté, Raymond, 121-3, 126-9, 138-9.
Lalonde, Marc, 201.
Landlord-tenant legislation, 211.
Landlords, 178.
Lang, Otto, 176.
Lang, Ronald, 189-91.
Langdon, Steven, 173, 192.
Language issues, 180, 181, 225.
LaPierre, Laurier, 77, 79, 81, 84, 86, 94.
La Presse, 64.
Laskin, Bora, Chief Justice, 207.
Latin America, 119.
Laurier, Sir Wilfred, 46.
Lawrence, Allan, 114.
Laxer, James, 92, 96, 97, 124, 127-8,
   129-30, 135, 172, 215-17.
League for Social Reconstruction, 12.
Le Devoir, 41, 60, 65, 76, 122, 181.
Left wing, 19, 20, 24, 44, 89, 90,
   94-5, 107, 233.
Lenin, V.I., 4, 10.
Lépine, A.T., 7.
Les Gens de l'air, 180.
Lévesque, René, 160, 181, 201, 204, 207.
Levitt, Kari, 91.
Lewis, David, 13, 19, 24, 28, 43, 64,
   75, 86, 91, 92, 94, 95, 106, 169-71,
   173, 185, 186, 202, 206, 226, 228;
   as federal leader, 128-9, 137-8, 141-2,
   145-7, 155-64;
   as leadership candidate, 123-8;
   and 1974 election, 165-7.
Lewis, Michael, 106, 186.
Lewis, Stephen, 53, 75, 83, 86, 88,
   108, 109, 110, 181, 183, 186, 215;
   and elections, 114-7, 177;
   and the Waffle, 130-5.
Liberal party, 5, 6, 7, 9, 11, 14, 21, 29, 33, 47-8,
   50, 56, 75, 97, 101, 111, 120, 127, 145, 146,
   148, 151, 155, 156-8, 160, 171, 176-8, 180,
   181, 183, 186, 187, 193, 195-9, 201, 204, 205,
   213-15, 219, 220, 223, 225, 227, 235;
   in British Columbia, 49, 107, 140, 161,
   178;

and elections, 34, 38, 40-2, 44, 64-5, 66, 80, 82, 84, 141, 162-3, 164, 195, 196, 199, 208, 219, 220;
in Manitoba, 68, 99-100, 154;
in Ontario, 57, 72, 115-7, 176, 177, 183, 208;
in Saskatchewan, 51-2, 69-70, 111, 113, 114.
Lilooet (B.C.), 69.
Lloyd, Trevor, 71.
Lloyd, Woodrow S., 33, 51-2, 70, 87, 107.
London (England), 21.
London (Ont.), 135.
Loubier, Gabriel, 83.
Lougheed, Peter, 117, 159, 174, 196, 209, 226.
Lumber industries, 178.
Lyon, Sterling, 183, 184, 207, 208.

Macaulay, Robert, 53.
McBride, Sir Richard, 140.
McCormick, Sam, 221.
McDermott, Dennis, 97, 109, 191, 194, 206.
MacDonald, David, 30.
MacDonald, Donald C., 48, 50, 71-3, 87, 88, 108, 109, 116, 130, 198.
Macdonald, Sir John A., 5, 198.
McDonough, Alexa, 202, 204, 222.
MacDowell, Laurel, x.
MacEachen, Allan, 197.
MacEwan, Paul, 111, 202, 204, 222.
McGill University, 44, 45, 77, 89, 91.
Mackenzie, Robert, ix.
Mackenzie Valley Pipeline, 159.
Maclean's Magazine, 81, 188.
McMurtry, Roy, 207.
McNaught, K.W., x, 78.
Macphail, Agnes, 11.
Mahoney, William, 18.
Majority Movement for Freedom and Private Enterprise, 161.
Manifesto for an Independent Socialist Canada — see Waffle Manifesto.
Manitoba, 36, 46, 69, 73, 87, 88, 103-5, 149, 152, 162, 165, 171, 174, 180, 183, 192, 196, 205, 207, 209, 214, 225, 234;
elections (1962) 47; (1966) 68, 99; (1969) 99-103, 114; (1973) 153-5; (1977) 183; (1980) 199; (1985) 225.
Manitoba Club, 184.
Manitoba Federation of Labour, 186.
Maple Leaf Gardens (Toronto), 43, 65.
Marchand, Jean, 64, 180.
Market Opinion Research Ltd., 114.
⸳ Ray, 209, 226.

Marxism, 9, 106, 181, 235.
Media, 216, 217, 219.
Medicare, 170, 183, 227.
Medicare crisis in Saskatchewan, 46-7, 67. See also Health insurance.
Memorial University, 111.
Menihek (Labrador), 202.
Mercier, Honoré, 5.
Methodists, 10.
Michels, Robert, 87, 169.
Middlesex South by-election (1969), 108.
Miike, Martha, ix.
Millard, Charles, 18.
Miller, Frank, 223.
Mincome Programme, 148, 179.
Mineral Resources Ltd., 151.
Minimum wage, 183.
Mining industries, 178.
Minnedosa (Man.), 99.
Mission-Port Moody (B.C.), 211.
Mississauga, 155, 163, 172.
Mitchell, Donald, 108, 130.
Monetarism, 191.
"Mongrel enterprises", 149.
Montreal, 36, 37, 43, 45, 60, 75, 78, 84, 90, 121, 124, 126, 129, 158, 180, 181, 193, 214.
Montreal *Star*, 27.
Morin, Roland, 121.
Morris, Joe, 187, 189.
Mortgage rates, 153, 164, 167.
Moscow, 11, 199.
Mosher, A.R., 13.
Mount Royal constituency, 64.
Movement for an Independent Socialist Canada, 135, 155.
Mowat, Sir Oliver, 5.
Mulroney, Brian, 214, 215, 216, 219, 220, 221, 222, 225, 227.
Multinational corporations, 172, 192.
Munro, John, 186, 187, 211.
Munsinger, Gerda, 67.
Murray, "Ma", 69.

NDP Now Group, 123, 126-7, 135.
Nakitsas, George, 217, 219.
Nanaimo (B.C.), 45, 76, 105.
Nanaimo-Cowichan-The Islands constituency by-election (1969), 87, 88.
National Committee for the New Party, 20, 21, 23, 28.
National energy policy, 159, 225.
National Housing Act, 163.
National petroleum corporation, 159.
"National Policy", the, 5.
Nationalization 149 150

Nationalism, Canadian, 96-7;
  Quebec, 76, 90, 119.
Native people, 55, 129, 178, 183, 206, 223.
"Ned Ludd", 163.
New Brunswick, 36, 120, 123, 138, 199,
  202, 204, 222.
New Deal (United States), 7.
"New Deal for People", 113.
New Democratic Party, 5, 9, 27, 28, 29, 30, 49,
  50, 51, 79, 80, 98, 103, 117, 119, 120, 124,
  145-6, 147, 148, 151, 169-74, 176-81, 183-7,
  191, 193-9, 201, 202, 204 11, 213 17, 219-23,
  225-8, 230;
  campaigns (central) 185; (1974) 169;
  (1979) 195, 196; (1980) 198, 199, 209; (1983)
  217; (1984) 219;
  constitution and structure, 20, 25, 27, 45,
  59-60, 89, 229-31, 233;
  conventions, vii, 190, 191, 206, 229, 231
  232; (founding) 22-8, 37, 44, 57, 124;
  (second) 44-5; (third) 60-1; (fourth) 75-8;
  (fifth) 88, 94-5, 107, 127; (sixth) 124-8;
  (seventh) 155-6, 160; (1976) 172; (1983)
  213, 217; (1985) 227, 234;
  elections, 33, 53, 55, 113; (1962) 35-8;
  (1963) 40-4; (1965) 56, 61-7; (1968) 81-5;
  (1972) 141-3; (1974) 165-7, 170, 186; (1975)
  176; (1979) 195, 196; (1980) 199, 200; (1981)
  204, 208; (1984) 219, 220, 227, 235;
  federal council, 159, 171, 215, 232;
  federal office, 51, 61, 63-4, 67, 79,
  85, 170, 173, 188, 206, 231;
  finance and organization, 35, 41, 61-2,
  67, 79, 82, 85, 88, 97-8, 115-6, 137, 170,
  185, 192, 194, 199, 229-31;
  and labour, 22, 23, 29-31, 32, 35, 37, 50,
  97, 107, 108-9, 131-2, 174, 185, 187-91,
  208, 230;
  and leadership, 85, 105-6, 124-5, 128, 171,
  173, 198, 207, 232, 233;
  membership, 229-231, 234;
  and party discipline, 232;
  and policies, 23-5, 34, 43-5, 63-5, 76-8, 82
  85, 88-91, 94-5, 100, 126-9, 151-3, 173, 195,
  198, 199, 215, 217, 229;
  and principles, 3-4, 44-5, 88, 91, 235;
  and provincial councils, 232, 233;
  and women, 206, 209, 217, 219, 227, 230,
  234;
  and youth, 155 230.
New Democratic Party of Alberta, 75, 117,
  174.

New Democratic Party of British Columbia,
  55-6, 105-6, 107, 140, 148-153, 179, 188,
  210;
  and elections, 49-50, 68-9, 106-7,
  139-40; (1975) 179.
New Democratic Party of Manitoba,
  148-153, 188, 213, 214, 234;
  and elections, 47, 68, 99-103, 153-5, 183.
New Democratic Party of New Brunswick,
  123, 138.
New Democratic Party of the North West
  Territories, 174.
New Democratic Party of Nova Scotia,
  111, 163, 202.
New Democratic Party of Ontario, 28, 50,
  53-5, 64, 67, 71-2, 91, 96, 115, 132,
  137, 155, 177, 178, 183, 208;
  and elections, 47-8, 71-3, 115-7, (1975)
  177, (1977) 183;
  leadership, 88, 107-10;
  and Waffle, 130-5.
New Democratic Party of Quebec, 36-7, 38,
  41, 45-6, 57-9, 63-4, 76-8, 83-4, 126,
  140, 142, 205, 214;
  conflict with federal NDP, 119-24,
  128-9, 138-9.
New Democratic Party of Saskatchewan,
  51-2, 107-8, 111-3, 148-53, 176, 188, 204,
  209, 234, and see also Co-operative
  Commonwealth Federation,
  Saskatchewan.
New Democratic Party Waffle Group,
  97-8, 123-5, 129, 130-5, 136-8, and see also
  Waffle Group.
New Democratic Party of the Yukon, 173.
New Glasgow (N.S.), 141.
New Labrador Party, 111.
New Left, 89-91, 95-6.
New Party movement, 19-22, 23, 24, 27,
  28-9, 33, 38, 50, 96.
New Party clubs, 21, 28-9, 50.
New Party Founding Fund, 23, 28.
New Westminster (B.C.), 199.
New York, 151.
New Zealand, 17.
Newfoundland, 36, 110-111, 193, 196, 199,
  202, 230;
  and elections (1985), 222.
Newfoundland Democratic Party, 110-11.
Niagara Falls, 28, 189.
Nickel Belt constituency, 61.

Norquay, John, 101.
North, the Canadian, 183.
North American Air Defence Command, 24.
North Atlantic Treaty Organization, 22, 44, 95, 213, 227.
North West Territories, 143, 151, 174.
Notley, Grant, 75, 117, 176, 205, 210, 213, 225.
Notre-Dame de Grace constituency, 64.
Nova Scotia, 14, 21, 36, 111, 163, 196, 199, 204, 222.
Nuclear weapons, 24, 34, 39, 40.
Nystrom, Lorne, 171-3, 205-7, 216.

Ocean Falls (B.C.), 150.
October crisis (1970), 119-22.
Official Languages Act, 101.
Oil companies, 164, 174, 205.
Oil development, 176.
Oil prices, 157-8, 196.
Oliver, Michael, 28, 45, 121.
Olympic games, 180, 193.
Ombudsman, 103.
Ontario, 5, 6, 8, 13, 14, 15, 21, 34, 36, 46, 87, 120, 131, 155, 177, 192, 196, 197, 199, 200, 204, 206-9, 220, 223, 230;
    elections, 47-8, 69, 71-3, 111, 115-17; (1975) 177, 181, 183; (1980) 199; (1985) 223, 225;
    northern, 38, 84.
Ontario Federation of Labour, 131.
Ontario Hydro, 148.
"Operation Candour", 50.
"Operation Freedom", 27.
"Operation New Canada", 79.
"Ordinary Canadians", 217, 219, 222, 227.
Organization of Petroleum Exporting Countries, 157.
Orillia (Ont.), 134-5.
Oshawa (Ont.), 48, 54, 117, 132.
Oshawa-Whitby constituency, 86, 169.
Ottawa, 23, 44, 48, 69, 100, 129, 143, 151, 169, 171, 172, 176, 178, 186, 188, 200, 207, 208, 228, 231, 232.
Ottawa River, 3, 173.

Pacific National Exhibition Coliseum (Vancouver), 65.
Palestinian state, 212.

"Paper entrepreneurialism", 192.
"Parallel campaign", 194, 198.
Paris (France), 90.
Park, Eamon, 18, 62.
Parkdale constituency, 81.
Parliament, 7, 11, 22, 156, 157, 171, 189, 190, 196, 197, 200, 204, 205.
Parti Québécois, 121, 122-3, 160, 167, 180, 181, 193, 201.
Parti Socialiste du Québec, 45-6.
Patrons of Industry, 8.
Patullo, T.D., 140.
Paulley, Russell, 68, 87, 88.
Pawley, Howard, 205, 208, 214, 225.
Peace movements, 233.
Peace River (Alta.), 117.
Pearson, Lester B., 34-6, 39, 44, 56, 65, 66, 79, 80.
Peckford, Brian, 204, 222.
Pellerin, Jean, 41.
Pelletier, Gerard, 64.
Penner, John, 75,
Penner, Roland, 208.
Penner, Stephen, 130, 135.
Pennikett, Tony, 223.
Pensions, 146, 147.
Perrault, Ray 83.
Peterborough, 22, 31.
Peterson, David, 223, 225.
Peterson, Tom, 101.
Petro-Canada, 209.
Petroleum export tax, 154.
Pharmacare plan, 148.
Phillips, Edward G., 55.
Picard, Gerard, 41, 57.
Pincher Creek-Crowsnest by-election (1966), 69.
Pinney, Marjorie, 53-4.
Pipelines, 158.
Pitman, Walter, 22, 109, 110, 117.
"Platform of Principles", 9.
Plumptre, Beryl, 147.
Policy Review Committee, 173.
Political Action Committee (CCL), 17.
Populism, 8.
Port Arthur (Ont.), 61.
Port Colborne (Ont.), 31.
Potash, 153, 205.
"Power to the People", 128.
Prescription drugs, 148.
Prince Edward Island, 36, 163, 226.

"Principles and Objectives", 44.
Privatization, 235.
Progressive Party, 208.
Progressive Conservative Party, 5, 6,
    7, 14, 29, 31, 34, 38, 39, 41, 47-9,
    52, 54-5, 61, 65-6, 75, 78, 80, 82,
    97, 99-100, 101, 102-3, 117, 127,
    139, 140, 145, 146-8, 162, 176-8,
    181, 183, 184, 187, 193, 195-7, 199,
    206, 209, 211, 213-5, 220-3, 225,
    226;
    in Alberta; 117, 159;
    in British Columbia, 140, 161, 178;
    and elections (1962) 34-8; (1963) 39-41;
    (1965) 61-66; (1968) 80-82; (1972) 142-3;
    (1974) 156-7; (1979) 195, 196; (1984) 219,
    220;
    in Manitoba, 153-4, 208, 210;
    in Ontario, 72-3, 114-15, 116-17, 176, 183,
    208.
Pro-nuclear policy, 208.
Protestantism, 7, 52.
Provincial constituency association, 233.
Public Order (Temporary Measures) Act
    (1970), 120.
Public housing, 100.
Public ownership, 227, 235.
Pulp and paper, 178.
Puttee, A.W., 7.

Quebec, 15-16, 22, 29, 38, 43-4, 46, 56, 63, 66,
    83-4, 119-21, 140, 159, 160, 162, 167, 180,
    181, 190, 193, 196, 200, 201, 204, 207, 219,
    225, 226;
    and the NDP, 22, 24-5, 36-8, 41, 43, 45-6,
    57-9, 64, 76-8, 120-2, 124, 126-7, 165, 181,
    196.
Quebec City, 36.
Quebec Federation of Labour, 22, 25, 36,
    167.
Quebec Pension Plan, 77.
Quebec strikes (1972), 4.
Queen Elizabeth II, 207.

Racial prejudice, 171.
Rae, Bob, 193, 197, 206, 208, 223,
    225.
Reagan, Ronald, 193, 222.

"Realpolitik", 146.
Recession, 153, 191, 206, 209.
Referendum of 1980, 204.
Regier, Erhart, 38-9.
Regina, 13, 36, 38, 44, 108, 113, 174,
    206, 213, 217.
Regina Manifesto, 213.
Reich, Robert, 192.
Rent controls, 178, 179.
Rentalsman, 105, 210.
Renwick, James, 54, 88, 108.
Representation, 231.
Republican Party (United States),
    114.
Resolutions, 231.
Resources, 61, 150, 153, 161, 167, 205,
    207, 222;
    industries, 150-1, 183, 211;
    provincial control of natural, 205.
Revolutionary Marxist Group, 155.
Rhodes scholarships, 13, 108, 124.
Richards, John, 155.
Right-wing, 183, 210.
Rivard, Lucien, 67.
Riverdale constituency, 55-6, 72, 75;
    by-election (1964), 53-4;
    motion, 134.
Robarts, John P., 47-8, 56, 72-3, 114.
Robin, Martin, 9.
Robin Hood, 165.
Robinson, Svend, 206.
Roblin, Duff, 47, 68, 99, 100, 149.
Rodriguez, John, 207.
Rogers, Bruce, 81.
Romanow, Roy, 108, 174, 204-7, 209.
Ross, Walter S., 106.
Rotstein, Abraham, 93.
Rowley, J. Kent, 131.
Roy, Maurice, Cardinal, 37.
Royal Commission on Taxation, 18.
Rural policies, 152.
Russia, government of, 4, 198.
Ryan, Claude, 79, 119, 122.
Ryerson Polytechnic Institute, 173.

St. Catharines, (Ont.), 14, 30, 131.
St. John's, vii, 222.
St-Jean Baptiste Day (1968), 84.
Salaries for housewives, 116.

Saltsman, Max, 54, 76, 93, 196.
Samis, Iona, 131.
Sarnia (Ont.), 158.
Saskatchewan, 13, 14, 22, 25, 28, 36, 38, 43, 46, 66, 75, 84-5, 87, 147-53, 155, 159, 165, 167, 170, 171, 174, 176, 179, 205, 206, 209, 213, 215, 226, 230, 234;
elections, 51-2, 69-70, 111-13, 123; (1975) 176; (1980) 199.
Saskatchewan Co-operative Commonwealth Federation, 13, 15, 33-4, 54, 55, 103-4, 150, 160. See also New Democratic Party of Saskatchewan.
Saskatchewan Oil and Gas Corporation, 151.
Saskatchewan Power Commission, 174.
Saskatchewan Waffle, 108, 130, 134-5, 155.
Saskatoon, 43, 70, 108, 162, 209.
Sauriol, Paul, 60.
Scarborough (Ont.), 39, 172.
Scarborough West constituency, 81.
Schefferville (Quebec), 221.
Schreyer, Edward, 66, 86, 88, 99, 103, 171; as premier, 103-5, 106, 147-9, 151, 153, 154, 160, 183, 184, 186, 191, 234.
Schreyer, Lily, 172.
Scott, F.R., 19, 121.
Scott, R.V., 50.
Scotton, C.A., 79, 124, 215.
Seafarers' International Union, 30.
Sears, Robin, 199, 207, 215.
Sefton, Larry, 18, 97.
"Self-determination", 122-3, 126-7, 129, 138-9, 232.
Selkirk constituency, 86, 100.
Senate, 186, 204.
Separatism, 78.
Sexism, 171.
Shaw, Lloyd, 202.
Shulman, Dr. Morton, 72.
"Sixty Days of Decision", 56.
Skelly, Robert, 226.
"Slates", 232.
Smallwood, Joseph R., 21.
Smiley, D.V., 78.
Smith, Ralph, 7.
"Social contract", 213.
"Social Corporatism", 190.
Social Credit, 13, 29, 44, 49, 68-9, 101, 106-7, 117, 140, 145, 165, 174, 178-80, 193, 196, 209, 210.

Social democracy, vii, 192, 235.
"Social Democratic Party", 27.
Social Democratic Party (Germany), 87.
Social Purpose for Canada, 23-5.
Socialism, 3, 4, 9, 10, 11, 27, 34, 44, 45, 50, 57 61, 70, 71, 75, 92, 93, 100, 101, 106, 109, 121, 130, 132, 140, 210, 230, 234, 235.
Socialism Canada Seventies, 91-2.
Socialist Caucus, 213.
Socialist International, 215.
"Socialized medicine", 46-7.
"A Society of Friends", 228.
Solidarity, 211.
South Indian Lake (Man.), 100, 101.
Spadina (Toronto), 208.
Spadina Expressway (Toronto), 115.
Sparham, R.D., 50.
Speakers' Notes, 63.
Special organizations, 230.
"Special status", 59-60, 63-4, 76-8, 127.
Spenser, George V., 67.
Stanfield, R.L., 79-80, 120, 142, 143, 163, 166, 187.
"Stay" option, 152, 183.
Steuart, David, 111-12.
Stevens, Geoffrey, 147.
Stevens, Len, 186.
Stewart, Clara, x.
Stormont by-election (1974), 177.
Strachan, Robert, 49, 50, 68-9, 77, 87, 105.
Strikes, 174.
Stupich, Dave, 152.
Sudbury (Ont.), 31, 72, 230.
Supreme Court of Canada, 190, 207.
Surveys, political, 71, 114-6, 139, 161, 162. See also Gallup polls.
Sweden, 192.
Swedish labour federation, 189.
Syncrude, 174.
Syndicalism, 10, 189, 190.
"System", the, 54-5.

Tantramar (N.B.), 202.
Tax reform, 217.
Tax-sharing formula, 43.
Taylor, Charles, 44, 59-60, 64, 76-7, 81, 83-4, 86, 89, 91, 93, 171.
Taylor, George, 108.
Teamsters' union, 30.

Television, 195.
Templeton, Charles, 53-4.
Tenants' groups, 226, 233.
Thatcher, Margaret, 193.
Thatcher, Ross, 51, 54, 55, 69, 71, 111, 113.
The Pas (Man.), 100.
Third World, 173.
Thompson (Man.), 31, 68.
Thompson, T. Phillips, 7.
"Three Wise Men", 64.
Thurow, Lester, 192.
"Tories" — see Progressive Conservative
   Party.
Toronto, 14, 18, 31, 37, 38, 43, 48, 53,
   65, 68, 83, 114, 117, 134, 143, 159, 172,
   173, 193, 194, 219.
Toronto *Telegram*, 91.
Toronto Trades Assembly, 18.
Trade unions, 227, 230, 232, 233.
Trade Unions Act (1872), 5.
Trades and Labour Congress, 6, 8, 9, 18.
Trail (B.C.), 31.
Trotskyism, 30, 49-50, 55, 92, 135, 202, 230.
Trudeau, Margaret, 167.
Trudeau, Pierre Elliott, 25, 41, 64, 80-1, 84,
   89, 90, 100, 113, 119-20, 121, 127, 143,
   156, 158, 162, 165-7, 174, 176, 178, 180,
   181, 186, 189-91, 193, 195-201, 204-8,
   214, 215, 219, 221, 223, 225;
   and controls, 187-9.
Trudeauphobia, 205.
Turcott, Garth, 69.
Turner, John, 141, 147, 163, 164, 165, 174,
   186, 187, 198, 215-17, 219, 221, 223.
Turtleford by-election (1961), 33.
"Two nations", 25, 57, 65, 77-8, 127.

Underhill, F.H., 12.
Unemployment, 21, 23, 153, 191, 192, 226.
Unemployment insurance, 145, 227.
Unions, 3-6, 20-3, 157, 161, 185, 186, 194,
   209, 223;
   and controls, 196-7;
   and leadership, 187, 194;
   and Liberal Party, 14, 186;
   and New Democrats, 23, 38, 44, 71,
   72, 101, 108-9, 137, 231;
   and Waffle group, 97, 131-3. See also
   Trade unions.

Union Nationale, 83.
United Auto Workers, 18, 30, 97, 109, 191.
United Electrical Workers, 30-1.
United Mineworkers of America, District 26, ,
   17.
United Packinghouse Workers, 18, 185.
   See also Canadian Food and Allied
   Workers Union.
United States, 6, 7, 10, 103, 114, 150, 157,
   160, 192.
United Steelworkers, 18, 30, 31, 72, 97, 111,
   121, 133.
Universal social programmes, 221.
University of British Columbia, 78, 156,
   206.
University of Toronto, 71, 92.
University of Toronto Press, 23.

Vancouver, 13, 14, 37, 65, 69, 86, 107, 140,
   148, 152, 155, 156, 160, 166, 206, 228,
   232.
Vancouver-Burrard constituency, 43, 69.
Vancouver Island, 10.
Vancouver *Province*, 49, 139.
Verville, Alphonse, 7.
Vichert, Gordon, x, 132.
Victoria, vii, 29, 118, 211.
Vietnam, 76, 90, 96.
"Voluntary taxes", 193.

Waffle Manifesto, 92-4, 95, 107, 114, 127.
Waffle movement, 92-5, 96-8, 109-10,
   122-8, 135, 137-8, 141, 155, 215;
   in Ontario, 130-5;
   in Saskatchewan, 108, 130, 134-5, 155.
Wage and price freeze policy, 187, 210.
Wakefield (Quebec), 91.
Walker, Robert, 54.
War Measures Act, 119-20, 134.
Washington, 39, 151, 217.
Waterloo South constituency, 76;
   by-election (1964), 54.
Watkins, M.H., 92-3, 95, 97, 135, 155;
   Report, 82.
"Way Ahead for Canada", the, 63.
Weir, Walter, 99-103, 107.
Weldon, J.C., 89.
West, the Canadian, 6, 8, 146, 147, 159,
   174, 199, 215, 220, 225, 227.

Westcoast Transmission, 151.
Westmount (Montreal), 56.
Weyburn by-election (1961), 34.
Wheat, 153.
White House, 193.
White, Robert, 228.
Williams, Lynn, 131.
Williams, Parker, 83, 90.
Wilson, Harold, 83, 90.
Wilson, John M., 109.
Winch, Ernest, 13.
Windsor (Ont.), 14, 30, 83, 131.
Winnipeg, 8, 11, 38, 47, 66, 88, 94, 108,
    124, 154, 163, 172, 200, 209.
Winnipeg Declaration, 20.
Winnipeg General Strike, 4, 10, 101.
Winnipeg newspapers, 103, 104, 105, 154.
Winnipeg *Tribune*, 105.
Wolf, Lawrence, 195.
Women's Mining Association, 179.
Wood, Henry Wise, 8.
Woodbine constituency, 53.
Woodsworth, J.S., 3, 8, 10, 11, 13, 17, 24,
    61, 78, 87, 146, 173, 228, 235.
Woodsworth Foundation, 50-1.
Woodsworth-Irvine Fellowship, 22.
Workers' control, 227.
Workers' Party of Canada, 11.

"Yankee imperialism", 40.
Yom Kippur War, 158.
York South constituency, 14, 64, 66, 86,
    165.
York University, 86.
Young, Walter, 44.
"Young Turks", in the NDP, 75, 87.
Yukon, vii, 223.

Zakuta, Leo, 15.

221

DUE DATE